Zimbabwe, a passion shared

To Luise Liesl Pohl
† August 2009
the invincible

NO NEED TO FLEE ANYMORE

To Lucien Delchambre
† December 1965

ZIMBABWE, A PASSION SHARED

PATRICE DELCHAMBRE

MOSAE MONDO

First published in The Netherlands in 2010 by Boekenplan, Maastricht.
Third, revised edition 2015

ISBN 978 90 8666 282 1
Nur 600

© 2015 Patrice Delchambre
© 2015 Uitgeverij Mosae Mondo, Maastricht – The Netherlands
www.mosaemondo.nl
www.booxstore.nl

Cover design and editor: Mosae Mondo, Maastricht – The Netherlands

All rights reserved. No part of this publication may be reproduced, stored in a retrieval system, or transmitted, in any form or by any means, without the prior permission in writing of the publisher, nor be otherwise circulated in any form of binding or cover other than that in which it is published and without a similar condition including this condition being imposed on the subsequent purchaser.

TABLE OF CONTENT

Introduction 9
Chisipite Harare 11
Granny Betty's story – Betty Townsend- Coetzee 19
The letter 23
Shapes of womanhood – Claire Ingram 27
We are testing the network 35
The sorrow of Zimbabwe – Hans van Hooreweghe 37
Heat, water and history 45
History of the Chitepo family – Nomusa Chitepo 57
My life at Fairhome as a day mother – Louise Bingandadi 63
United Nations Day at the Harare International School 67
Saturday – Sabbath 73
Never give up! – Assia Post-Bouzidi 77
Colours of the rain or the song of every Shona mother 85
My life as a house manager – Charity Musingairi 87
Love in the time of cholera 89
About a lot of fear and a great job – Veerle Lens 93
Christmas Holidays 99
Scents of Africa – Marijke Legerstee- Alcock 103
Woman of Power 109
Chidemoyo Mafarararikwa's poem 111
Fairhome and Fair Trade 113
Happiness comes unexpectedly – Mia Moers 119
Corals, crocodiles and queues 125
Japanese showering – Emmanuel Ruben Neves 129
Basil on the operating table 135
Poem by Ian James 143
Woman 145
Big House, Small House – Harare 1976 147
A new start – Esther Steijn 149
End of the month drinks and more rain! 153

The night of the cholera *157*
My life as a Shona artist – Itai Derere *159*
Victoria Falls: Mosi-o-Tunya *163*
Returning Home – Paddy Hobley *165*
Poem for Hilde, A Far-Off Friend *171*
Half Dutch, Half Zimbabwean – Wilma Hoefnagels *173*
Measles and schools *179*
Word, Vision, Song, Spirit – Kundisai Mtero *183*
Sleep? *187*
Pamella, a mother with three boys – Pamella Sithole *189*
11 and 12 February 2009 *193*
To Stay or Not – Graham Dunbar Bogdan Acutt *195*
Never at home *203*
Homesick for Africa *205*
Shangaan Sheila – Sheila Bell *207*
Fifteen hours on the bus *211*
It's a small world in Zimbabwe – Thomas and Bruno *213*
Hakata, or the Full Moon Stones *223*
Zimbabwe: Nirvana for the nihilist – Bengt Post *225*
The summer song of the yellow weavers *233*
Party Time *235*
And now what *243*
End of 2012 *247*
There is a crack in everything – Bengt Post *249*
Waiting for the winds of change *253*
And now, so many years after the beginning – Aad van Geldermalsen *257*
Chengeta Primary School *265*
The Jacaranda tree of Zimbabwe *267*
The Flame Lily of Zimbabwe *269*
The Ndoro of Zimbabwe *270*
Useful Addresses *271*

Introduction

In *Zimbabwe, a passion shared* I want to tell you about the Zimbabwe that the reader does not know from European reports nor from travelling journalists. It is about Zimbabwe from within and about the Zimbabwe of today. In this collection, I give us, women and men, the opportunity to write about the way we see, feel, taste and experience life here. This is different for everybody and each of us tries to rise above the new daily tragedies of this country.

We stand by each other whenever life sometimes seems to become impossible. This is how new connections and surprising friendships are born.
I know all the people who have worked on this book personally and have a special connection with each and every one of them.

The people I have invited for each individual chapter also represent a special group in this local community: the business woman, the mother, the teacher, the singer, the confectioner, the home-study director, the project coordinator, the daughter of a slain freedom fighter, the single mother of seven, the NGO accountant, the musician, the women responsible in Fairhome orphanage, the artists, the travel agent/Rotarian, the hairdresser, the entrepreneur, and many more.

Everything is written with love and passion for this crumbling country.

A story about how people go and search for friendship and succeed.

Chisipite Harare
September - October 2008

My name is Patrice Delchambre. I am the daughter of the late Lucien Arthur Alfons Delchambre and Luise Liesl Pohl. The daughter of a very handsome, dark Flemish military man and a beautiful, blue-eyed, German refugee.
A daughter born out of a passionate relationship that had to remain secret for many years. I have a brother and four sisters. As we always used to say: *the Delchambre clan: people of flesh and blood.*
Thanks to my eldest sister, Evy, I had the chance to attend university. I am the second in a family of six, with Dirk, Myriam, Carla and Chris as my other siblings.
My full name is Patrice Alice Hector Delchambre and I design corals.
I live in Zimbabwe.
Zimbabwe is underneath my salty skin.

My husband, a very special man, is Aad van Geldermalsen, epidemiologist, sailor, glider pilot and father of the most beautiful children below the equator: Alies, 27, Sanna, 24, Sytse, 21. Aad dedicated his heart and his time to Africa and earned the respect and friendship of our *local brothers* as they are called here. My best friend, my husband. He has more Shona and enlightened ex-Rhodesian friends than any of us might expect in this little world.

Twenty-seven years of Africa, seventeen of which were spent in Zimbabwe.
Six countries after 1977 and three children later, I often look at the old Saint Nicholas poem I received from Peter in 1979.
"Patries on the move again. The world is your home."
This little verse, put on a red and black collage, has always travelled with me. Travelled with me as a loyal companion on whom I could call and who has always silently agreed with me.

When I turned forty, I decided on two things; life starts now and this woman is going to live her dream and study fine arts in the capital, Harare. Decision number one: I was done with all of the income generating projects for women in the compounds of the commercial farms surrounding Bindura, the district capital of the Mashonaland Central province.

I was done with development aid as a primary motive for my presence in the bush in yet another country and in my existence beside my husband.
I was going to reinvent myself and start over with the three kids in a modest house with an adjoining Portuguese cottage and a fair bit of land.
Nice and shaggy, much to discover in the silence of a close that leads nowhere. Three children who can finish their secondary education in one and the same quality school.

The second decision was a small spelling adjustment and at the same time a homage to the murdered leader Patrice Lumumba: from now on Patries is Patrice.
Done deal.
A glimpse back in time.

As a seven-year-old, I was already dreaming of this life's journey to Africa. The catholic upbringing at the strict Our Lady Visitation, the sisters of the Love Order, with the little nuns busily travelling back-and-forth, gave me the first, typically sixties insight into Rwanda, Burundi and Congo. This turned out to be based on compassion for these poor, savage heathens: collecting silver foil, crocheting baby clothes for all those little curly headed one-year olds and up, knitting baby socks and caps for the non-curled natives. It never occurred to us to even question Africa's weather conditions.

'Don't you want to study?' our dad, whom I loved to bits, asked.
'You don't want to study? Not a problem, I'll open up a bar for the six of you and we'll call it *The 12 bare bums.*'
Thus, the scaredy-cat became an unpopular study head, a grade chaser and I planned a future for myself, far away from my home-town of Leopoldsburg.

'Talents are not to be wasted and buried', my Evangelical mother told me. Would I be able to bury them temporarily, I wondered doubtfully? Store them until after Africa, for example?

But Africa was what I wanted, even later, after our college time and the effort and dream of a freed Zimbabwe. That was it. I wanted to work, but most of all enjoy. So there!

When, 33 years later, I was selected, after auditioning, to feature in the film *Congo*, filmed by the way, in our very own highlands – a beautiful mountain range near the Mozambique border – filming was stopped repeatedly. Both my Shona counterpart, as well as the entire film crew could not stop laughing, because my line as the Flemish wife of a colonial

plantation owner 'Jef, why are these natives so restless?' could not leave my throat without a burst of laughter.
The film portrayed the period of the Belgians' large-scale evacuation from the former Congo, in which some of us actresses were murdered.
At night we all sat nicely in the charming hotel of Chimanimani – the largest mountain range in this country – after having a real blast with our eternally connected African brothers. The schizophrenia inside of me harbours the Prussian rigidity and the French *laisser faire*. The star-sign of Virgo completes the disaster. The Flemish workhorse inside of me will not get the better of me. My catholic upbringing often dips the moments of happiness, relaxation and pleasure in a sauce of guilt, whether it concerns work, passion or leisure.

But still, all I want to do when there is a full moon is dance in the African night with my female friends. These friends, there have been so many over the long years, both locally and internationally, become the chain of your daily happiness. They have become family in this extraordinary global life in which our true family lives so far away.
Friends are family in this existence, you often hear. Do we often dance in the African night? We sure do. We did that in Somalia, Zambia, Lesotho, in Cape Town and in every special Zimbabwean spot during a full moon. The Hakata bones with its two male and two female symbols were tossed up and our future, prosperity and success were predicted. And, far more than dancing during a full moon, we care for each other here. When we are together, little is needed to perfect the dance of us, crazy women.

The balance of seventeen years of living in southern Africa's former paradise, Zimbabwe, makes someone think. The picture looks different every time, depending on the presence or absence of water and electricity, cash, affordable food in the shops or relationships with colleagues at work or within the art world and with all the more consequences for our Shona compatriots. The sadness of it all.
For now, I keep the scales balanced like reversed Magdeburg hemispheres and I thank the lucky stars.
The multi-cultural education, provided to 60 different nationalities at our International School of Harare, is about to enter its tenth year. A passion. Designing ceramic objects at home is an equally important passion.

Passion within the Rotary means putting away charitable feelings in order to set up projects with potential, a vision and a future of self-reliance.
Sustainability is the new fashion, so consultants, who come and go and who are sometimes twenty years younger than my husband, tell me.
They use impressive, new jargon, often without any sense of reality or understanding Africa, let alone Zimbabwe.

Finally, for several years now, one night a week, I have a home restaurant. Dear friends who run a travel agency suggested this to me ten years ago, but necessity means pressure and routine means grind. So all the freedom and creativity is now up to me. This week two nights, the next maybe none at all. And mind you, never more than ten diners a night.

The invited guests did not notice the concept as such, except for the quality of the meals and the presentation of the table at our modest, little home, now with a garden with home grown palm trees, oleanders and lavender.

This way, it does not feel like work, but more as a passion and cooking as the most transitory form of art. As long as everybody around me enjoys! Every single meal is allowed to be a work of art.

Five years ago, this mini-restaurant was immediately dubbed *A Taste of My Life* by my children. But five years ago, the situation was also more simple: we enjoyed our own, local cheeses: the fragrant Vumba, named after this mysterious mountain region. We used local chutneys and atchars. The meat was affordable and the imported fish from Canada, Cape Town or Mozambique was available everywhere.

Now, nothing is left of the local produce. Confiscation of the remaining farms continues with happy abandon. Done by chaps who call themselves war veterans. Most of them were still in diapers or rags, historically speaking, because just maybe it was their father and mother who once helped free the country. Maybe not; war veteran is the most tainted word in Zimbabwe. So, we import food *en masse* from South-Africa and from Europe for ourselves, our staff and our local friends.

Our little home remains cool in recent days. The breeze is unusually late, but ensures cool air in this hot month of October. On the same cement table that only this afternoon was used to wedge the soft, grey clay, sushi is rolled, homemade pesto tried out with a glass of cool, white wine, Zimbabwean vegetables processed into a creamy soup, traditional African dishes mixed with oriental spices. Wild red berries from Isphahan soon adorn the steamed Himalayan rice. Art and cooking are my passions at an equal level. Come for dinner and the chef will take care of fine dining for a few in a place where less than 20 kilometres away people are dying of hunger.

Or cholera. Or aids.

The fine dining is perhaps a refuge, just like I take refuge in art. Refuge and relaxation are close together as concepts, I think. Nevertheless, I am often happy and relieved and absolutely relaxed with the wonderful results of both due to their therapeutic character.

Do I have the right to take refuge?
Art is cheaper than coke is what I always say.
Superficial living is not possible here, with the daily, incredible devaluations, suicidal politics and lightning-quick stockpiling of food. Sometimes, I drive to my Harare International School crying when I see how broken this beloved land is.
"Cry the beloved country."
Fortunately, Paolo Conte sings along with me as if he is in the back seat. This is how I pass the large gate of our International School every morning at five past seven sharp, happy to see how the old and trusted Security Guards always spring to attention and greet me happily. Even more so when the musical choice of the day has been approved. You always take care that your windows are open on both sides when driving through. Yesterday's Madonna appeared to be okay, today's Goldfish they do not like at all.
'Morning Mam, I am fine. And you?'
'Fine thanks, Garikai, when is my peanut butter for Fairhome ready?'
'Anytime from now Mama.' In Zimbabwe, this could mean anything.
'Thanks *Shamwari*.' Or: 'Thanks, friend.'
'Have a nice day.'

Meanwhile, it has been raining since the first of October, in the shadow of the wind. Thousands of purple blossoms are shed by the mighty Jacaranda trees. A festive entrance: that is how this purple-coloured lane that leads to the largest campus of our school feels.
I enter my little office, take off the large sunglasses – the definition of my jaw line is more or less missing – I apply my make-up and once again have the happiest face here. You should know that it is only ten past seven in the beautiful morning.
Little Miss Sunshine of our school, is what the vice-principal's wife calls me. The sun? The comedian by day and crying wolf by night. Not always, mind you. When she is not dancing, that is. At full moon.
As long as my eighty-eight students benefit from it by day, is what I always say.

I mean, I live in Africa.
These past years, my head also lives in Europe with my three children, my best and most accomplished three works of art ever. My head lives in that little apartment near the Maastricht Market, where two of the three are, and in Amsterdam.
My three children move between The City, as they call it (what?), and the *Kumusha*, or The Village, Home, or the Rural Areas of Maastricht. The soft south has welcomed them, half Belgians or half Dutchmen or African globalists, warmly. Their typical accent, which everyone is trying to place, quickly changes to English when they are together.

Thanks to the voipbuster system, mom is often asked to read this or that recipe over the phone, because the love of cooking is inherited by all three of my offspring.

Zimbabwe is under my skin.
My best, darkest African friends, the sons of the soil left one by one over these last years. Those friends taught me the ways of Zimbabwe as they saw it and, most of all, as they lived it. To them, coming back is not an option. On average, they keep five to fifteen family members alive and they themselves often perish due to homesickness in their new country.
I now design sympathy funeral cards using dried and pressed Jacaranda leaves almost monthly because there is always a death highlighting the fact that the average life expectancy is only 34 years.

Some of my expatriate colleagues at school use Zimbabwe as a transit. In three, sometimes two years' time all sites were visited: the world wonder of the Victoria Falls, the Zimbabwe ruins, the Highlands, and the luxurious *lowveld* lodges.
Several new American teachers of this school year think everything is terrific between July and September but show the first symptoms of a burn-out less than three months later, despite comfortable accommodation, generators, water tanks, electrical gates and alarm systems, all maintained by the school.
However, others adjust in no time at all, often with little children and try to make Africa their home, never mind how temporary it is. These people are the kind who go camping everywhere and integrate totally.

My Flemish friends are at a different phase in life or another African country keeping a different pace and live too far from here to come over. These friends from my former European life have agendas filled to the brim or are recovering from relationships that took too long.

My children, raised here, have stored their African youth in twelve picture books. I rummage around their rooms as sole visitor *à la recherche du temps perdu*. By now, that small, romantic cottage not far from the main house has changed into an office, library and mini-hotel intended for numerous consultants that will have to take the clay inside and kiln outside the kitchen for granted. My new passion, over the last eight years, next to art education, the twelve street kids, the fine dining and friendships, is to refine my own work.
My corals in local clay get more complicated as time goes by. They symbolise the desire for the ocean or the unattainable, the embodiment of the freedom and timelessness. Yet, the corals' curls have to be perfect. Oh well, you can never be fully satisfied, right? The largest corals are baked in a cadmium red glazing. I am concerned about this endangered organism.

My eldest students diligently research the status of the world's corals before we start this new art project at school, which this year will be called *"Endangered coral reefs"*. Art and work, everything mixes together.

Zimbabwe.
"This was once my palace. Now it is my prison." – Lady Jane Grey.
I just quote her, the good woman – *the nine day Queen*.
She should come *here* for nine days.
Here. What was once my palace, is now my prison.
The most beautiful African country, crushed, raped, abused while the world watches and waits and waits. Oh no, the world has forgotten Zimbabwe. Or better said: the world press. Afghanistan, Obama, Tibet, China, everything that is more sensational for the evening press is chosen as more important as the June 2008 elections.
Leaving is no longer possible.
Or, leaving is not the solution.
Staying is no longer a choice.
This is what I call a new start,
so fresh and refreshing as the smell
of homemade rosemary bread,
as bright as the purple snow of the Jacaranda,
as hard as the carmine red of the Flamboyants,
as soft as the gentle colours of the Frangipane blossoms,
bright, hard, and soft.
This is Zimbabwe.

This is our beginning, to introduce the most beautiful country with the sweetest people ever, done by 25 people with stories out of 25 lives.
At the same time it is a way of contemplating in honesty, reflecting on our lives in the brightness of morning light and when the fireball sun has sunk, on Sun- and Mondays.
Standing still, no longer running, not panicking, but opening up your head and heart for new energy.
Standing still more often.
Listening. Watching.
Caring for your friends in these times of tension.
Dealing with the increasing difficulties as well as enjoying the gratitude of the small, daily successes.
And find out why Zimbabwe is underneath our skin, baked in and grown on to us.
Like no other country, like no previous African country.
No expensive scrub will ever get these layers off.

BETTY TOWNSEND- COETZEE
GRANNY BETTY'S STORY

My name is Betty Townsend nee Coetzee. I turned 90 in September 2009! I am living in a senior home called Pleasant Ways, in Harare, very close to my beloved grandson Gary.
As I am in my late eighties I can say I have seen Zimbabwe growing and changing rapidly. I do feel the pain in the eyes of my people around me.

Let me tell you my story.

I was born in 1919 in Watervalboven in the north-east of South Africa. My mother, Maggie Thompson, was Scottish and had cared for her parents for many years before marrying my father relatively late in life. My father, Hendrick Coetzee, was a Guard and later an Inspector on the South African Railways. He was transferred to South West Africa (now Namibia) where I started primary school and later to Pretoria. By the time I reached Senior School we were living in Johannesburg, where my father retired and set up as a building contractor.

I left school at 16 and went to work at a large Johannesburg drapers firm called Paramount and in my spare time I did a bookkeeping course and then moved on to work as a bookkeeper. When I was 20, I married a miner, Jack van den Berg, and we had two sons, Billy and Allen. Jack died in an underground rock fall in 1949.

On the 13th February 1950 Jack's parents drove me and my two little boys up to Rhodesia to start a new life. Accommodation was very difficult to find in those days and for several years we moved from one place to another, house-sitting for people who were going on a long leave to Britain.
Around this time I was introduced to the sport of bowls and took to it like a duck to water. I often travelled to South Africa representing Avondale Sports Club and Rhodesia in bowls competitions. My name is recorded on the club Roll of Honour.

In 1964, when I was 45, I met, and with great joy, married George Townsend who worked for the Rhodesian government in the Ministry of Agriculture as an expert on tobacco.
My sons, Billy and Allen, had attended Prince Edward School for senior school and there Billy joined the Cadets and went on to follow a highly

successful career as a paratrooper in the army. In 1977 he died in a rocket attack on the eastern border of the country. His widow, Jean, and their two children moved down to South Africa.

My son Allen married young and his wife, Diana, died of an asthma attack in 1966 when their son Gary was only a few months old.

Poor Gary's mum, this sweet Diana, was not even 21 years old. Allen moved away to Umtali (now Mutare) with the baby to escape the sad memories of Salisbury but would travel up to see us every couple of weeks. When Gary was 8 months old I told Allen that I thought that my grandson was showing signs of being an anxious and unhappy baby and that I thought he should allow me and George to give him a home. Allen agreed with relief. It was quite an adjustment to be looking after a young baby again after so many years but Gary has been the love of my life and brought me so much joy. At that time I was working for Central African Building Society (CABS) and I was able to leave Gary with a very caring day-mother while I was at work and collect him at 4:30 when I finished for the day.

When Gary was three years old Allen married a lovely girl called Ria who proved to be the daughter I had never had. They had a little girl, a sister for Gary. But within two years they were divorced. This divorce in no way affected the loving relationship I have with Ria to this day.

In 1968 George and I bought land in Eastlea and built ourselves a house. Gary went to primary school at Admiral Tait Primary and then went on to Churchill High School, where his artistic talents became apparent. He left school to train as a hairdresser in London at Allan's International Hairdressing School and at the same time studied interior decor. Sadly his hairdressing career was brought to an end in a car accident in which his elbow was crushed but he returned to Harare and worked for a number of years as a partner in the firm of Ash Interior. More recently he has joined the Harare International School as the manager of all aspects of the staff housing. He is respected and loved by everybody at school and I am very proud of his accomplishments. In his free time he is still a popular design consultant!

In 1974 I retired from CABS, at 55 but I was continually asked to come back and fill in at various branches around the city when there were staffing gaps. It did not suit me to be on call in this way as I really wanted to spend more time in the garden that George and I loved.

Eventually we came to a most satisfactory arrangement where I would only work during the busy last 10 days of each month at the main branch in the middle of town.

In 1990 George and I felt that the house and garden in Eastlea were becoming too much for us and we sold it for a good price and bought into the Molly Williams Trust where our convenient little cottage and garden suited us down to the ground. In 1994 George died of cancer.

The balance of the money for our Eastlea house had been very carefully invested and brought me in a good return. At this time however, Zimbabwe began its dramatic economic decline. The returns from my investments became almost valueless, the levy for my cottage went rapidly from $ 70 to $ 7 000 a month and my initial comfortable pension of $ 10 000 a month ceased to be able to support me. I was nearing bankruptcy. At this point my daughter-in-law Jean, Billy's widow, urged me to come down to South Africa and I converted the last of my Zimbabwean money into Rand at the very disadvantageous rate available at the time and went to join her. I was very grateful for the fact that eventually George's pension had been converted into a Pound Sterling pension (because he had made his pension contributions in Pounds) and I was entitled to a £ 36 per month pension, paid quarterly in South Africa.

When I got to Jean's in Midrand however, I found that she had not investigated what would be involved in my finding accommodation and the months dragged by with the possibilities proving either far too expensive for my limited budget or with waiting lists that would mean I was unlikely to get a place for years to come. Meanwhile my relations with Jean soured miserably and I found myself in an increasingly impossible situation. This was such a stressful time that I developed shingles.

Eventually I found a shared room in a Salvation Army institution that favoured accommodating ex-Zimbabweans but fortunately I was only there for 3½ months before I was given a home by my beloved ex-daughter-in-law Ria and her husband in the granny flat of a house that they had just bought in Sabi. That day in 2004 when Doug and Ria came to fetch me, remains one of the happiest days of my life, right up there with the day I married George Townsend. I pointed out to them that the date was the 7th December, George's birthday, which made it an extra special day for me. I loved everything about living in Sabi. It was heaven.
Sadly this glorious time of living with Ria and Doug in Sabi could not last. In 2007 they had to sell their house and Doug now manages a conference centre.
I was heartbroken to leave but my compensation is that I am now close to my dearest grandson, Gary, who organised me this place at Pleasant Ways, an Old Age Home just down the road from where he works.
Gary pays my way here and is unfailingly thoughtful and loving to me. I have been here now since May last year and have settled in very comfortably. Hence, my life is really about Gary and me!

The home is well run despite the many difficulties of running such an institution in Zimbabwe. It has a most beautiful garden and the recent heavy rains have turned the lawns into a lush green carpet. Flowers and trees are blossoming!
Despite my age I still have many friends, visitors and acquaintances. Gary's friends all call me "Granny".

Gary is constantly popping in to see me, bringing me the medicines I need, extra food and special treats like sweets, grapes or other fresh fruit. He used to give me Zimbabwean currency to buy myself little things but now it has to be US dollars as the local currency has become worthless.

The staff at Pleasant Ways is kind but suffer like any institution to provide us with the daily food and the medical care. All my companions have to be assisted nowadays through friends and relatives. Some of them suffer as their grandchildren are living in the UK and seem to be totally oblivious about our current daily devaluating situation here. Often dear Gary tries to help them out as well.
Friends of his take me to church at the Highlands Presbyterian Church every Sunday, where I have been a member for decades, have helped with the flowers, and was the treasurer of the Women's Association from 1980 to 2002.

Regularly I am grateful to spend a sunny Sunday with Gary at Aad and Patrice's place. In their lovely garden, full of palms, Jacaranda and lavender, I enjoy my gin and tonic whilst the "young ones" ask me about the past, the days of yore and the stories I so enjoy telling over and over again. I enjoy their keen interest and the cooking and feel refreshed and cheerful when Gary drives me home again to Pleasant Ways.

I am sad that I can no longer read as calcification has developed in my eyes that the doctors cannot do anything about but on the other hand I enjoy watching the TV set up in my bed-sit and I have some flowers like roses and day lilies growing on the edge of my little garden that give me great pleasure.
The daily sunrises and sunsets are unforgettable and make me forget the situation we are all trapped in. I am very grateful for Gary's love and support and for my health and the fact that I am still able to take a long walk every day.
Daily I pray for the country and my wish and dream is that for the coming year the change will come and the people will stop suffering.
May Zimbabwe be soon the jewel of Southern Africa again!

THE LETTER
JUNE 2006

Letter for the King
Letter for the Minister of Foreign Affairs
Letter for the press
Letter for the Belgians

Your Highness the King!

My name is not Tonke Dragt, who wrote the wonderful *Letter for the King*. My name is Patrice Delchambre, I am Flemish and I thought I was proud of that fact. It is with great dismay that we learnt that our Embassy in Zimbabwe will be closing soon.
We are about to say goodbye to Ambassador Boudewijn Dereymaker and his unique and hard-working colleagues.
Your Majesty! Can you imagine what it feels like to have lived in Africa for 25 years, to have raised three children, and felt supported by the services of an embassy?

I am re-reading a letter that was sent from here to our King Albert in Belgium.

Can you imagine what it feels like to live in Zimbabwe at the moment? Can you imagine what it feels like when we have to say goodbye to this embassy in Harare, with all its staff, diplomats and incredibly loyal, local staff? Can you imagine what it feels like when we can all say that this was the very best embassy in twenty-five years of living abroad? Can you imagine what it feels like to live without the service, friendliness, dedication and efficiency of a very good ambassador?
Can you perhaps imagine what it feels like for all elderly Belgians for whom Zimbabwe, after wanderings in Rwanda or Congo, was to be the new and protected *Heimat*? Do you know what these elderly Belgians have to cope with at the moment? Do you know what it feels like to be active in a "pyramid emergency response system" of volunteers for three years and be able to contact and support each other weekly through a radio network?

Do you know what it feels like to know we cannot prepare ourselves properly for the more grave situations that are hanging over Zimbabwe's head?

Your Majesty, to us it seems that Zimbabwe is, politically speaking, the last place you would close down an embassy right now.
Budgetary reasons, we assume?
My family members love to travel and travelling is in our blood. Thus, we have seen a lot and love to visit embassies in each country to register ourselves. This Christmas, we stayed with friends in Luanda.
I count on my fingers how many countries and capitals there are in Africa that are, in our opinion, more expensive than this small embassy of ours. Harare's houses are modest, cost of acquisition and/or rental are lower than in most surrounding countries.
Every expatriate and Belgian knows this.
Your Majesty, we are halfway through 2006 already. What difference do ten years more or less make? For you? For us...everything!
What does it matter to be of service to Belgians for a few years more, so that we can function well in a country that is dramatically falling apart? We are already *and* unfortunately more than halfway down the road to a suicidal Zimbabwe. The situation, economically, politically and also mentally no longer needs to be explained.
The course each of us has taken has made us realise that our Embassy is desperately needed here, the pyramid system is essential, the support to all Belgians is vital. At this moment, we Belgians feel abandoned.
Forgotten.
And this in a country that is abandoned by every god and of which most of the population watches depressed and apathetic. The farmers have lost their farms. The Belgians their embassy. The Shona their soul.
The pyramid work and all its support disappears, everything crumbles. Are we, Belgians, of no importance here? Of no real or economic importance?
Your Majesty!
If you know what all of this feels like, then only one question remains!
We ask you and beg you, please reconsider the Minister of Foreign Affairs' decision.
Please accept my humble, yet concerned, greetings.

Patrice Delchambre
Hathaway Close, 2, Chisipite,
Harare
Zimbabwe

That was early June, 2006.
The reply to this letter, hand-delivered to the Palace, I received on June 26, 2006. My name misspelled, but this could happen to any dear old principal private secretary to any king. It is fantastic that a reply was even written! Right?

C/TD/P533.211|

Dear madam Delachambre,

I have the honour to have been ordered by the King to inform you of your letter's arrival on June 26, 2006.
The monarch has duly noted the contents of your writing.

Sincerely,

J. van Ypersele
Principal private secretary to the King.

It is now two years later.
Nothing remains of the original, fully developed pyramid telephone cascade system. However, a new core group has formed on the initiative of the Pretoria embassy in which Walloon newcomers, without experience with the old system, also take part.
By writing emails to the Gentlemen in Pretoria, I have really had to draw attention to us Belgians here, because between the departure of the charming last Belgian ambassador in 2006 and mid-October, last year 2007, everything remained quiet.
Last year, we celebrated the fifteenth of November in our garden, on our own initiative, in the presence of "the gentlemen from Pretoria" and next week we are holding this reception again in Pangolin Lodge, close by in a suburb called Borrowdale. At this lodge, run by my friend Marijke Alcock, living is wonderful if you want to work in peace as a consultant and love privacy at the edge of the city. Several hotels have already closed due to lack of water, or still open for a little while to rake in some cash. The stench there is indescribable.
A Belgian military attaché sometimes visits to explain to us Zimbabwe's situation. Should it come to an evacuation, the French will put us in their aeroplane, we are assured.

If you realise that the radio handsets distributed by the Belgian government are hardly working or not working at all, you wonder how the Belgians, young and especially old, can ever be notified or evacuated. The network of cell phones has been hopeless over these past months. If the borders are ever closed, you wonder if a military aeroplane would even be allowed to land here. Our question, whether the medical emergency kit, flown back to Brussels with the closure of the embassy two years ago, is allowed to return is a closed matter, the attaché tells us. We should not dream. Great, my husband, a medical doctor, has offered his services to the Belgian Delegation yet is ignored.

At least we know what to do. Just in case.

CLAIRE INGRAM
SHAPES OF WOMANHOOD

My name is Claire Ingram. There have been other names.
I was Claire Saul in my girlhood, skipping and singing along with the breeze on the farm as it caressed golden love through my curls.
My parents were from Scotland, where my mother's heart never left, and where I laid her to rest not long ago.
I had two brothers and a beloved sister and we grew up on an isolated farm in central Zimbabwe.
I followed my father over every inch of our land, my footsteps smudged within his, absorbing his lessons, dancing my tomboy girlhood in wide open spaces, on a farm where horizons were familiar because we owned them, where sunshine glowed on all things good, where my soul and myself were one.

My womanhood started as Claire Rothschild, when I married and moved from the farm to a high-rise flat in Hillbrow, frightened by claustrophobic, jostling crowds, apprehensively unprepared for the life gently nudging in my womb. I was on foreign terrain, in an unfamiliar tribe. I focussed my energy inwardly and greedily enveloped my unborn daughter in complete, absolute love.

Jess was born and as I gazed in spellbound awe at my firstborn, I felt, for the first time, completely woman. I immediately understood the unconditional love that my mother had always embraced me in. With this womanhood, I realised too, an unfamiliar passion within- an overpowering urge to nurture and protect, at all costs- even at the expense of my own life.

I carried my son alone once he was conceived.
The marriage was broken, as was my heart. Nic, my son, as tiny as he was, taught me the strength of endurance. My womanhood dictated, nay demanded, that I remain steadfast in order to protect, to nurture. After heartbreaking but immensely valuable lessons learnt from this marriage, I began to contemplate life from the periphery, as a divorcee and single parent.
As a failure, I thought then.

"The sun has receded and winter has come. Just as the leaves have been swept off the trees, so too has my soul been stripped. It is now a grey, cold rock, unyielding, impenetrable. With the onset of spring, will it bloom again?"

It did. My womanhood embarked on a new path when I became Claire Ingram. As Steve's wife, I was able to refocus my energy outwardly this time, and it was safe to shower him with all my love. This I did wholeheartedly.

We celebrated the births of two more daughters, Jayd and Holly, and our family moved back home to the farm- to my place on earth, where the roots of familiar and well-loved *Msasa* trees mingle with the roots of my girlhood. There, we endured hardships and successes, terror and love. All of it, we braved together.

We shared adventures on the back of Steve's bike.

We pondered problems with heads bowed together.

We grieved, we laughed, a lot.

It all seemed so fragile, too good to be true.

This womanhood, so drenched in love, was soon to be shattered.

I was brushing my teeth one morning, when, looking out the window, I spotted a figure skulking in the bush, cowering with menacing nuisance and dark intent. I scanned for more, and there they were, blended in our African bush. They were stealthily advancing towards our house, towards my family.

Steve was at the other end of the house and the eight young schoolchildren, who were boarding with me, were all still fast asleep. He came through and together we watched, the fear pulsing in the static between us. This was the start of a journey of terror. Over the months we were confronted with terrible, terrifying menace and torture. Eventually we had to abandon the farm for fear of our lives. Our friend Alan had recently been murdered on his farm next door, so we knew that this menace was darkly real.

We threw my parents' possessions into whatever containers we could find, and the trucks drove 30 years of accumulated memories, clutter and valuables away, amid clouds of dust and ululations. We then packed up what remained in our house, although I insisted that the house remain curtained and furnished for our return.

That was never to be.

We moved into Harare, battle-weary, bewildered, and defeated.

My womanhood now was reduced to a hollow, parched shell and I could feel my soul rattling around, caged within an empty prison.

I longed for our home, our place on earth, my freedom of space and spirit.

Then Steve died. At the age of 42, he had a freak accident and broke his neck. He refused treatment, not wanting to burden his family. He died a humble, noble, bravely gallant man.
Without him, my womanhood donned the heaviest, most suffocating mantle imaginable. I was left bereft, swirling in mists of excruciating sadness, howling into a bottomless hollow of anguished grief.
My children watched me closely and soon, the fear that was etched in their faces roughly shook my numb, bewildered womanhood awake.
I began to realise that their response to this horror would reflect directly from my own. I have come to appreciate that success in life is measured by the gallantry with which appalling experiences are survived with grace. My womanhood suddenly became streamlined with singular purpose, to nurture and protect our children on both of our behalves.
I became a widow, a widow with intent.

Two weeks after Steve died, my parents and brother were held hostage and were subjected to two days of beatings, torture and terror. My father was humiliated shamelessly. My mother dived onto my brother whilst he was being mercilessly beaten with logs from the fire. She sustained injuries that she was not even aware of, in her quest to protect her son. The heavy mist that I was enshrouded in began to swirl slowly.
Again, my family was under threat, I had to rouse myself.

I nursed my mother as she gradually took to her bed more and more, always stoically Scottish, never complaining, always completely committed to her love for us. My womanhood mothered my mother. I soothed her, I stroked her beloved face, I called her by her pet name –the name that her mother used to whisper to her- "my wee lamb". Without words, she had my assurance to carry her torch, to shine her gentle light. I kissed her goodbye, my lips dry then, gone from my womanhood in a gasp, was my mother's complete, unconditional love.

By this time, my sister, my soul's best friend, my confidante throughout our girlhood and now as women-sisters, was becoming gravely ill with cancer. I nursed her with every fibre of my being. My womanhood was mother, sister, protector, desperate healer.

I wrote to her, keeping vigil at her bedside, finely tuned to her every breath.

I massaged you through your labour
with Sarah,
pregnant myself
I soothed your pain
and excitedly reassured you.

*Now I massage your agony
this time without any reassurance
of hope or recovery.
This time,
the only assurance
is death.*

*I walked behind you
as your bridesmaid
gazing in pride at your beauty
your smile
your radiance.*

*Now I trail after you
as your nursemaid,
catheter instead of bridal train.
And I gaze aghast at
how thin you are
how weak
how sick.*

*I stood with you at your 21st
feeling as if it was my own party.
I was so excited for you.
We greeted your friends in unison
and danced the night away,
celebrating.*

*Now I stand guard
at your bedroom door
feeling as if it is my own death.
I greet your friends
and usher them in
with whispers and tears
and I sob the night away
in desperate, helpless desolation.
We used to stick posters up in our room together
and giggle over gorgeous guys.
Now we ponder over
medical files together,
trying to make sense of this madness
trying to find a way to conquer this bastard.
No giggles now.*

We used to count down the days
until our birthdays,
excited beyond ourselves
for the big event.

Now we are counting down the days
until your death,
dreading your departure beyond all explanation
beyond all belief
beyond all injustice.

We used to phone each other
from wherever we were
pouring love through the lines
and asking to send love to friends.
Now I whisper to you,
still pouring love
and I ask you
longingly, secretly
"Please, say hi to Steve."

I used to gently prick your feet
with needles,
taking out thorns,
reflecting on the day that we had shared.
Now I prick your arms
with needles of morphine,
to ease the agony this evil, gluttonous cancer is inflicting on you.

We used to share perfumes
Anaïs Anaïs and Impulse
the room like a bouquet of roses
Now you smell of muti and ether
and dressings and morphine
and traces of a deeper, darker, sinister smell the smell of death.

When my sister died, my womanhood, already orphaned, became desolate. However, being a custodian of her three beautiful children relieves my grief and enables her to extend her love to her children through me.

I have started writing, partially therapeutically but mainly in order to try and pass on some of the lessons I am learning.

I am teaching in Harare, where Patrice is a colleague and a dear friend.

I do not know what guise my womanhood will come to do next.

What I do know is this: My womanhood is not to be denied or ignored.

It is to be encountered, acknowledged and honoured, held in high awareness. In holding it in this way, I have come to know a deeper silence and stillness, a wisdom deeper than I would have thought possible.
And all of this in the midst of raging storms.
I am emerging from an ocean of grief, from the sorrow of many deaths, from the inevitability of chaos and tragedy.
Within the aftermath of the triumph of destruction, I know that within every adversity is the seed of an equal or greater benefit.
Life is to be lived, laughter to be laughed, joy to be enjoyed.
My womanhood has embraced the tremendous triumph of life.

Singled out...

I remember watching, when I was married to dad, a documentary on single parenting. What stuck in my mind was the report of how duo-parents generally operate and co-operate with their children. An analogy to a playground was made, where a couple was standing under a jungle-gym, watching their child climb. The mother was anxiously coaxing the child to "come down, that's high enough..." while the father was encouraging the child "come on, man, it's fine – go up another step". I am very aware, as a single parent, of having to establish a balance, within myself, as being both mother and father. It is hard to do this, because I have to, at times, push aside my maternal "coaxing- down" (which shouts the loudest inside me) and then summon up courage to tell you to "go higher", even if you do not want to.

I remember one such day – not in a playground, though. It happened in the middle to the bush in Hwange. Holly and I were bird watching in camp and the guide, Roderick, walked past with his AK slung over his shoulder. He had been driving that morning with us and had impressed us with his uncanny eyesight and bush knowledge. Holly watched him walking past and ran up to ask him where he was going. He said he was going to the nearby pan to have a look at the game. Holly leapt in the air and asked if she could please, please go... Immediately my maternal voice shouted "no". But another voice objected to my initial response.
I want to instil in you guys a love for fun, for adventure, for "one step higher". Of course, this is without being reckless.
Maternal recklessness is far, far inferior to that of her counterpart. I let Holly go, and then ran after them on the path to quiz Roderick: 'Are you sure, sure it is ok for Holly to go with you (Mr. armed guard)?'

He reassured me and off they walked down the path, tall, golden grass brushing them on both sides, dust scuffed up and hanging luminously in the hot, hot sun, her sun-white ponytail in stark contrast to that casually-slung AK.
I turned back, my mum voice screaming at me.
Then I sat at the gate, waiting, chewing, searching the road, my heart in my mouth.
What if, what if, what if?

I heard their chatter long before I saw them returning, ecstatic, with tales of tall giraffes and zebra stripes blurring in the distance.
This is a day my girl will remember for the rest of her life.
A day of African savannahs, wild herds, adventure.
I weighed up the balance of parenting, and today, I acknowledged that I am not a bad dad!

goofingram@gmail.com

WE ARE TESTING THE NETWORK
6 NOVEMBER 2008

I am testing the different communication networks one after the other today via two mobile handsets and via the landline.
Nothing, *nada*.
Waste of time.
Once again messages are not getting through and often you need to dial twenty to thirty times before you can reach someone at all. I try the international operators on the 966 number but immediately get an answering machine croaking: "Your call has been placed in a queue. Please hold or try again later." I hold and that same sentence gets repeated about fifteen times and then everything stops as I am cut off. I try some friends in Cape Town, and kids and mums in the Netherlands and Belgium through the landline and on the two cell phones lying around the house. After three quarters of an hour, I give up. There are probably no international lines today.

Through the school's email system, we receive word that later on, there will be no more paper at ZESA, the Zimbabwe Electricity Supply Authority, and at Tell One, the national phone company.
This means that you need to call them to request your bills. Ordering bills, "No ma'm, that is no longer possible. No, ma'm, no more fuel either", not just printing paper. The question is what is the magic number you need to call to settle all bills. "No, you cannot pay in US dollars, either. But ma'm, there is no Zimcash available at the moment. We can't help you."
We leave it, for today. They will find us, I hope. The next day at work I hear that all the phone lines have been stolen for the copper for the fourth time in two years. And when I come home, the landline has ceased working completely as well. And this lasts for ten long days.
Welcome home.

HANS VAN HOOREWEGHE
THE SORROW OF ZIMBABWE

Johan Verminnen sings about Brussels while I am driving through Harare. I am singing along in the car, but my mind does not wander off. When driving around this city you'd better set your mind on the traffic. Traffic lights often do not work. And when they do work, you must take into account the fact that red lights are often ignored in this country.
Holes in the road wear out not only your tires but also your rims. The blazing headlights of oncoming traffic are not dipped, thus making you blind, running the risk of mowing someone off the road, driving off the road or colliding with the person driving in front of you who did not switch on his rear lights or who does not have any rear lights at all.

Better not to drive around in this town at night, is what they commonly say over here. My friend's son drove his car into a lamp post recently. A write off. The car, that is. The lamppost had been a total loss for a few years. His son could have lost a lot more as well.
In Zimbabwe, you are allowed to drive a car at sixteen. In Zimbabwe, you can also smoke weed, get behind the wheel, stone drunk and ignore all speed limits without running the risk of getting a serious fine.
Combine all of this and sooner or later, you get an accident involving a teenager.

"In ruins I don't know you, oh, you have changed strangely..." it seems as if Johan Verminnen is reading my mind. This city has been my home for twelve years. Twelve years ago, this city was deserving of its name, *Sunshine City*. Cheerful shopping streets, nice restaurants, art galleries and craft shops, where tourists enjoyed the many beautiful things offered by this country. Now, twelve years later, you could almost call this city a ruin, even though the sun is still shining and the Jacarandas are losing their flowers at this time of the year, camouflaging the collapse with a beautiful purple blanket.
Then you wonder whether every country in Africa is doomed to decline from the moment of gaining its independence. In Zaire, they started this process earlier, thus succeeding in ruining everything sooner.
Zimbabwe is no exception to this rule. They just set to work a bit later here. Nothing new to me, but still unexpected.

Before I, together with my wife, a three-week-old baby and his almost two-year-old brother, moved to Zimbabwe to start up a small business. I lived in Mobutu's Zaire: five years of making plastic shoes for a few adventurous Brugesians and five years of keeping a tea factory running for an Antwerp baron. Finally, the genocide in a close neighbouring country made life for a Belgian in Kivu impossible.

Ten years in total, during which time I came to the same daily conclusion that the same standards and values did not apply in Zaire as in Belgium, where I used to teach at a technical school. Ten years did not suffice though to make clear to me that this was not only the case in Zaire, but in almost every country on this continent.

Harare.

I arrived in January 1997, suffered all fears of the newly self-employed and lived through the first crash of the Zimbabwe dollar in November. President Mugabe was under pressure to pay his war veterans a considerable bonus without having drawn up a budget. Back then I regularly listened to the car radio. In those days, there were still interesting DJs who played fun music. The only thing on the radio nowadays is the president's party propaganda and music to the beat of crushing maize into flour. When I heard on the radio about the fast decline of value of the local currency, I could not believe it. I had just lived through ten years of hyperinflation in Zaire. I did not need this in Zimbabwe. When leaving Zaire I had told everyone there how beautiful and stable Zimbabwe was. The land of the future, an example for Africa! The business had just taken off, loans were being paid off and the future was indeed looking magnificent! "This will not happen." I can still hear myself saying out loud in the car. But it did and it still is.

It has been approximately ten years now that I have been battling the zeroes. When I arrived in Zimbabwe, three Zimbabwe Dollars were worth one American Dollar. Meanwhile, they deleted three to ten zeroes from the local currency on the silly slogan: "from zeroes to heroes". This heroic action did not, of course, amount to nothing. It boils down to getting five-followed-by-25-zeroes Zimbabwe dollars for one American dollar. Do not ask me what to call five followed by 25 zeroes. Moreover, no-one has any interest in this completely valueless currency. Now we all do our transactions in American dollars. Way easier and less risk of losing money. It has one great disadvantage, it is illegal and you could end up in prison. Could, that is. Nowadays, most state officials have become so corrupt that it is possible to buy your way out of any unpleasant situation.

I have known days when I handed clients a bill for a thousand euro, albeit in Zimbabwe dollars, and two weeks later that same amount was paid in Zimbabwe dollars. Painfully, that same amount in Zimbabwe dollars was then barely worth ten euro. Hard to keep a business running on that basis

but certainly worth running the risk to start illegally working in foreign exchange. The problem with these American dollars is the lack of small change on the market. Recently, I received a packet of gum as change for half a dollar and I had to select something two dollars worth more in the store as change on a five dollar note. Or fifty South-African rand. Because, regardless of the exchange rates, one dollar is worth 10 rand in Zimbabwe. Easier this way! Frustration, anger and fear at the business take its toll on life at home. Especially when running the business together with your wife. "Never going into business with your partner" only gets a meaning once you are in business with your partner. But there are even worse circumstances which can thwart the development of a happy family life. Over the years and in spite of difficult working conditions, we did succeed in buying our own house and our family in the mean time comprised of four children. By the end of the nineties, you could buy a house over here for the same price as a four-wheel drive vehicle, so I sold the car and bought a house instead. A house with a pool similar to many houses in Harare. In this pool, Nathan, our youngest at just two and a half years old, drowned, one Sunday morning in winter, May 2004. That morning, I was not home. I received a call from my wife screaming down the phone. I did not understand any of it so I raced home to find my drowned child in her arms. Both were soaking wet. In Zimbabwe, you cannot count on an ambulance showing up at your door shortly after calling them. Here, you need to put your wife and child, while hoping he is not dead, in the car and drive to the hospital, as quickly as possible, honking your horn, driving through red lights, driving into another car. Once there, you need to walk into the hospital, holding your motionless little boy in your arms, and go straight to the emergency room. Here you stand at the operating table, next to someone whom you think is a doctor.
"Ah, Hail, doctors," Willem Vermandere sings.
And then you hear that your child has deceased.
I have been wearing contacts for twenty years, even though my eyes are too dry; *keratoconus*. It can only be remedied through a corneal transplant or by wearing contact lenses.
Transplant? No thank you. I'd rather bear the contacts. Wearing them has never been as comfortable as in those days.
Burying a child in Zimbabwe?
You cannot bear burying a child on a cemetery in a remote corner of Harare. You only need to have visited a cemetery here once to know this. Your child deserves somewhere nicer.
In Zaire, we were all expats. In Zimbabwe, I lost that expat feeling somewhat and my circle of friends consisted more of "people from here". One of these friends owns a beautiful piece of land in Juliasdale, a hamlet in the mountainous East of Zimbabwe.
Kerry proposed burying Nathan there.
"That's what friends are for", they simply say here.

After the shocking discovery that they, all too obviously, performed a post-mortem, my wife and I dressed Nathan, put him in his coffin, closed the coffin and put it into the boot of the car. This is all possible in Zimbabwe.
Here, you put your deceased child into the boot of your car and you drive 250 kilometres to bury him in your friend's garden.
On our way to Juliasdale, we were stopped by the police asking us what was in the boot. After explaining that we were going to bury our child, we were allowed to simply drive on. By my father's request we played Willem Vermandere's *Runeke's litany* during Nathan's burial. Willem Vermandere, a well-known West-Flemish artist and, together with Toon Hermans, my father's favourite artist, composed this song for his deceased grandchild.
West-Flemish music in the East of Zimbabwe.
It took a long time before the realisation of what had just happened hit me and I started thinking things through. In this situation, you gain another perspective on life and it also has a baleful influence on your relationship. You keep wondering why your wife was sitting in an unknown man's lap while getting a loving massage on the evening after the funeral.
During the first 25 years of my life I had rarely been confronted with death, even though my family was large enough: my parents were still alive, along with four brothers, a sister, about thirty uncles and aunts, and about seventy cousins. The chance of bereavement statistically was rather large. It goes to show that man needs his luck in life. In Zimbabwe you experience what death feels close by. Burying a Belgian child in Zimbabwe. A truly Belgian child; Flemish father, Walloon mother.

The Walloon mother I met in Zaire. It could not be otherwise, since I did not speak sufficient French while living in Belgium to pick up a Walloon girl and my father read *'t Pallieterke* (a fiercely pro-Flemish weekly).

But you take charge of your life all over again, even though it has changed. And even though your relationship has taken a terrible knock, one day you are back in that same hospital in Harare, this time to welcome a child into the world. A girl, her name was Léanne. Two years ago, I had three sons and one daughter; suddenly, I had two sons and two daughters. And then family life in Zimbabwe needs to take over again. There are no school buses or trains here and your child cannot cycle to school, to the scouting or friends.

Several schools, vast city; you can easily drive 100 kilometres a day in order to get the children where they need to or want to be.
Here, you need to pay several stores a visit in order to come up with a decent meal. Then you get home and there is neither electricity nor water. When this happened twelve years ago, this would be a news item: The next day the electricity company apologised publicly for the power cut in a

certain municipality. It was not necessary to apologise for the loss of water, because there never was much – Zimbabwe knows long periods of drought. Despite this, there was always water that could be drunk straight from the tap. For months on end, not a drop comes out off the tap in Glen Lorne, the suburb in which I am now living by myself, situated just outside Harare, in a valley, with snakes in the garden, monkeys in the trees and a neighbour with a well. The neighbours, are a family by the name of Mugabe but apparently no relation to "the Mugabe". Mister Mugabe does not want to supply the neighbours with water from his well. Mrs Mugabe, however, allows it. A whistle from the Mugabe family's gardener suffices to make my gardener swing into action the moment Mister Mugabe has left the house. Then the garden hose is slung across the wall and my water tank gets filled with water from Mister Mugabe's well. I would like to thank Mrs Mugabe for this, but I cannot because Mister Mugabe might sense something amiss. I do not wish to cause Mrs Mugabe a beating and I cannot make do without water.

Electricity is another problem. When I do not have any, the Mugabe family does not either. On these occasions you cannot sling a cable across the wall. Then you need a generator.

In Zimbabwe, they have open coal mines and power plants running on coal. They possess one of the largest dams in the world with all the works to produce a lot of electricity. Yet, more and more generators are switched on in this city. Few Zimbabweans lie awake worrying about global warming. Most are tossing and turning in their beds while wondering how to survive the next day, how to pay for tuition and how their country will fare. It happens to me as well, the tossing and turning in bed. However, it is better than tossing and turning in a bed in Belgium.

My father used to be a bird lover who guided people through the coastal nature area called "the Zwin" for years. This was his passion, together with music. Listening to music, writing music, conducting music, playing music, recording music. Anything to do with music. In his office there was always music playing in the background. He was a school principal and thus he could afford it to listen to music at work, albeit more quietly than at home. At home, you sometimes got the impression that he had invited Aalter's brass band for a rehearsal in our living room. No wonder my mother started taking yoga classes. Six children, most of them obsessed with music, and a brass band conductor in one house compels a housewife to find peace somewhere.

Now, the children have all left and no more wind or percussion instruments are being played. Yet, she continued her classes and Paula has become a yoga instructor. She is kept busy. Clearly, more and more people in Belgium need rest and meditation.

Back to my father. Years ago, he jumped out of bed in the middle of the night and into the ditch to record the song of a nightingale.

Hubert Van Hooreweghe died almost two years ago, but the song of the nightingale died long before that. Actually not his song; the nightingale was no longer. The little creature must have died a poisonous death or, like myself, have decided that there are more beautiful biotopes in the world than in Belgium. Despite rarely being confronted with death before, during the last four years I got more than my fair share. My mother-in-law also died shortly after Nathan passed away. But I do not miss my mother-in-law.

The night is seldom quiet in Zimbabwe.

I have a bird in my garden, a night jar someone told me, who sings almost all the way through the night even though his song is not as beautiful as the one offered by the Belgian nightingale. The crickets and frogs in Africa make sure that the night is filled with sounds and that helps when you have trouble sleeping.

Once, we took a plant from Zaire for my father-in-law. By the way, he is still among the living. There probably were some eggs of a Congolese cricket left in there, which, after hatching, suddenly provided the Walloon summer nights with an African accent. It lasted until the Walloon winter set in but that was a long time ago.

So I sometimes toss and turn restlessly in my bed, alone. Thankfully not too often; I am a solid sleeper but, like so many in Zimbabwe, I sometimes wonder how it will go on. I make Belgian pralines in a country where people die of starvation, cholera and AIDS, while seeing my children every second weekend. And I am a family man.

Meanwhile I have become more acquainted with the unknown man massaging my wife the evening after Nathan's funeral. Less so with me than with my wife, whom I can almost call my ex-wife.

Getting divorced in Zimbabwe.

A farce, just like everything else in this country. Earlier today, I was at the Supreme Court. The receptionist was eating cooked maize with his hands, picking it out of an enamelled jar. Guaranteed made in China, similar to most pots and pans which can be found here with bursting enamel. While there was something in front of him on the table resembling a register, he did not write anything down. I think due to the fact that he did not have a pen.

A Shona conversation lasting a few seconds with my lawyer of which I did not understand a thing and we were allowed to proceed. Through dark hallways, since there was no electricity. Maybe this was for the best,

because then you notice the almost complete lack of the parquet floor significantly less. Somewhat similar to a jigsaw puzzle, but with the majority of pieces missing. It was raining and there must have been a hole in the courthouse roof because water was coming down the stairs. All the way down the stairwell were stacks of files, soaking wet. I suddenly imagined myself slipping on the stairs of the Supreme Court and breaking an arm or a leg. Would you be able to carry this to justice?
Madam Judge made us wait for her again.
Only for half an hour this time.
Last time for two hours.
Last time she apologised.
She claimed not to have received a 2009 diary yet and thus she had been unable to note down the appointment.
I saw her driving again in a Mercedes, last model S-class. She drives around without number plates. This lady is supposed to decide what will happen to my family.

Six months after Léanne's birth, I got a Walloon plead to leave the house. A result of the damage caused to a relationship by the pressure in this country and the loss of a child. I complied. Sadly enough, the Flemish still give in too often to the Walloons' wishes. The law prescribes in Zimbabwe that in case of separation, the children are to remain with the mother. A pity that my future ex-wife does not drink nor does drugs. Those are almost the only circumstances in which a father can gain custody over his children in this country.
My three children.

I used to have four, until the night she invited her boyfriend, the masseur. It was around Valentine's Day, you see. That night, he ran over Léanne. A summer evening in February in Harare. Léanne had just started walking and wanted to prove this with a walk in the driveway when *Sir* drove in. *Sir* had his head in the clouds and *Madam* had no idea where her daughter was at the moment she opened the electrical gate from afar. Love is blind, no question about it. I saw Léanne in the same emergency room of that same hospital.
I saw everything that I had lived through two years before all over again. For the first time in my life I pinched my arm in order to wake up.
I made the same announcement to the same three children as I had two years before. Only this time, it was a little sister and not a little brother.
We buried Léanne next to her little brother, now almost two years ago. Kerry allowed us to. "That's what friends are for."
Just like with Nathan, we put Léanne's coffin in the boot and brought her to Juliasdale. We were not stopped by the police this time and Willem Vermandere could not sing since there was no electricity.

Now I have two sons, Roderik and Mathias, and a daughter, Hannah, whom I would like to take care of, which a father is apparently not readily allowed to do in Zimbabwe. My children are now fourteen, twelve and ten years old. They were supposed to start the new school year last week. They are all in private schools. With a month's wages a state school teacher can buy a few pieces of bread. Not enough to support a family, but enough to go on strike.

Since the state schools are on strike, the government decided that the private schools should not open either. At best, my children can go back to school early next week but I can count myself lucky. Their mother is leaving for a trip for about three weeks and so they are staying with me. With or without school. My other two children whom I knew and loved are not coming back. The Zimbabwe I knew and loved is not coming back either.

But there is one big difference. Zimbabwe can come back, even while being different. This is a great country with great people.

In spite of all adversity, I have grown to love this country. I hope, and mostly do so for the Zimbabweans (I can still return to Belgium, even though the nightingale does not sing there any longer) that this country will rise from the ashes. Zimbabwe and its population do not deserve anything less.

My name is Hans Van Hooreweghe and I have written this because a friend asked me to. A friend who listened to my story over these last few years, maybe to the point of weariness.

A friend who immediately cleared her schedule and rounded up her friends to help me set up my business again after the mother of my children ransacked it.

A friend who just sent me a text inviting me for dinner.

As she often does.

She knows a bachelor's refrigerator is often empty.

Thank you, Patrice.

It did not do any good to my health; a packet of cigarettes and a bottle of wine per page!

hans@veldemeers.com

HEAT, WATER AND HISTORY
SUNDAY, 9 NOVEMBER 2008

This is our suburb: *"The place of too much water"*. This was explained to me by my Shona friends in 1994. And the pride we felt. Nothing was going to happen to us here, you see – *Eternal Water*.
I will tell you about the Chisipite of today. Sunday, forty degrees. No water out of the borehole and no electricity for three days.
In the distant past there were yearly floods in the area where these two cottages, now ours, stand. Early in the morning, during the winter months, there is a romantic white fog. During the rainy season everything feels wonderfully tropic and humid.

Our residence, a little over one acre, belongs to the upmarket area close to Harare. At the moment the nouveau riche are building everywhere like crazy. Megalomaniacal palaces. We have kept the two old, charming mini-houses in their original state, one with a Portuguese feel, the other in a Greek style, with round rooms. The past has not been demolished, nor has a new house been built; the grand luxury in neo-colonial English country style. Fix what was once old, lay down mosaic style floors made out of broken tiles in the Portuguese house. The Greek pillars that I found overgrown in the garden were used in the creation of the terrace of the second cottage. Walls brought down, round rooms built, bathrooms renovated and that was it.
The official 1930 title deeds mention that no one other than those belonging to a European race is ever allowed to live at this place, let alone become its owner. *Those were the days*. Sometimes I show it to my Shona friends over food and drinks. This was the Africa of the past, but no African was allowed to live on our property. In their own country that is.

Meanwhile, we are close friends with the large Nyadore family a little down the avenue, out of our close and up the next street. These were the first Africans who were finally allowed to buy land, as the first family, after the segregation, in not even the smartest part of town. This family has six children. Papa Nyadore, a devout catholic, later became a successful businessman and is mostly known for his integrity, generosity and love for the extended family system. Their eldest daughter and eldest son most certainly experienced the treatment of being smart darkies before freedom was granted.

Both were the first to be admitted to "white" boarding schools thanks to a bishop who saw how smart these happy rascals were. The children prayed however, on their bare knees every semester to be delivered from their suffering later in the sixties; their treatment in these "family oriented English boarding schools" was that terrible. Jameson, the eldest, is an introverted, quiet, private man. He is nearly fifty. He told me, during one of our nights on the town at the ancient Meikles Hotel, how he was treated as the one and only Black man living with all these Rhodies. Another human who explained the ways of the past in a painful way. But I remained seated, listening; shy with vicarious shame, feeling sick because of one of many anecdotes.

'Patrice, I still dream, how they grabbed me and pushed my head upside down in the toilets and how they flushed all their collected faeces around me, forcing me to swallow. Or drown in it.'

Thirty years later, Jameson returned to the local scene, not unlike dad, as a very successful and established businessman.

Jameson attended an "old boys" celebration at his old St. Georges, two or three decennia later. The boys, who did all this stuff to him, were there of course. They recognised him immediately by his tall, proud demeanour, dressed in an elegant and expensive suit, and they became not white, but ice-green and promptly stood up and disappeared from the "big reunion function" with their blond big breasted Rhodie women.

They probably went out to puke.

Jameson owns a lot of my coral and dish collection. Most of it, actually. The harm done to him will never fade away, however. Not even if I gave him a hundred of my corals. History's pain cannot be rewritten by one man. His arrogance towards some people I do understand.

Indeed. And you will be surprised by the amount of young families who still believe in this British school system seventy years later. Never think about an alternative, think about nothing. Snap the whip, with its vice captains and girls and their scary snitch systems. Caning, or corporal punishment. All this represses the ranks downwards, even more so in real life. Treat your darkies like in the old days and justify yourself by beating your wife. Reproduce knowledge; do not even think about analyzing. Learn by heart and question nothing.

On October 24, during an emotional African service in the catholic "Nazareth house", we buried Daddy Nyadore. His passing was unnecessary, as is the death of a lot of people here. If a hospital was able to apply just one pacemaker, he would still be among us. Probably. Who knows?

For a whole week, hundreds of people visited the family during the day and stayed until late in the night.

It was touching to be a part of these gentle people who, together, stayed with Mama Nyadore every moment.
From several shops food was delivered free for four long days in order to feed hundreds of visitors each afternoon and evening.
Jameson described his father's life and work in a touching way during the African service. And repeated the thing his 84-year-old father was so sad about in his final years: *'Three things are gone in this country: The Rule of Law, Democracy and Tolerance. Tolerance is the attitude of mind, the respecting of the outcome of elections.'*

Alas, alas.
Daddy Nyadore is gone.
It was too much for him as a very righteous man. The old pain around his heart and the pain in his soul. He, who loved his own Zimbabwe so much. He who had achieved so much.

Death is nothing at all.
It does not count.
I have only slipped away into the next room.
Nothing has changed.
Everything remains exactly as it was. I am I, and you are you, and the old life that we lived so fondly together is untouched, unchanged. Whatever we were to each other, that we are still. Call me by the old familiar name.
Speak of me in the easy way which you always used. Put no difference in your tone.
Wear no forced air of solemnity or sorrow. Laugh as we always laughed at the little jokes we enjoyed together. Play, smile, think of me, pray for me.
Let my name be spoken without an effort, without the shadow of a ghost upon it.
Life means all that it ever meant. It is the same as it ever was.
There is absolute and unbroken continuity.
What is death but a negligible accident?
Why should I be out of mind because I am out of sight?
I am but waiting for you, for an interval, somewhere very near, just around the corner. All is well.
I am just absent, but very close to you.

Is death nothing at all?
There is so much death in this life I always think.
And the water of our borehole, that I promised the family for the funeral, is now gone. The final hundred litres I delivered to the family, without knowing it would be our last drinking water.
Two years ago, we paid to strike a water well, 17 meters deep. So many thousands of US dollars later.

For two weeks now, the water level has dropped so dramatically in the area that many families are without a drop of water. Even though wells are being drilled like there is no tomorrow. No communication, no soil research.

The diviners, the water augurs, respected by every single water specialist are doing great business. Municipal water out of the tap, it is a rarity. For almost a year and a half.

We also enter day seven with no electricity. The candlelit nights seem shorter than ever.

Quickly, quickly. Quick as lightning. Action! Now it is Sunday.

Drag the tables outside and quickly ring up some friends. We will throw all the thawed, stockpiled meat and food on the *braai*.

The water out of the neighbour's borehole came in containers and buckets, but now there is also a large electricity fault in this part of town. So, it is not possible to draw up water. You get it from friends and you buy drinking water in the supermarket.

A person will go a long way to get a shower, a wash, and the only positive thing is that there is an increase in socialising.

The level of concentration during long meetings at school is a little lower than normal, but hey; we are all in this together. The absence of water after a period of five weeks of incredible heat is a concern, so is the almost weekly increase in prices at the dollar shops. The regular supermarkets are empty, clean and empty. Some of the numerous shelves look like strange scary art pieces.

I cannot even sell the clandestine pictures I took at the end of September to Dutch or Belgian newspapers.

Zimbabwe is out.

On Saturday, the soldiers apparently decided not to accept the long lines in front of the banks any longer and started to deal out beatings. When the army goes amok, we have got some interesting times ahead of us, right? You can only take out a minimal amount of cash from the bank, fifty US cents each day. That is, if the bank has cash! You can pay your gardener to stand in line and you can rush off to work. If you can get away from there! And pick up your loyal domestic in between, I guess. And the value of this amount you just cashed changes weekly? You will not even be able to buy a loaf of white bread with it. Zimbabwe must be the only country where the US value devalues regularly, meaning that prices keep soaring remarkably. Later that day, the devaluation is claimed to be thirty-thousand percent per day.

There is no way to turn it around.

This country is broken.

You confer with friends about who goes where for what over the next couple of days and in what amounts we buy for each other against which huckster prices.

In some places you can already pay with your expensive fuel coupons. Could it be that we finally understand the war stories our mothers and fathers used to tell us?

Around nine o'clock in the morning, the heat is sharp and stings.
The sky is clear blue. Even the wind is holding back.
The chickens, Bantum Bumps, walk jauntily past, led by a beautiful, brightly-coloured cock. The border collie and Pelle, the dumbest Labrador ever, do not appear to be bothered by the heat. It is just us who are trying to get used to not having water and electricity. Nearby, the generators drone, a migraine-inducing noise.
A quick swim in the small pool and then throw the last litres of water over myself in the little bathroom, a quick little shower. For days now, the house has been cleaned with chlorine water out of our swimming pool, but the large ants that pass daily and the first sand fleas are not bothered by it. Neither are the large Flat Spiders. The little lizards shoot back and forth around the little, red terrace, frolicky free.

From nine until one, all sweaty whilst listening to some music on the laptop, I look at the damage and think about what I can quickly fix up for *Fine Lunching*. In keeping with the Zimbabwean tradition a lunch is not finished before six/seven o'clock at night, so I have to prepare everything, make enough, defrost everything, it might not be enough? Kilos and kilos of meat, soup and canned vegetables and fish.
We call together our loyal staff: Eva, who has been with us for sixteen years, and Daniel and his wife Melody too. Tomorrow is a day off if they assist today, so they help joyfully and happily. And get a nice meal tonight. And the day off tomorrow! These Sunday lunches are more interesting to them then the Sunday Service "The Lord will provide" sermons anyway.

'Daniel, would you please light the *braai*?', I ask around twelve-thirty.
'That is fine. All the wood has been chopped and there is still plenty of charcoal from Zambia', is the answer with a roguish smile. His little girl, two years old, Rumbidzai, drags sticks back and forth.
In the mean time, Eva and I have cleaned all the vegetables, washed them in water in no time at all and put them in containers. Ants know how to find everything, even in an hour's time in this drought. The large red ones and the small, sharp, quick black kind.
Do not forget. Everything bites, that is why everything is ironed, sometimes too hot, which means your silk summer pants come back as brightly shining hot-pants.
I look outside where, curiously enough, everything still shines in the brightest tropical green colours ever: the palm trees, the hydrangea, the firs, the orchids, the pepper trees, the Jacaranda and the lavender and all the waving species of grass. It is impossible that the water has sunk away

so deep, I mutter. The vegetable garden was destroyed within four days, but hey, those twenty vegetable patches have no deep roots. Everything was scorched, gone by week's end. No crying over spilt milk.

Melody, the gardener's wife shoves tables together.
'How many today Madam?'
'Try to fit in ten to start with', I answer and quickly call a few friends who might just have woken up.
When I get to the phone, I reread an e-mail that I printed out after work. Because I cannot count or spell anymore: "The Cato Institute (www.cato.org/zimbabwe) has estimated inflation in Zimbabwe as from 6 November at 215 quintillion per cent.
That is: 215,000,000,000,000,000,000 %. This is a new record, surpassing Hungarian inflation in 1946 at a mere 20 quadrillion per cent."

Despite the situation, people are partying a lot this weekend.
The stress is shaken off; people are drinking hard, cursing hard and having sex. Hard.
Work hard, drink hard, swear hard.
Die hard.
Sometimes, I look like a Rhodie!
At least, I have learnt to swear like a Rhodie!
People sit with each other and share food and drink all the time. They discuss and analyse the situation. Or agree not to talk about it for an hour. And just cook something, like we did today, because you never ever throw away food here. The orphanage is an hour and a half away from here and the car is not working properly. So that is not an option.

I look at the set tables outside.
'Lavender flowers to decorate the cutlery?' Daniel's wife asks.
'Yes, please, Melody, and use blue paper serviettes today.' My grandmother's cotton napkins are still used, just like the hail-white embroidery done by the women from the cooperatives in the neighbourhood, but alas, you have to remain practical when there is not a drop of water around. I have trained Melody for three years now to assist Eva, but the beautiful girl is a true city girl and would rather spend her Sundays in bed or at a friend's, who will give her the latest Afro haircut, which often means eight to twelve hours of braiding. Setting a nice table is the only thing she manages after all this time of trying to teach her. And it does not get you dirty, right?

'Eva, shall we quickly marinate the defrosted meat?'
'Yes, but let's fry the fillet inside and let the men prepare the rest on the *braai*. They drink, they burn the meat.' A smart comment from my loyal old Eva.

She loves to stay with us and wants to help out every moment, because she knows Aad is building her a little house in the old Bindura township, an hour's drive from here.
'And we need to talk to the neighbour madam, Madam, because the dog killed another hen.'
Damn, and she was breeding nicely during the day, is what I remember. Our two dogs have an understanding with the cocks and chicks, but the neighbour's, Philip, disagreed.
Let's see.

The large cauldron with litres of defrosted soup looks fine: local spinach, some bitter, local celery and wafer-thin carrot slices. I cannot remember the how and why of this creation, nor why it tasted so soft in the end.
'Eva, please, will you cut the tilapia in fine long pieces to mix into the soup later?'

Tilapia is the only fish we have at the moment. We used to get the largest and most beautiful trout especially from the mountain regions of the wonderful Highlands and Nyanga. It is over. The snow-white tilapia bream can once again be found, however, only for about ten times the normal price. Quickly process it in the hot soup.
And then make some crackers. All kinds of crackers have been imported with a unique order through the school, early August. Importing ended up being a onetime policy to keep the staff happy. We ended up ordering all kinds of stuff we normally could not buy here nor would need in the future. Dog collars, cake mix to copy the Americans, white Haute Cabrière as if casket wine was not good enough anymore and Christmas Crackers, many dozens out of fear that Christmas would not be celebrated in Zim anymore.
Crackers with imported Danish cheese, the price is outrageous, but sometimes people just give in. After all, we are not members of an expensive sport or health club as in Europe, is what I always say.
The cut up fish is bathed in a marinade of lemon spices and olive oil. Whatever I can drag with me in my hand-luggage each time I visit my children in Europe, I take with me. Kenya Airways is competing with Ethiopian Airlines and offers each client forty-five kilograms.
Which is what I arrived with at the airport early October with a relaxed face, apart from the fifteen kilograms of hand-luggage and sweat that was dripping away underneath my neck hairs, because every customs officer was going to stop me and shove me in a booth, right? Just so they could tax everything for 100 %? It had to go wrong for the first time?
No, the gods were with me. More than they were with the Chinese.
Traditional Shona warrior were dancing happily in the arrival hall for at least one hundred freshly imported Chinese immigrants, so I skipped along with two heavy suitcases and bags filled with new laptops and

passed by the customs offices. Look at the result. Moulds to make chocolate. Himalayan and Nepalese rice, sushi rice, Spanish white beans, large lentils, black Indonesian rice and mixed spices.
Illegal olive oil, the pure stuff, from some castle in Sicily. All the dried foods I would not even buy in Maastricht in twenty years. Let alone think about. Oh well. I want to run my little restaurant creatively and cooking is relaxing, right?
So, tilapia with some bizarre herbs or strange berries in the soup.

And then. Another course?
Since Sheila and Paolo Barduagni are coming, I have to finally beat my Shona friend's Italian husband at his own game. Will I be successful? I jerk open the fully filled supply closet (the woman from Doris Lessing's The Golden Notebook would me proud of me) and take pasta shells off the shelf.

Penne a la vodka now becomes *Shells a la vodka*.
Simmer heaps and heaps of ripe, mellow tomatoes for two hours in a large casserole dish. A handful of mixed herbs is allowed depending on your mood. Or some fresh basil from the garden.
Cover the cold olive oil with freshly squashed garlic. Make sure it's cold, my previous Principal, Mr. Maggio, taught me, otherwise you sear the outer skin and the flavour does not come out. For numerous Saturdays, he taught me how to cook traditional Italian dishes. Everybody's dream is the *Silverspoon*, the infamous cookbook. Is it a dream? I often yawn at cookbooks, cannot follow a recipe properly. From *The Naked Chef* to *the South Beach* diet. Cooking has to be artful and creative. It should make people smile and relax in this element of our lives.

'And that is what everyone does and, thus, is not what is meant to happen. Don't you dare', I still hear him say. 'Garlic is gold, so put it cold in the oil and slowly heat it together. It's either onions in the tomatoes *or* garlic. Never both, you understand?' Okay, I have always humbly listened to the traditions of the Italian mamas and their Italian sons, in Zimbabwe, that is. Meanwhile, the finely chopped tomatoes simmer right through my mutterings and I secretly throw in a handful of dried French herbs anyway. Yup, from the G.B. supermarket of Leopoldsburg.
In Belgian Limburg.
Where my old mother lives.
Who taught me how to cook.
Flemish, French and German recipes.
Except, I never paid proper attention.
But *soit*.

After simmering softly and long enough everything is blended with a hand mixer until the red colour changes suddenly into pinkish red and later creamy red.
How I love red.
Red corals and Italian red.
Flamboyant Zimbabwean red.
Freshly mixed pepper and enough salt.
This makes the real, classic basic sauce. Simple and authentic.

The shells should be boiled *al dente* and drained the moment it is to be served. No sooner.
White wine is great with it. But these guests are still drinking Leffe after the soup. It is unbelievable, but near us a home business has opened. All sorts of drinks are imported, as long as you pay in US dollars. New shops are mushrooming everywhere.
The Leffe is cheaper than the local beer because the sell-by date is May 2008 and nobody feels guilty buying this heavy Flemish beer.
The police often raid this shady store, after which another bribe has to be paid somewhere in the city and the garage can open again.
'Stella Artois', I hear Aad telling our guests later, 'Stella Artois, Amstel and Heineken and all sorts of South-African beers and liqueurs are available just 'round the corner!'
Like that, we all help destroying the local economy.
For every service, every car-part, every commodity as they call it here, the most extreme rates are charged. Over the past weeks, the greed has increased so much it sometimes makes me sick. I sometimes pass up my shopping out of anger and give the last of my cash to an old man behind me, who clutches a half loaf of white bread in his weather-beaten hands.

Suddenly it is all ready: marvellous table, the nice, blue tableware made by fellow ceramist Marjorie Wallace, fresh, mauve bougainvillea in thin vases, lavender between the napkins, tear stones and shells between the plates.
'I get sick and tired of your perfectionism', my husband says. 'Can't it be more simple? Relax, it's almost forty degrees outside, go sit down for a second, darling.'
I do so immediately and I pop open one of the last six good bottles of Haute Cabrière. Definitely not a Chateau Migraine, we thought.
We work hard.
We live hard.
The country is hard and every week it seems to become harder.
However, on this Sunday, the Flemish workhorse still wants the same: despite spontaneously calling up a lot of people and inviting them, the table settings and the food still need to be works of art.
It takes a while before Aad and I get a group of invitees together. The irony is that a *major electricity fault* in town disabled most suburbs and

everyone is busy throwing their defrosted supplies on the *braai* and calling each other. Trying to. You need to endlessly dial the same number over and over again. Or hope your text messages come through. Sometimes this only happens 24 hours later.

Friends trickle in, carrying swimming gear and more booze. More wine, children and coincidental visitors. On a Sunday like this, you eat calmly and slowly. In between each dish a few will dive into the swimming pool. The pine seeds from the Albert Heijn supermarket decorate the last salad with lettuce and cherry tomatoes from a dying vegetable garden. Earlier, our Paolo was lyrical about the Italian vodka sauce, so now I can completely relax. From now on, all the men are responsible for the continuation of the *braai,* course of the menu.
Grey clouds are building up like angry old pears, but the clear-blue sky conquers and claims victory an hour and many filets, T-Bone Steaks, Lamb Chops and *Boerewors* later.
Moreover, Olive enters my little studio and buys two large pieces of art: the Carmine-red Celtic Chalice and the Royal Turquoise dish, both unique pieces and I want to hang on to them for one week longer.
'Sorry Olive, they are a part of my soul. Can we talk about this? You will have to leave them with me for a week before I can let them go.'
The Ugandan friend with her brightly-coloured, beautiful African outfit understands.

This Sunday is over, cannot be taken away from us anymore and ends with business unexpectedly. Despite the whole Zim situation I am happy and proud, my works are spreading out over the world.
While all ten guests are recovering during the serving of ice cream and exquisite Belgian pralines, made by our friend Hans, a few Congolese latecomers make their entrance.
Very relaxed, wide robes and so proud of themselves that it makes me quiet. They heard of our party and decided to join.
Why not. Have a seat.
Just like this, I organised a fifty-third birthday party for Aad. With a little band and at least sixty people. Around half past two the next morning half of Congo came round. How the bush telegraph worked we did not know. But it worked. That was a fact.
This might be a final alternative to the failing network!
It's half past six into the warm night.
Our troubles seem far away and life seems sweet.
Night falls quickly in Africa.
The scents sensual and heavy.
They will soften your words.
Night falls quickly in Africa.
The last bottles pop open.

Children sleep peacefully
around the quiet pool.
Night falls quickly in Africa.
Quickly a few cups of espresso
with pralines from Chocolate Hans.
Night falls quickly in Africa.
Look up, there is the black sky-curtain.
The shadows of the Jacaranda become darker.
The stars quickly bring in the new moon.

'Where on earth is it so beautiful as here?' sigh the guests.
Nowhere and everywhere where man feels at ease of course.
Right?

The gate is closed and locked.
The border collie barks into the quiet night.
Once again, we forget to set the alarm.
No rain again tomorrow.
The sky is far too clear.
Another week of heat and drought.
You'll see, you'll see.

NOMUSA CHITEPO
HISTORY OF THE CHITEPO FAMILY

My name is Nomusa Chitepo. My father is the late Herbert Chitepo. My mother is Victoria Chitepo.

Returning at independence in 1980 after almost two decades of exile in East Africa was a mixture of "home-from-home" happening, as well as a new experience on many levels, not least socially and culturally. The whole country was bathing in euphoria and great expectations as everyone celebrated this historical event. This was what we had been waiting for; as children growing up, all we understood was that one day, some day, hopefully sooner than later, we would be "going home" to that special land to be called Zimbabwe. No longer would we be referred to by locals as *wakimbizi* or refugees; no longer would we have to learn and speak this "foreign" language, being *KiSwahili*; and forever we could live as a family once more, no longer separated by our father's absence while he was gone to fight the war of liberation.

Reflecting on life and events after the thirty years since, at once combines feelings of pride, joy, sadness, nostalgia, disappointment, disillusion and more and yet no loss of hope and faith in the anticipation of that other future for our country.

Our small family left Southern Rhodesia in 1962, and grew in size from three to eventually six children, four girls followed by two boys. Our father had been invited by Julius Nyerere to be the first director of public prosecutions in the newly independent Tanzania. The initial years were characterised by a life of comparative privilege, especially having arrived from a country where the yoke of racial segregation still prevailed. Thus, we enjoyed multiracial schooling from the start and benefited from all the trappings of private education and middle-class living – music and ballet classes, an ocean liner trip, weekends at the beach, not to mention domestic helpers and chauffeur!

This lifestyle was to last for only about four years, after which our father left Tanzania to be based in Zambia to head up the planning and execution of the armed struggle for liberation. We moved into a much smaller dwelling at the local university where our mother started to work for the family as a Residence Supervisor, the first of a number of jobs until she settled on teaching, primarily to afford her time with her children during our school holidays. Although we did receive a little financial support for our education from sympathetic organisations, to supplement her meagre income we made and sold peanut butter and lemon curd, raised chickens, grew spinach for sale and also knitted booties and bonnets for new-borns to sell at the hospital maternity wards. I must add that my younger siblings put in a much larger share into these endeavours as I had, by then, gone to boarding school!

Never did we believe that this existence could or would be permanent. We were basically away from home temporarily, until Zimbabwe could be. None of us knew *exactly* what Baba was up to, just that it was important enough for this dream to materialise, and we would see him whenever and as often as he could make the time and the journey to visit us. I do recall one day at school when I was twelve years old, my (mostly white) classmates were comparing home backgrounds and what their fathers' occupations were. My input that my father was a barrister, was met with a response by one girl that I was lying and that he was a "terrorist". My fury saw me launch a padlock into the back of her head and yank a fistful of her hair out until I drew blood. Such was the pride of our father implanted deep in our young beings. And also we knew my father was a freedom fighter, not a terrorist.

Beyond the love and bond of family unity we shared (made stronger by being "foreigners, refugees"), was the steadfast message from our parents of the importance of our education, and above all, the lifelong goals of self-pride, self-reliance, determination and independence that we must strive for. The two of them did occasionally differ somewhat though on the means to those ends. When I announced that I wanted to pursue a career in computers (very new then), my mother's viewpoint was *'what if you meet a spouse from a small town with no computers'*, whilst in contrast, my father's attitude was *'if you meet a small-town man, you take him to where the computers are'.*

Consequently, we returned to Zimbabwe bearing no glass ceilings, and oddly, with little anticipation of inter- or intra-racial diversities, social rules, mistrusts or tensions of the scale we were to find abundant. That blacks had not many years prior been "allowed" to move into previously "whites only" suburbs, did not help absorb some of the revelations.
Try and join a sports club to join their hockey games? No...whites only! Try to enter that night club in a northern suburb? No...whites only! Want to have a look at this apartment advertised for rent in the Avenues? No... sorry, just been taken a.k.a. for whites only! Job-hunting in the private sector with a couple of university degrees in your back pocket? No... sorry, over-qualified! So let's try bars for black people. Oh dear!

Wearing trousers and dangly earrings and smoking as well, are you not looking for a red light district?! But to top it all; *"Your surname is Chitepo and you don't speak Shona? Come, come now!!"*

The consolation prize for these early trials and shocks was getting to work for the brand new independent government, and where better than right where it felt most significant – I joined the ministry of finance and economic planning, whilst my sister joined the ministry of foreign affairs. What satisfaction and honour that brought us. Mother was doing greater things than us of course, at ministerial level. Needless to say, the elation of being back lived on wildly. Some friends and school mates from East Africa visited this beautiful Sunshine City and were wowed by the beauty, cleanliness, development, efficiency, and altogether "western-ness" of the place.

Sadly, though, we had returned without our beloved father. He had been assassinated five years previously in a bomb blast in Zambia. He would never share this promised land. The perpetrators of the killing were to remain a subject of enquiry, debate and contention.

Coming from Tanzania it was different to have supermarkets, clothing shops and banks. It was difficult to understand how Zimbabweans could complain that there was no rice on the shelves for examples, with so many other options to choose from such as pasta, potatoes. It was strange to have to adhere to dress codes in public places such as hotels, and in the workplace because I had never come across such in Tanzania. People were not permitted to wear shorts, jeans, sandals or sneakers after 6.00 PM in hotels and bars. There were still shops and areas that had previously been for white people only. One day, my sister Zanele and I went into the famous Saunders department store and in the elevator, two white women were discussing the hail that had recently destroyed the tobacco crop, commenting that this would never have happened before independence. It was evident that people were still taking in the changes that had occurred in the country as this was just the beginning of independence.

One fine morning, whilst driving a government car on duty a good two years on, there was a traffic jam that led to an altercation with some random white guy who was meant to give me way, and I refused to budge. He launched into a loud tirade of racist and sexist abuses. The last thing he expected was that I would lodge a case of criminal injuria against him and have him found guilty and made to pay a fine, though very nominal in my view. Most surprising however, were the reactions of my black compatriots to the newspaper front page report about the incident and subsequent law suit. They said that I had behaved as if I was precious, after all, who had not been insulted by a white man?

Despite everything that would suggest otherwise, I did eventually find a landlady who had crossed that racial-occupancy unwritten regulation. It was still early eighties, and how different a cost of living then, to what we later came to survive. So "cheap" was renting my furnished, one-bedroom flat, I was to find myself at odds as to how to spend my salary. So, back then, I was able to pay my younger brother's private school fees and still have cash to spare. How one could manage that now, the mind boggles. Not much later, and in a better-paying job, it was time to buy and move into one's very own home. But not after having to countersign the legal documents for transfer of ownership confirming that I was indeed a "spinster" (beyond marriage at age twenty-seven?) and not needing my father to be my legal guardian.

A couple of years later, that very issue had barely been legally resolved with women being granted full rights, when my baby girl joined me in this world. Yes, single, unmarried. She was born very premature, at a time when paid maternity leave had not been fully resolved. Lo and behold, I had to repay five weeks I owed my employer for leaving work upon her early arrival, booked to be due eleven weeks later. I apparently over-stayed my time off for motherhood while she was still in hospital, and was forced to take unpaid leave. I wonder how many mothers today would believe my story.

The racial landscape gradually but steadily changed before our eyes as those whites who couldn't take the heat, left the kitchen. Our children were integrated in schools and in the workplace, and our sporting teams were making their marks in various disciplines worldwide. Blacks were taking positions as captains of industry, our leadership was the envy of free Africa and our leader revered as an international statesman. We witnessed the arrival of a unity government, more women in public leadership and civic society, and in general the people of Zimbabwe taking full personal charge of their destiny. So it seemed, so it is said to have been.

The 1990s arrived and heralded the so-called economic recovery pro-gram. Those years of exchange control fell away and central control of economy took a back seat. *Bureaux des change* sprung up all over and it was a *free-for-all* currency market, for those with the means of course.
Suddenly next year's model cars appeared on the roads and property developments were springing up around Harare. However, there was evidently no change though for the masses, except backwards. People began to recall pre-independence life as being easier, even better.

And *backwards* steadily we slid, moving through food price riots and confrontations with the police and armed forces, increased political dissent and the advent of a daring opposition to what had become a one-party state. In the later nineties, we sensed the build-up towards a new democracy simmering nervously below the surface of the socio-political landscape.

Over that period, I found myself self-employed, not by design, but it happened after other plans and hopes were dashed. In retrospect, it was for the best for me and my daughter Chiyedza as I was able to offer her what I consider the richest opportunities possible educationally, culturally and in the sporting field. She was unable to comprehend why each time I broke down in tears when – first at age eight – she was selected to take the lead role in the first locally produced feature film and again the following year, to become the first black girl to represent Zimbabwe in springboard diving. She would later prove to be an accomplished violinist. Admittedly, they were trying years, with weeks or months passing with no work contracts coming through. But oh, so rewarding.

Not all went so smoothly on the family front. We lost two siblings, a brother and sister, their loss a decade apart, both in very tragic and emotional circumstances. It hurts to this day, and probably forever will. The greatest strength to bearing the pain, without a shadow of a doubt comes from our mother, the most stoic, principled, loyal and loving soul on earth. My family grew with the addition of my late sister Zine's young daughter. She has since and forever will be my gift, my *Zawadi,* as her name translates from *KiSwahili.*

Election fever gripped the nation as the century turned. It was however accompanied by a new zeal, that of land redistribution. Yes, I understood the *"raison"*, for after all, my own father had long stressed this issue as being the heart of the struggle. I could not, however, buy into the methods used to achieving this end. This was not made easier by the mistrust born and the chasm that widened in the relations that had since been fostered between me and white now-dispossessed family friends made mainly through my daughters associations. Not the neatest way to deliver the latest agenda.

With my family of three now, we strode into the later years of the twentieth century. Every single year everybody proclaimed that the following year would be better than the last, as Zimbabwe witnessed fuel shortages and spiralling record-breaking inflation rates. But the year 2008 had to take the biggest prize. Who would have predicted that we should endure a full year of food shortages, completely empty supermarket shelves, no cash available, trillion dollar bills, electricity outages, barter trade, paying school fees using fuel coupons, prices of goods changing before you get to the till, importing basics from South Africa – the list was long. Latterly, when all options seemed closed or unachievable, we figured a brand new governing arrangement might be the only way forward. So here we are today, in a sprint to the finish line with a government of national unity. Winners all.

With a measure of embarrassment, but no regret, I have to admit that I can only relate experiences from the long-life position of privilege. I have not told a story of leaving the rural life for town, or one from the township to the suburb. But these have been my parents' stories. A friend, on reading this, pointed out that my life of supposed privilege came with its disadvantages and pain. But I have recounted the truthful story of a fairytale homeland that truly exists, a unique homecoming, the land of my birth and the land of tomorrow.

LOUISE BINGANDADI
MY LIFE AT FAIRHOME AS A DAY MOTHER

My name is Louise Bingandadi, but people call me simply Lois.
I am Shona.
I am tall, strong and dark in complexion.
I am a single mother of two children.
My home place is Mutare, near Mozambique. Mutare is the gate to the world and on top of one of the most breathtaking mountains in the Eastern Highlands.
From various places one can behold what we call "World Views". Once you see them, they are forever on your mind. You are high, you behold the whole world and you think that all your problems have been swept away with the wind, because of the beauties that nestle forever on your minds! Forever!
The people are proud and independent.
They do not like what is happening right now here in Zimbabwe.

MAY I TELL YOU ABOUT MY LIFE?

It is hard, we struggle to survive and we dream of a change that will ensure us better lives. Right now we are very sad and often do not see any way out anymore!

I was born in Mutare in 1967 and just turned forty-one years old.
My mother had ten children and we grew up in the rural areas of Zimunya.
I am the daughter of Josephat Bingandadi and Everjoice Mutezo.

My primary education was obtained at Gombakomba Primary School and I finished my secondary education up to form two in Harare. Today I am a qualified pre-school teacher and I have taught pre-school children for about three years back home in Mutare. I have a secretarial certificate, and am a professional tailor.
I have a Zimbabwean passport.
If you want to organise a passport these days, you have to sleep many nights on the streets in front of the office, just to stay in the queue and line up until one day it might be your turn. Even then, luck is not ensured!

I was married to Aleck Mubani who passed away in 2002.
Together we got two children: Ian James, born in 1996 and Portia, born in 1998. Ian James is in Grade 6 and Portia in Grade 4. They are both extremely bright children.
It is for them I live. And survive.

Both my parents are still alive and in Mutare.
My dad is Mozambican, my mum Zimbabwean, born in 1923 and 1930. Dad is a pensioner, he worked as a driver for Anglo American and served the company for sixty years. His pension does not get him anywhere today! My mum is a tailor and she can farm. She inspired and taught me. She encouraged me to become a self-employed woman!

In the year 2000 I went back to live with my parents, as my husband decided to get married to another woman. The children were two and four years old. I looked after them and helped my parents working in the fields. I managed to survive by sewing bedspreads and seat-covers. I accepted any job in order to make ends meet and would work in other people's households. Apart from being a domestic I also did part time washing and ironing for others again.

In the year 2003 I had a very special and important dream.
In this dream God told me to start attending St. Elisha Apostolic Church and pray there. So it was because of that dream that I joined this church. I became one of their best singers. I started teaching other single mothers good behaviour. Since my husband passed away I never re-married and Ian James and Portia are therefore half orphans.

In August 2008 I attended a Church Congress in Mhondoro and that is where I heard that at St. Elisha Orphanage in Selous, near Ngezi, 125 kms away from Harare, they were in desperate need of a day care mother to look after the orphans. On the 6th of September in 2008 I joined the orphanage and I really like the job.
The pay is symbolical, only ten dollars a month, but I get food and have a bed to sleep in. I feel pity for the children that have no one to care for. Some of them learnt to survive on the street. Relatives, neighbours or friends heavily abused some of them. They are not healing, I can see. Some survived too long on the streets, learnt to steal for survival and feel a little tied up here with a roof over their head, but they are a happy bunch altogether. As long as we receive food!

I believe in working with them because there is a God somewhere that will bless me one day and my own children. I love these kids that were dumped five years ago in the bush in the Operation Clean up, and I consider them my own. One day I hope my worries will be over too.

Right now I teach the children on a daily base because the local school has been closed three months ago. All the teachers ran away. Patrice supplies me with books, games, clothes, art materials and teaching resources. And food on a regular base! She helped us with developing the garden near the river. The girls find huge shells that she takes to Harare to her own art students!

St. Elisha Orphanage is also called Fairhome.
We are living in a house that used to belong to one of the farm managers that had to desert the farm years ago. The tobacco barns are no longer used since the school that was located there, has closed down.
The former Belgian Ambassador's wife helped us with shelves in the bedrooms and with lovely furniture.
We have chickens and our outside kitchen hut is lovely. When we sit there at nights we can see the stars from everywhere!

We try to study and learn and read with all the children during day time. Often there is no water and no electricity.
We have three girls and nine boys. Two ran away, they had been living too long on the streets to be confined to a house. They were two handsome and clever boys. I am sure they are true survivors. But I worry about them.

My most important dream is to be able to leave Zimbabwe one day.
I will need proper employment since my children are very bright and they deserve decent education.
I hope my life and the life of all the orphans and the street kids will be better one day.
We live in hope.

If you feel you would like to support one of my eleven boys with the school fees, please contact me through pdelchambre@gmail.com
Many thanks!

UNITED NATIONS DAY AT THE HARARE INTERNATIONAL SCHOOL
21 NOVEMBER 2008

It is Friday morning, five thirty. I open my eyes and ask Aad for my cup of Rooibos tea. He always wakes up earlier than I and the Aljazeera journalist is already yelling in the television room.
I think of my friends.
Of their waking-up and what their first thoughts might be.
I wonder about how they open their eyes and their day starts.
Their hands reach for the light switch: power or no power?
Their hands turning on the taps: water or no water this morning?
The lines on our faces. Do tropical years count double?
I think.

About Assia having a full programme with two sons at two schools, miles apart; about Marijke's twelve cottages being fully occupied and having to play hunter gatherer earliest of all of us in order to make a full and praiseworthy lunch magically appear on the table.
About Eric, who will need to fire his gardener since hectolitres of water were being sold clandestinely at the gate, for big bucks, during weeks of absence.
About Claire, who prepares her day before seven o'clock in her classroom while being responsible for seven children at home. She always smiles.
About Kundisai with whom, during Rotary meetings, I prepare the programme of the A Capella African Voices choir.
About Louise, who is starting a reading programme with my ten street kids about 125 kilometres from here.
About Hans, who will start on the Christmas decorations in his Belgian coffee and bonbon shop and taking three children to two different schools between ten past six and ten past seven.
About Andre, chairman of our Rotary Club, with whom I need to discuss the situation of the 12 street children, and who, in his mind's eye, is getting his son Paul into a school in the Netherlands.
I think about each one and about the others whom I have not talked to in a while. About my new friends in Maastricht who follow us closely with worry.
Ready. Ten minutes of contemplation. I am late! Get on with it!
Erheb dich du schwacher Geist!

'Morning Garikai, Happy United Nations Day!' I wish my friend the security guard at the gate. The camera zooms in on my old RVR.

'Happy United Nations Day, Patrice. Here are your twenty five pots of peanut butter for Fairhome. Freshly ground by my wife!' he answers proudly.

Freshly ground, that is what the day feels like at ten past seven. Freshly ground, because there was a storm the whole night long. The floodgates opened.

Unfortunately, those who needed to be washed away by this nightly mini tsunami remained. But swept clean and steaming in the morning light, the school looks more than brand new. I drive in and inhale the familiar scents of the trees and bushes on campus as if for the first time. The guinea fowl chase the peacocks and do not mind the first ground staff strolling in. As if a problem-free day arises from the old Zimbabwe. Angels are dangling in the last Jacaranda. They will start throwing new slates and slate-pencils down. That is what it feels like.

'Isn't it the perfect day?' my colleague greets me, parking next to me, next to the great art room. But a dark and heavy buzzing right next to us makes us hold our breath.

Damn, damn.

The mimosa blossoms on the big old tree sag heavily, and we notice that thousands of bees have settled in this tree.

Danger! Soon, the yelling, cheerful students, dressed in national attire will be coming in!

'David!, Daniel!' I call the two heads of maintenance on my mobile and they come rushing towards me with red-white tape to fence off our classrooms.

'Thanks madam, do not worry. For sure they are not killer bees,' they joke. The sharp morning light hurts my eyes.

'I know guys, but it is a festive day today and with everybody on campus the swarm still might want to attack.'

We experienced this once in 1993 when looking for bushmen paintings and disturbed a bee colony in a cave. We had to run for our lives with Sytse, six years old, on my hip and dragging Sanna along through the bush. Alies was running ahead like an antelope. She has always been a good runner. Meanwhile the bees were swarming around us and stinging where they could. I still dream about it.

Meanwhile, my students are also swarming in. Dressed up. Cheerful. Boisterous.

Sixty different nationalities representing our school. I restrain myself while my proud boys and girls are coming up to greet me. Song e Kim is wearing the most beautiful Japanese outfit, no doubt belonging to her mother, with heavily stitched silk from top to bottom. She looks twenty-six instead of sixteen.

She bows. I bow back respectfully and she teaches me the welcoming rituals of her culture and in her language. There will be no teaching. Our classroom is being used to practice body art: flags, symbols, anything and everything that can be applied using body paint to the arms and face. The computer is playing national anthems!
The young afro-American girls are dressed cheerfully and daringly. The African youngsters turn up in their fathers' traditional garments. Impressive, these loose Arabian robes, the beautifully decorated sandals.
They look proud and smile haughtily.
This is their day!
The future is theirs.
A thousand colours in traditional patterns, thousand butterflies on the Indonesian wraparounds, the robes covered with symbols, the Nepalese batiks. This day in Zim is worth a thousand suns to me!
Here I am, in my simple French outfit from a boutique in Maastricht. Just like that. You do not want to see me in a Belgian flag wrapped around my butt as some of the parents did three years ago, do you? Or dressed like a Flemish peasant? Or like a carnival Gilles de Binche? I can joke about this with the French, German, Dutch and Flemish youths in their language, but that is where it ends. No doubt the Asian and African top them all with their colourful traditional costumes.
'Miss Delchambre, where is your Belgian outfit?' asks the tall Kadijah from Mauretania, dressed in very soft shades. You can tell she is a daughter of the Royal family: posture, charisma, magical eyes. Pride.
'Sorry honey, we might be nationalistic Belgians living abroad but certainly not chauvinistic. I feel European in Europe today! But I promise you, we have organised three chips fryers and you will taste Belgian chips in a paper bag. Homemade mayonnaise!'
Louis, the only other Belgian at this school, and I were crazy enough to make this promise.
Preschoolers too are looking their sweetest in their kaftans, kimonos, Cossack pants or Spanish boleros. The little ones trip regularly on the soft lawn that one is allowed to walk on for the occasion. Beautiful, traditional dresses are seldom practical. Older brothers or sisters are grabbing the little ones forcing them to behave.
Everyone greets and yells and laughs.
Kilometres of tables encircle the classroom blocks and are set with dishes according to countries and continents.
Parents of the parents association are busy receiving and organising the traditional dishes of each country. It looks wonderful. Obviously, all the mothers are also dressed magnificently. Next to our classroom, Ethiopia's and Zimbabwe's dining tables are fortunately adjoining, as every year.
'Morning Sunshine Goddess. How are you today?'
I only meet her once a year. The most beautiful woman amongst all mothers. Not as dark as the Shona, but darker than any coloured or Indian

skin; not brown but golden. Royal appearance. She organises, together with her husband, traditional Zimbabwean food with a staff of approximately ten domestics; enough for a hundred visitors. Generous!
All fine dark traditional vegetables, *mazondo* (knuckles and bones), tripe, *trotters* (pig joints), chicken and filet. And of course great steaming dishes with *sadza*, boiled maize flour, our staple food. Local spinach with fresh peanut butter sauce and wild vegetables are steaming in wooden bowls. Every year, she turns up in a new, enchanting outfit, South-African Zulu style with European medieval cut. Miss Sunshine smiles radiantly and lets me taste some wild vegetables which were shipped in from the Chimanimani Mountains. In-between sour and bitter, heavenly. In-between sorrel and purslane?

At ten-thirty we accompany our classes to the Performing Arts Theatre, the spacious Greek auditorium.
'Let us get the flag bearers organised according to alphabet', yells the admission officer. We help out and it goes smoothly.
In the foyer, all the selected little ones are lined up neatly, ready to proudly, parade the long and heavy national flags down the stairs and up the stage. The Principal welcomes students and parents, gives a brief introduction to the day's festivities and then the Elementary's different children's choirs perform at their best. Thirty-five violinists between the ages of, yes, four and twelve, play the Zimbabwean National Anthem next. We rise.
Subsequently, sixty students, one after the other, stride downwards and onto the stage. Not one child trips while holding the flag this year and every child greets the audience in his or her own language. Every flag bearer receives roaring applause. Twice, I rise together with my befriended colleagues: for the Belgian flag, for the Dutch flag.
It takes a full thirty-five minutes for all the flags and students to pass, two per flag. Finally, everyone jumps up under a roaring whooping and *ululating*, the African way of cheering one's approval or praise.
We are all united when the Zimbabwean flag is hoisted slowly.
Handkerchief out of your purse, woman.

A lot of crying during the National Anthem.
'Patrice, look.' I am being nudged.
'You notice how many people refuse to sing, how many men hold their right hand onto their bosom but keep their lips tight?'
'I know, I see.'
I cannot say anything more, overcome with emotion.
Sadness is in the air with parents, with staff; everyone who has a job at school is present.
Maphias, the school's bus driver, puts an arm around my shoulder.
'It is going to be alright, love. Soon.'

'Yes, Maphias, *inshallah* you mean!'
We get up.
'Come Maphias, time to get the kids back, time for food.'
We wait for all the classes to be guided neatly outside and then the Principal waves: 'One flag left behind on stage! Belgium!' My eyes fill up with tears yet again.
That's never happened before!
That's an omen!
Nervous wreck.
Silly goose!
'Thanks! For ten years, I have been waiting to carry the flag and finally...' I joke quickly, while taking the long, heavy flagstaff.
The two tiny Belgians, four and six years old, were the first to run straight out of the auditorium to the three deep fryers being lined up by mum and dad.
Photos are being taken by several parents next to several flags. People greet, kiss, cry. Four hundred and twenty students, all staff including gardeners, all parents and visitors queuing for sixty different national dishes. Music everywhere, cheerfulness everywhere.
I miss last year's Pied Pipers. Instead, all of the Indian girls are performing a gracious dance in the middle of the big lawn.
Waiting is a true pleasure today!
A plate of sushi, some Zimbabwean wild vegetables, *tsunga*, Indonesian snacks and I am done.
'Louis, give me the stapler', I shout. He is frying the chips while I fold and staple the chip bags.
'Cocktail sauce or plain mayonnaise, darling?' mama Celine asks my Senegalese colleague, Daniel Badji.
Multi Culti!
This is our day!
We smile.
Celine and I like each other, but we almost never meet. They work for the European Commission, I work at school.
I fold chip bags at a horrific pace.
Grab a sexy Kuwaiti final-year student by the collar and shove the stapler in his hands.
'Food for work, darling!'
'The queue for the Belgian chips is the longest!' whoops Celine.
Sure enough and our most valued customers are Congolese, Rwandese and Burundi! Arms locked with Japanese, Nepalese, Swedish and Russian mothers!
With Paolo Conte on the backseat I drive home.
I want to call my dearest darlings in the Netherlands. Report.
Life is beautiful today!
But when I come home, the staff is waiting for me.

They look gloomy.
What? A power cut while all my work was firing in the kiln?
'No madam.'
All five thousand litres of water from the newly installed water tank have seeped away during the night.
'Excuse you me?'
How is that possible?

No complaining but bearing
and praying for strength.
Forty degrees.
I open the fridge peevishly
and throw a bottle of white wine in the cooler.
I set two glasses.
Call a German friend.
Same story for her.
Getting a divorce on top of that! Poor thing!
She is a tough cookie working very hard for an NGO.
Within five minutes she drives into Hathaway Close.
'TGIF!'
'Thank God it is Friday!'
'Der kann mich den Buckel runter rutschen.'
'Entweder oder.'
'Zum Wohl.'
'Zum Wochenende ohne Wasser, Schatz.'
He can jump in the lake!
This way or the other!
Cheers!
Cheers to another weekend without water!

SATURDAY – SABBATH

Together with some colleagues we worked late yesterday evening.
A new ambitious Principal, new homework.
And it was a Friday.
A bit daft probably.
But necessary.
Besides teaching, meetings, acting as advisor, in service planning, community work and strategic planning, we receive a new assignment despite the daily stress: rewriting the entire curriculum.
See now?
There you go.
When will we just slide that in?
In desperation, we agreed to work together for one evening a week for a few hours.
Two years ago, we had to pull this off with the previous busy bee as well. Months and months of work. When finished, that Principal Mr. Maggio was offered a job at the International School of Florence.
Speedy Gonzales knew best!
Goodbye – *Auf Wiedersehen.*

This new Principal darling has also seen the light.
There we go!
'Despite the stressful and difficult circumstances, I count on you as a professional bunch of people.'
No buts and no negotiation after this faculty meeting.
Thankfully my three children have left.
Feeling sorry for the young colleagues at school!
And there was me hoping to design a new coral this weekend...
Forget it!

On Saturday I feel shattered.
Train-smashed.
Depressed.
Trying to avoid shopping for four or five days helps.
Especially not searching for something in particular.
The US dollar prices are ridiculous anyway.
Two friends of ours drive 40 kilometres out of town to collect a food order for all of us at a cheese farm. Another friend buys the rear end of a cow

somewhere in the rural areas. A third tries to locate wine. A fourth hears a rumour about affordable goats.
Just go ahead.
Faites vos jeux.
Je ne peux plus.
Six weeks ago, we transported ten kilos of Tilapia fish from the Kariba Lake; a four-hour drive.
This weekend, I will not be doing a thing, all tasks have been divided!
Inspecting the pantry.
Getting lettuce from the neighbours.
And going to the hairdresser's with a little bag of shampoo and conditioner. These days the water is provided in buckets...

Dazzle hair design. Sure!
I'm feeling dazzled when I stumble in at half past ten.
More due to fatigue than for any other reason.
Bag containing shampoo, conditioner, hair serum.
The generator is throbbing; the water is ready in jerry cans, I notice.
Neither power nor municipal water; sometimes you get asked on the phone to wash your hair at home before you come.

Nyasha is washing my hair and I notice in the mirror how swollen her legs are. It takes almost two hours for her to get into town from the location or the township in the morning. The minibus fares differ in the morning from the evening. And they are even more expensive in the evenings when it is raining, she says.
'Patrice, it is because there is no fuel and no cash. So those drivers with fuel can ask you to pay whatever. What can we do? We need to get home and get to our children.'
She is in charge of eight children. Four of her own and three from her deceased sister. Single-mindedly, she continues to plod on. Do not mention the regime to her. She fears being arrested again like in June, due to supporting the opposition. She was carried off to the bush, interrogated, beaten up and only found three days later by villagers. They came upon her by accident on their way to the river. They nursed her, washed her and three days later, when she was able to walk again, brought her to Harare in the middle of the night.
Sally, the business manager, pays someone full time on a daily basis to buy cash here and there in order to send the workers home in the evenings at the discretion of the mob of minibus drivers.
I close my eyes.
My soul shrinks.
A fan of shame unfolds.
The clam shuts.
I remain silent.

'But listen, I hung your old curtains and *Sekuru* (the old man) is very happy with them', she carries on cheerfully and she massages my scalp like no other. I have known Nyasha for fifteen years and she knows my children from visits in the past.

I relax under her hands. Massaging the scalp after hair conditioning is an old custom here and, as a result, I fall asleep within two minutes. Right away I dream that I am in a small restaurant called "Witloof" in Maastricht, together with all my children and four friends from Maastricht's Rotary Club. A short dream. The dream of lust and longing. In a ceramic shell of safety and security. Sinking to the bottom of the ocean between the corals.

But fair songs do not last long and fair dreams are even shorter!

Jenny is blow-drying my hair.

An unknown heavily draped lady sits down heavily next to me. Jewish, I think. All that bling bling jewellery, as badly decorated as a British Christmas tree. That expression. Do I know her from somewhere?

A second later I do not need to wonder anymore, because she starts telling me her life story as if I invited her for it. Anyway, I happen to sit next to her, right?

'Yes, Jewish I am but listen; now I am born again Christian.'

'Oh for Jove's sake', I think and I doze off in an English daydream. But she carries on regardless.

Either she is high on *mbanje* or some other stuff, or she is just plain extrovert. Or jolly borderline. Or she moves from hairdresser to hairdresser and removes her self-punishment robe and flogs herself pleasantly.

'Has your rubbish also not been collected now for six weeks?' I attempt.

She cannot hear me. She is on Cloud Nine or "Train Seven" and it is too late.

'When I lost my farm three years ago I thought the Lord had punished me for my sinful life', she rattles on. Meanwhile, I am awake again.

'Yes. I had a lover for more than ten years. Black, tall, handsome, sexy, beautiful. Full-breed. No darling, not my gardener. I am not that type. Just someone I happened to meet in a bar. I became a loose woman! Hair down, enjoying life every secret second of the day! Then I confessed it all to my hubby, who has always been such an understanding man. Sure. He lost the farm and still attended Mass every Sunday all the same. A true believer, a farmer for God my darling! Totally in the Lord!

But then, when I just thought we had patched up things, I became a full-blown lesbian, at least I thought so and when she betrayed me, I fortunately fell in love with Buddhism which is such an embracing religion. I meet lots of interesting people there.

Then I became obsessed with some lady who preached Crystals, Passion and Beauty, a bit too expensive to maintain, so then I turned Catholic and now finally after all these wanderings I found my true love: I am a born again Christian! I am floating with love!'

Well, I noticed that.
I was under the impression that only Shona men were genetically unfaithful. The Rhodies are also pretty apt. This story is not new to me. The search for truth and religion is a shared concern in Zim. And the hairdressing salon is indeed the safest place where everyone can let their hair down. I am not ready to pay yet and, mind you, in Dollarland where we are all dollarized, there is no change. The change pays for the next session which I book with pleasure for the coming Saturday.
The heavy bosomed lady from the outpourings above suddenly kisses me on the cheeks.
'God bless you my child. Your aura radiates!'
In the meantime, the next lady has taken my chair.
'Shit man. My nerve!' she yells. And then to the hairdresser who, tired, does her hair up in a ponytail: 'Make the best of it, Jenny!'
A Rhodie woman of not yet thirty. Pretty, slim, blond, aerobically trained. Maybe fifty kilos?
'Make the best of it, my husband told me he has a girlfriend.'

I rush out.
Into the air, into my garden, among the lavender, the ferns and the orchids.
The Secret Garden as my garden is often called.
Tables and old chairs, little hideaways everywhere.
My garden.
Your secrets are safe.

ASSIA POST- BOUZIDI
NEVER GIVE UP!

My name is Assia Post, nee Bouzidi, married to Bengt Post and mother of Sander Salah Madiba (11) and Daan Saad Thulani (9).

I have lived in Zimbabwe for the last 13 years. It is not easy to summarise this epic journey. Attempting to synthesise and above all to characterise a life so full of events of all kinds, so intense and unpredictable in one chapter, is impossible. Regardless of my approach, the result will always do injustice to the truth. Trying to convey my impressions of a country that has been so misunderstood like Zimbabwe is a daunting task and I simply do not have the time to concoct the perfect recipe – one day perhaps. For the moment I will focus on one aspect of our lives here and try to render it as vividly as possible.

In 1996 I arrived in this wonderful country, with Bengt and our friends Bernard and Dorien. Our decision to start a completely new life, so radically removed from what we were accustomed to, was an easy one. All four of us were ready for a new adventure.

Sander and Daan were born and raised in Harare. Both are true sons of Africa, free in spirit, full of life and open to everything and everyone. This becomes especially obvious when we are in Europe visiting our family and friends. For such free spirits, adjusting to the confined spaces of Europe, for example realising that jumping up and down and running around in my mother's small flat just might disturb the neighbours next door, upstairs and downstairs, does not come naturally. Riding the escalator in the department store, up and down, up and down, with a wide-eyed enthusiasm as if it were the latest in rollercoaster rides, just might attract some attention. How do you explain to them that they are not supposed to throw their plastic candy wrappers in the bin reserved for paper only or that they have to put on their shoes when they go outside to play? We try and go to Europe once a year and regularly visit Belgium, The Netherlands and Switzerland. And each time, the kids' eyes fill with wonder as soon as we get off the plane. To them, Europe is one big amusement park: the cars – look, an Audi Q7!, the supermarkets – look, there are products on the shelves!, the sports shops – look, they have 350 different types of soccer shoes!, everything is exceptional and incredible.

At home, life is rather different. Barefoot the whole day in our huge garden, gathering insects, picking wild fruits and cooking over a wood fire for a surprise lunch. Our four dogs, three cats and varying number of rabbits, add to the impression that we are surrounded by nature.

It must be clear by now that it is Assia the Mum speaking in this chapter. Bengt and I have always been in complete agreement as to our priorities in life. When Sander was born, I stayed at home to take care of him. Two years later Daan arrived, which gave me a few more years at home. Just to let you know that I am well-versed in my subject: my boys.

These last few years, life in Zimbabwe has changed dramatically; as I am sure you are aware of. When we decided to come to Zimbabwe, childless, it was with nothing else in mind than immersing ourselves in an African adventure with no expectations other than that it would be very different from what we were used to. We have now come to a point where certain basic requirements must be in place for us to continue with our adventure. To us those basic requirements are security and education.

Contrary to what one might read in the western media, I have never at any moment felt insecure or in any kind of danger. I often go for walks on the huge farm next to our house, I go out by myself at night, I drive into town and I travel long distances, without any fear that something terrible might happen. No sweat, no panic. I never worry about myself or about my children. I feel at home here, feel comfortable with everyone here, locals, immigrants and expats, as do almost all of those around me. So requirement #1, security, is fully met as far as I am concerned.

Second requirement, for which there can be no compromise, is education. Zimbabwe still has one of the highest literacy rates in Africa. Education was traditionally considered very important. For the first twenty years it was indeed free and open to everybody, resulting in a school attendance both in urban and rural areas that became the envy of the rest of Africa. *Mayor*, who has been working for us for the last eleven years as our nanny and maid, passed her 'O' levels; *Lovemore* the taxi driver is a qualified mechanic and *Tendai* the cashier at the supermarket has a degree in electrical engineering. Zimbabwe, the Cuba of Africa. People here are very educated compared to, for example, South Africans. It is one of our tragedies – great education, but no jobs. Unfortunately the education has suffered in the last ten years, as has everything else.

The educational system here has traditionally been English, very English. The curriculum, the uniforms, the discipline – all straight from the former colonial masters. Our kids' school for the last seven years, Heritage School, is no exception.

The school day starts at 7 'o clock, often with Assembly in the Main Hall.

As the Headmaster of the school enters the hall, all the children stand and chant, in unison: 'Good Morning Mr. Tapera and everybody else!' This is followed by the weekly prize-giving for good behaviour, effort and sports. At the end of Assembly, the children wish all present a good day and proceed to their classes like soldiers to their barracks – in perfect formation and silence. To me, it still boggles the mind how they manage to keep such a huge number of children perfectly in check.

Then the school day begins as it begins in any school anywhere. The subjects are the same: English, Geography, Maths, History, Science, but also Shona, the most widely spoken language in Zimbabwe. At 9:30 there is a half-hour break. At 1 PM, the children are given 15 minutes for a quick lunch and to get ready for an afternoon of extra-curricular activities, mostly sports. With that little time, you can imagine that the kids' lunches often come back untouched, just a little hotter and smellier than when they were packed in the morning. The choice of sports is also very English of course: tennis, cricket, rugby, hockey, football, Scottish dancing but also swimming: all self-respecting private schools and quite a few government schools have their own swimming pool.

Having been raised in the Belgian school system, it took me some time to understand and appreciate the particularities of the English system and I remain sceptical about some aspects. Corporal punishment is still in vogue here, being the most difficult to accept, especially since neither Bengt nor I ever raise a finger. Although I am against corporal punishment, and thankful that our children's behaviour has so far not led to any spankings at school, I must admit that I appreciate their and their friends' discipline and good manners.

The uniforms: white shirt, grey shorts, white socks – long in winter, short in summer –, black shoes, blazer striped in different shades of blue and a touch of gold. All topped with the obligatory colonial floppy hat against the scorching sun. Pretty standard, really. When you dig deeper, so to speak, it becomes comical though. The devil is in the detail. Underwear must be white – no prints – in traditional jockey style: no boxer shorts or strings allowed! But I must say, all the kids look very elegant in their impeccable uniforms and a great advantage is that at 6 in the morning there are no discussions about who is going to wear what. Not being the nicest person when I am fresh out of bed, I am grateful for the school uniform – no difficult discussions or decisions while I am still half asleep. Also, no child gets beaten up over his expensive Nikes or his Dolce & Gabanna jeans. That's the great advantage of the school uniform: although it doesn't come cheap, it makes everybody exactly that: uniform.

Okay, so much for the uniform. Now let's move on to the hair! Boys' hair is not supposed to touch the ears or the shirt collar.

In our tropical climate, where hair grows more quickly than in more temperate zones, this means a haircut every four weeks or so. At 10 dollars per cut per child, I am considering training as a kid's hairdresser and starting my own business!

Sander and Daan have both thrived at Heritage School. It offered everything a child (and a parent) could wish for. Beautiful grounds, great teachers, management that listened to the children and their parents, great sports facilities, including a 25 meter pool (actually 24,5 meters, the result of a minor calculation error).

But gradually the growing crisis in Zimbabwe is affecting not only the socio-economic and political situation, but also education. Millions of people leave the country, no longer able to support themselves and their families here. Everyone is affected: first of all the commercial farmers, their workers and their families. But of course the crisis trickles down to businesspeople, doctors and other professionals, labourers, and alas, also teachers. Teachers' salaries do not keep up with inflation, and the level of education slips slowly but noticeably, while its cost skyrockets. As a result, there is an exodus of teachers and hundreds of thousands of children, no longer able to afford the fees, are seeing their future being snatched away before their very eyes.

Before long, our children are saying goodbye to one friend after another, as they leave for the UK, Australia, Canada, and South Africa.

And soon they are seeing one teacher after another leave, as they change schools, jobs or countries. By now, we have bid farewell to a good portion of the friends we made through Heritage School as well as many of our Dutch friends. The toughest goodbye is when Bernard and Dorien announce that they are leaving Zimbabwe for South Africa, where Bernard has landed a job with the IFC, a division of the World Bank. We came to Zimbabwe together and our boys grew up with their children Max (12) and Malaika (9), who they consider almost as brother and sister. After having lived our dreams together for nine years, our paths finally separate. Thankfully, Johannesburg is not far, and we see each other a few times a year, as do our children. Sander's first ever solo trip was from Harare to Johannesburg to visit Max last year, his present for his 11th birthday.

The founder and Managing Director of Heritage School has had enough and decides to return to the UK with his wife, who headed the Junior Department. They are soon followed by their son, who was the Facilities Manager. Not surprisingly, the school now goes into free fall and suddenly we are faced with barely qualified teachers and a management that seems more focused on maximizing income than educational quality.

Despite so many people leaving, we are determined to stay. But that means that we need to revisit requirement #2: education. We can no longer leave our children at Heritage School, we must find a solution. Sander and Daan are the only children left in their classes who have been at Heritage since they started school. Apart from those children who have left the country, all their other friends have left Heritage for one of the other private schools that have managed to maintain a good level of education: Chisipite Girls School, Hellenic School and St. John's Boys School.

Now, every time I put my kids in the car to drive them to school, I am gripped with panic. I need to get them out of Heritage and into Hellenic or St. John's. In his last three grades, Daan has not finished a school year with the same teacher he started with. Miss Webber goes, Miss Munhuwei comes, Miss Hlatwayo goes, Miss Mwaita comes. All with different approaches and frankly, each a bit less convincing than her predecessor. Miss One wanted active participation from the children, Miss Two did not want any interruptions during class, Miss Three encouraged children to be independent, Miss Four preferred followers, Miss Five had a weak spot for boys, Miss Six found them a nuisance. Poor Daan. Neither he nor his classmates knew what was expected of them anymore. And Daantje can do with some clear direction!

For Sander it was different. Not as many changes, but the change that did come was quite a shock. Not finding anyone to replace Miss Seven towards the end of the second term, the school called Miss Eight out of retirement.

Miss Eight had an impressive resume that included the best schools in the country. In fact, it included a lot of schools – it seemed she never spent a considerable amount of time at any of them. Rumours began to spread that she was perhaps a bit too trigger-happy.

Now I am not one to believe everything I hear, especially not when the information is second or third hand, so it isn't until a beautiful day in October that I discover the painful truth. It is 3:15 PM and time to collect Sander. After waiting for an unusually long time, I finally see him coming out of the Junior Department building, clearly dragging his feet. I can tell from afar that something is wrong – perhaps a fight with a friend, a poor grade. I give him a big hug and ask him how the day had been, as I always do. The grunt I receive in response confirms my suspicion. I insist and ask if anything happened. All of a sudden I see tears welling up in his eyes and before long he is crying wholeheartedly. In between sobs, he tells me that Miss Eight had grabbed him by the ears, smacked him on the back of the head and humiliated him in front of the rest of the class, the reason being that he had forgotten to bring his Maths book for the second time, despite having done his homework and having handed it in.

I will spare you the details of my immediate reaction in the Headmaster's office and my discussion with Miss Eight.

Basically, I told the Headmaster and Miss Eight that if anything like this happened again, my reaction would be as Mediterranean as myself.

The urgency of finding a new school for Sander and Daan is now all too apparent. After several conversations with Bengt and consultations with friends, we finally make a choice – we want our boys to go to St. John's.

St. John's is a boys' school (Primary and Secondary), reputed for its strictness and discipline, but also for its longstanding quality of education. Although we were not necessarily in favour of a boys' school, St. John's solid and stable reputation and the fact that it is the only local school to offer the International Baccalaureate, convinced us that it was the best choice. In any case, now that the choice has been made, we need to get them accepted. An aggressive strategy is required and you can rely on Assia for designing and implementing such a strategy. This is a defining moment in our family history – it is war out there: we will fight to death and no prisoners are to be taken!

Phase 1: Fill out and hand in application form, together with Birth Certificate and latest Report Card. I go to St. John's and ask for the application forms. The secretary who receives me is not the warmest person I have ever met; a hair's breadth from rude. She tells me that I am the 2,347th desperate Mum she has spoken to in the last six months and gives the impression that she has seen about 2,346 too many, if not more! But this is crucially important, so I try and remain as friendly and polite as I possibly can. After explaining procedures, the secretary makes it clear that there is not much point in putting the children on the waiting list for the junior school, which already contains 700 names. Perhaps I should consider other schools, such as Gateway or even Rusawe, a boarding school. My optimism and determination suddenly seem utterly ridiculous to me. How did I ever think that I could just walk in here and book places for my two children – some kids have been on that waiting list for 2-3 years already.

I leave with the application forms but without much hope. The next day, I hand in all the required documentation and try and convince the secretaries that my case is very different from the other 2,346. After all, my boys are exceptionally intelligent, athletic, extremely good looking and multilingual. They will be fantastic assets to St. John's, really! I even offer to give French classes – French teachers are a rarity in Zimbabwe. Perhaps I could meet the Headmaster in person to argue my case? Out of the question, the Headmaster has no time to speak to parents of children on the waiting list and we cannot make any exceptions. It is clear that this is going to be tough, long and drawn-out war. I have to follow the line of differentiating my case from that of all the others, regardless of their merit. I need to fight my way into the Headmaster's office so that I can personally present my case. But how to get past the secretaries who guard his office with an impressive array of weapons? What are they hiding? How can they be disarmed? I start reading up on war strategies on the internet.

Okay, let's take a step back. I managed to get through Phase 1. Now I need to break down my offensive strategy into tactical moves. Tactical move number #1: make friends with your enemies. Using any excuse I can invent, I start visiting the secretaries/gatekeepers on a daily basis: the first time to make sure that my application forms have been well received, the second time to ask whether they need anything else, the third time to offer to submit more Report Cards of Sander and Daan, next to remind them that if the school needed a French Teacher, I would be more than happy to be considered. And so on, until one day, I meet an old teacher of Sander's, Mrs. Bredenkamp, who had moved to St. John's in the previous year. Mrs. Bredenkamp had been Sander's Grade 4 teacher at Heritage, and she loves him. On to Tactical Move #2!

I ask Mrs. Bredenkamp for a meeting during which I explain the situation to her. She promises to discuss Sander's case with the Headmaster and I leave her office with a tinge of hope. Solution in sight, *Inshallah!* On my next visit to the secretaries I ask to call Mrs. Bredenkamp who assures me she has spoken to the Headmaster. I continue my daily visits, hoping to perhaps one day run into to the Headmaster by chance. During one of these visits, I meet an old teacher of Daan, who has also left Heritage for St. John's, halfway through the year. Rather guiltily, she asks me how Daan is coping with the new teacher. Without being too untruthful, I tell her that he is not coping very well – after all, it is the third year in a row that he has had a change of teacher and this is why I pay daily visits to St. John's, in the desperate hope that I can take my children out of Heritage as soon as possible. Dear Ms. Hlatwayo, she obviously feels for me and proposes to arrange a meeting with none other than the Headmaster, Mr. McKenzie. Bingo! It is 1 PM; the secretaries are out to lunch. Double Bingo! This is my lucky day! Jenny Hlatwayo leads me into Mr. McKenzie's well guarded fortress.

I introduce myself while realizing that I have managed to break into Mr. McKenzie's office without firing a shot. Time for Tactical Move #3. A voice inside me tells me to beg, to implore, to go onto my knees and plead for a place for my children. But my pride and temperament command me otherwise. Mr. McKenzie tells me that, pure coincidence, he had already heard my name mentioned that same day. I tell him I am not surprised, having pulled out all the stops to get my boys in. And I tell him that, when it comes to my children, I am a very determined woman. The meeting goes so well that I leave the office with McKenzie's promise that Sander is in. A few days later, I call the secretariat to tell them of my meeting with Mr. McKenzie. The news that I managed to scale the walls of the McKenzie fortress unnoticed by the secretariat does not go down well at all.

After suggesting that I must have managed under a false pretext, otherwise it is absolutely impossible to manage a meeting with the Headmaster, my friends the secretaries have no choice but to face up to the horrible truth: someone, a foreigner nonetheless, has managed to break through their defences. I succeeded, despite their seemingly superior arsenal; the first battle has been won. Assia 1 – Secretaries 0. Or is it? A few days later I find out that Sander's place was given to someone else. Did the secretaries have anything to do with it, unwilling to accept defeat?

Now I am worried, really worried, and afraid that I have made two real enemies, two enemies for life and have ruined my chances. Until the day that I receive a phone call from my friend Emma Frost, who is on the St. John's Parents Committee and former Heritage parent. I had contacted her also a few weeks earlier and asked if there was anything she could do. Emma brings good tidings, but there is one condition. The good news: Sander has been accepted and starts in a week. I don't believe my ears; it is too good to be true. And the condition, what is the condition? Emma tells me that the secretaries are well aware that I still need a place for Daan, but they do not want to see me – they want me to stop harassing them. Victory tastes very sweet indeed and it costs me no effort to promise that I will not bother the secretaries any longer. Two months later, a day before we leave for the Christmas holidays, Daan is also accepted, for January 2009.

Finally, Requirement #2 has been fulfilled – both Daan and Sander are at St. John's and should be in good hands until they go to university. And while I smile a very satisfied smile, I am reminded of the French saying: "God wants what woman wants." What a great experience, what a discovery to realise that even goals that seem insurmountable, tasks that seem impossible, are no match for determination and optimism. The idea that I am in control of events and not vice versa is a great feeling that gives me a lot of strength. The boys are very happy, the secretaries have become friends, believe it or not, and my conversations with my friends are no longer frustrated monologues about school.

Having put this behind me, I now have the space to face my next challenge: I want to get back to work. After so many years of this or that temporary job, no job at all and one year as an assistant French teacher at the International School, I am eager to re-enter the job market – no easy feat in a country with an estimated 80% unemployment rate!

I am not yet sure what I want to do, but I have a few ideas.

All I can say is: Beware!

Assia is on a mission.

assia@thulani.net
– Translated from French by Bengt Post. –

COLOURS OF THE RAIN OR THE SONG OF EVERY SHONA MOTHER

Weeks of waiting
Slowly the heat builds up
Past the huts
Past the hills
Past the pen
And past the water well
Past the chirping
of the crickets
the heat sneaks
past your shadow
and gushes off the rocks.
In creamy clouds
In angry thunderheads
Into a dark blanket
Slow and still,
a motionless beast.
All shades
red and sienna
Scorched earth
rainy month
that is your name, November!

Waiting for the sweeping
The swinging and the swaying of the branches
Of our old *Msasa* tree
just before the tired fireball sags
orange she descends
into the dusk
and in the last light
all bougainvillea melt
into one colour

The purple, rose, red, lilac plum-red
And now a storm needs to blow
and moaning
trees need to crack
and let all hell break loose
No lightning as in Africa
No rains as in Zimbabwe
luring us both
outside
in the deep of the night.

And in complete darkness
do you smell the rainy colours
soak inside of me
and breathe along with me.

I will throw the *Hakata* moonstones
for you
Your future
in my palms

With the first rays at dawn
When the grass starts singing
When you run
out of my arms,
straight towards
the silver smoke
of the first wood fire
Tomorrow
Sunday
Surely there will be
a new Zimbabwe
my sweet son!

CHARITY MUSINGAIRI
MY LIFE AS A HOUSE MANAGER

My name is Charity Musingairi.
I was born in 1962 at Mutare General Hospital, the last born out of four boys and three girls. All my sisters are still alive and married. Three of my brothers have died.
I grew up in Manicaland, in the high density suburb of Sakubva. I was a good student.
My parents could, however, not afford the school uniforms so I was unable to attend Zhamba secondary school. Uniforms and shoes are the killers of the old system for the very poor of today.
My parents – a father, policeman with the city council of the, at that time, Umtali and my mother, housewife and peasant farmer, still managed to give us a good life. We were able to afford the basics in life and a few small luxuries at public holidays and Christmas.

As a young girl I enjoyed netball and going to the cinema to watch movies, especially adventure movies and listening to country music!
My grandparents were living in Mutema village, in Chipinge. That is what I call my rural home. They died during the liberation struggle of Zimbabwe.
At the age of fifteen I sought employment and became a domestic, supporting my family as my father no longer worked. My parents moved to Chipinge and I started living with my older sister.
I realised life was not going to be easy with only a primary school education. Some girls my age were studying; I had to earn a living for all of us. I pulled through and decided to stop comparing my life to that of other girls. I accepted my fate and understood how lives and people were different.

I had been working for three years before I met the love of my life, in Sakubva. Israel was my husband to be and father of our first son. I moved and built a new homestead whilst my husband had to stay in Sakubva because of his job with the Manica hotel. He used to visit me whenever he could and I gave birth to a second son. We left as a family together to Harare with Israel's new job.
In St Mary's, in Chitungwiza, we found a house to rent. Finally we were able to live together as a family and it made us much closer to each other.

My father died and my mum needed a lot of emotional and financial support from us. During the rainy season we would help her ploughing the fields.

In 1987 I gave birth to our last son, at St. Mary's clinic. Through the Seventh Day Adventist Church I started helping orphans and older needy people. I felt good reaching out to others and be of assistance to them. I still enjoy doing this community service.

In 1994 I started working again and was accepted once more as a housekeeper. This time I was accepted into a very kind Dutch family. I had to leave my own children in the care of a maid in the township.

I commuted and made long hours, covering forty-five kilometres to and from work every day. There was no other choice as I had to supplement my husband's salary and support three growing sons.

In 1998 my husband passed away, a difficult time for all of us in the family. We coped however and pulled through and did move forward.

I am still active as the house manager as the family has moved back to the Netherlands with their two children. I look forward every year in October when they all come and live in the old house during the children's school break. I work now as the head of all the staff at our workplace and do enjoy my responsibilities.

I love my country Zimbabwe. It is quite beautiful with many wonderful areas. Not many of the Shona people can afford to see their own beautiful land.

For my part, I really feel privileged to have seen our Great Zimbabwe, the Victoria Falls, Hwange National Park, Matopos, Imire Game Park, the Nyanga mountains and our own Domboshawa rock formations just outside Harare.

And how many domestics can say that?

LOVE IN THE TIME OF CHOLERA

It is Sunday and it is December.
The Flamboyants paint the lanes in red.
Rose red,
blood red.
Every colour graces my land.
In the rural areas
the planting season has started.
The first rains are celebrated
with *chibuku* beer.

It has been boiling hot for two weeks now.
Nevertheless, *Sinterklaas* did not skip Zimbabwe and I am told that the *Zwarte Pieten* were very kind[1].

We are at Chocolate Hans' home, together with some ceramicists, a chef and a landscape architect as well. Our friend Hans, has just returned from Belgium where he bought raw materials for his special *métier*. Children are running wild outside, on bare feet, butterfly-cheery and free. The smoke of the wood fire spirals upwards, up the hills. Umwinsidale, just outside Harare, is one of the most beautiful regions at not even a ten-minute drive from my own house. You imagine yourself as being miles away from the city and miles away from reality. Although...
'Saint Nicholas does not really exist', Hannah informs me with a knowing smile and cheerfully skips off. Her two brothers roll their eye and look as if they see a lourie.
'I saw the presents in daddy's suitcase', she yells and her high pitched laugh gets stuck in the green foliage of the *Msasa* trees.
Africa is ours today and there is no work for a moment!
'Saint Nicholas knew that he could not find much in the shops; he needed help', we try hesitantly in order to support the holy man, but to no avail. Hannah disappears and we need to get her out from the wooden beams of the cottage three minutes later.

---

[1] In the Dutch tradition Sint Nikolaas and his helpers visit every year in December. The 'well-behaved' children will get presents. Sinterklaas songs and the composing of rhymes and verses are part of the fun.

Our agile and untamed little cat subsequently jumps off the nearly completed terrace into the grass and disappears into the bush.
At Hans' one cannot see where the garden starts and ends and there are no houses in sight. A few heavy showers during the last two weeks and everything seems to be dipped again in various lovely tones of green.

The grass is singing and the filet is fried on a wood fire.
Die ganze Welt is himmelblau.
We discuss the challenges of the past few days, the work and relationships in general, but we also laugh a great deal.
The chips cannot be fried yet, since the power is gone.
'That is how it should be,' I argue, 'if *you* don't have *I* might.' My kiln is filled and switched on and it needs power for the next eleven hours. What is more, my Christmas reports need to be done by this evening.
"Load shedding" is what the new electricity distribution is called.
Better believe it.
The garbage has not been collected for six weeks. Harare Drive, the main road encircling the town, is starting to have foul breath with heaps of illegally dumped rubbish on the sides. One often drives in low spirits passed people with vacant expression. They are looking for food in the remnants of other people's existence.

Worse is the fact that, as happens every year, cholera has broken out. Very severely in the suburbs Budiriro, Tafara and Epworth and other townships and this year, for the first time, officially in Harare city.
I provided our school nurse, Gail, with numerous documents from *Oxfam*, *Unicef* and the Ministry of Health in order to compile an information leaflet for all our workers. So she did and she gave a fine speech for our staff that now need to include cholera next to poverty, HIV, AIDS, flu, TB and such like to his life compendium.
The children hear us chatting about these problems. They know about schoolmates with staff that have become sick, but they do not want to hear about it any longer. To steer away from these issues, Hannah's brothers, Mattias and Roderick, show me the first *peachadilla* seedlings and the *Sinterklaas* meccano truck.
This month's movie *Alles is liefde* (Love is All) for the Dutch-speaking community really is not yet their thing. Love is like *Sinterklaas*: you need to believe in it, otherwise it won't work. The boys, I presume, no longer worry about the holy man and not yet with love, but they are very happy with their presents, and Sunday with dad.

My garlic courgette soup goes down well and the Flemish chicory tastes divine. Same goes for the filet, the most divine meat that is still available thanks to those last cows.

Fortunately the generator is located far away from the house and the music from the seventies makes us cheerful. The children eat well because dad's mayonnaise and the local oyster mushrooms in cream sauce taste superb as usual! It is now waiting for the small red *chanterelles*, but we decide we still need a lot of rain before they come out.

Despite publicity and mass education, the situation regarding cholera remains alarming. When we arrived in Zimbabwe in 1992, this was the priority item on the agenda of the job for my husband. So many years later, the problem has shifted from Mozambican border regions to practically every province in this country. This happens lately every November, when the rainy season starts. Unfortunately, we cannot consult the specialist on the subject today, since he has gone off for some much needed relaxation on his catamaran on Lake Chivero, three quarters of an hour's drive from here. Thus, he also misses the chocolate cake *à la* Chocolate Hans, cut by the boys shortly afterwards. What a pleasant family Sunday with friends, and the feeling we are all there for one another.
A fish eagle flies by.
How is that possible? Where is there any water around?
We remain seated in the dusk on the patio outside.
'Where will you be for Christmas?' Kerry, the chef asks.
'In Maastricht, with my children! I already fly on Saturday! My son turns twenty-one on Sunday. I will be flying Kenya Airways, via Nairobi and hopefully not via Lubumbashi like last time. But I am allowed 45 kilograms of luggage! What do you need? Mail me a shopping list. All of you!'

The comfort and closeness provided by friends is worth its weight in gold.

For Monday, we can handle anything: work, potholes, water shortage, power cuts, the car being damaged more after a visit to the garage than ever before, hours of queuing to pay your phone bill, collecting (or letting someone collect) your daily allowance of 3US in Zim dollars and cholera apparently becoming a seven headed dragon.

'Count your blessings!' we decide one again as one. Coffee, a last glass of wine and a quick bath at Hans', since our water tank is once again empty. Worries are for tomorrow.

VEERLE LENS
ABOUT A LOT OF FEAR AND A GREAT JOB

My name is Veerle Lens. I was born in Tienen and grew up in Landen. I had two brothers and was the eldest child in our family.

My mother's name is Joske Alewaters. She was a passionate geography teacher and (still is) an incorrigible perfectionist. My father's name is Stan Lens. He was able to link his sportive hobbies to a nice career as a sports teacher in the army.

Luk Raeymakers was one of my scouting friends in Landen. Later, we studied together in Leuven, lived in the same house with a handful of friends and stayed there after finishing our studies. We spent a lot of time in bars, to movies, theatre and travelling. We lived on my temp-jobs as a teacher.

After Luk ended his civil service, we were both offered a teaching job in rural Zimbabwe as Belgian NGO cooperatives. We got married and left "only for two years". That was 20 years ago.
Back then, life was relatively good for everyone in the promised land of Africa. Schools were built everywhere and teachers were paid pretty well. Moreover, there were parties almost every night at the local bottle stores. We lost our hearts to Zimbabwe and really wanted to raise children there.

And these children arrived. Rutger is 15 now. Lena is 14 and Jan is 12. They are great kids to whom we have tried to pass on the best of Europe and Africa. They have travelled a lot, are very social and feel at ease with people of any age and background. Thanks to Luk they are also three great footballers.

In the past 20 years, I have been swimming through a lot of interesting and challenging professional waters in Zimbabwe. But now I think I have found the job of a life-time. I develop methods for combining artistic self-expression with group counselling for *Orphans and Vulnerable Children.*
Besides this, I work together with local artists and counsellors of community projects in the least fortunate districts of Harare. As if that is not good enough, this job allows me to creatively connect everything I have studied with my work experience, hobbies, and professional and social contacts.

Monday morning, four-thirty, and I cannot sleep anymore. With great shock, I realise I have slept away an entire Sunday. Mostly out of necessity as there was no electricity and water. Doing the dishes is not possible, nor is doing the laundry or washing myself, let alone use the computer. For some reason, I did not get irritated and spent a nice day.

This morning, I realise that I will not get there like this. I am not able to meet (self-imposed) deadlines. The weekly acrobat try-outs at Streets Ahead and the *capoeira* sessions at Mavambo will end soon. There is not one letter put to paper and what is worse: the modules have to be done by the end of November.

We have found a way to link lessons in acrobatics to counselling by setting and meeting goals in our own life. Counselling is linked to *capoeira* through successful communication and interaction. Right now, it is all in my head, but it still needs to be put to paper. With every passing day, I fear I will have forgotten important information.

I promised to start with dance sessions at Chiedza in November. And it is already halfway through November. Fortunately, I visited an inspiring project last Saturday in Glen Norah. Under the supervision of an experienced artist/teacher, young girls come round weekly to practise old, traditional African music and dance to it – just as it happened 200 years ago.

An American acquaintance steadily believes that these projects can be perfectly linked to counselling. This way, ancient belief systems, customs and social values in the dances can be discussed in relation to its relevance to children today. Ritual music and dancing is about the place deceased ancestors take in daily life, harvests and festivals, the finding of a proper partner for young people, standing up for oneself, in war and in health.

I immediately made an appointment to discuss some issues the next Saturday, together with the teacher involved, some dancers and counsellors. Before that, I have to go to the library of the College of Music for a book that contains more information about the music and the dancing – a book that I will then have to read before Saturday.

I am worried about the Tanaka poetry sessions – these were interrupted and we cannot find any suitable dates to continue with them. I really would like to complete and document these before the end of December. I would have liked to plan some meetings to brainstorm about the possible use of hip-hop and expressive arts. But I will have to postpone this until January.

I am trying to figure out what I have to do today and in the coming days. Just keeping a family running is a lot of work. On top of that, Luk is not here to help out. He went to Zambia for his job (sigh). There are not enough days in a week. And then, of course, there is Patrice, who would like to see this chapter in her inbox before Saturday.

Out of sheer misery, I get up and sit on the patio, hoping that it will calm me down. The patio overlooks our large garden, of which you can only hope it will become quiet and deserted. Even at five in the morning, I cannot hope for that. Our night watchman is patrolling there in circles, coming very close to me. I repress the urge to just get behind my computer. If I try really hard, I can make myself think I am in my garden all alone.

At six it dawns and the children get up – feeling happy that we have got electricity. At ten to seven my car is filled to the brim with my own children, my gardener's children and our house keeper's children. I drive to five different schools and twenty-five past seven I am home again. The gardener opens the gate for me. I shower him with cheques to pay our monthly bills: water, electricity, property taxes, telephone, piano rental and cable television. All bills with extravagant amounts with many zeros that in most cases are not even worth 1 US dollar.

All these bills have to be paid in offices that are scattered all over town and all this has to be done during normal working hours. Moreover, there is a long line of people waiting to pay in front of each office. Our gardener will be busy for about two days. He jumps on his bicycle and pedals off. And I enjoy the only half hour in which I really do not meet anyone – nor in the house, nor in the garden. At eight o' clock, the housekeeper enters. Jane will mobilise the gardener two houses down to bring us buckets with water. His boss and madam have a borehole in the garden. I hope Jane flushes the toilet with those first buckets – turds have been piling up since Saturday.

Hopefully, we will have some city water soon, because the dirty clothes have also been piling up in these last weeks. Sometimes a few drops of water would come out of the tap, but not enough to run the washing machine. Jane promises to hand wash the children's school uniforms in the meantime. The mountain of dishes too will take her quite a while.

She busily walks around the house and I decide it is time to flee to the office. I know I should be thankful for all the loyal help in house – domestic help I would not able to be without. But the price I pay for that help is continuously too much for me: co-dependency and a total lack of privacy.

I pick up Rahim at home at a quarter to ten and at ten o'clock we are at *Streets Ahead* for the fifth puppeteering session. *Streets Ahead* is a drop-in centre for Harare's street children. The sessions support the children in dealing with social conflicts.

The children have made a list of the most pressing problems on the streets during the first session. During the previous sessions a number of these problems have been addressed: robbed and sexually abused by police officers, rape, pregnancy, abandonment and violence done by other street children.

Today, three youngsters are ready to enthusiastically create a short puppet play. Thirty others have come to watch, be entertained and they stay voluntarily for a counselling session of over an hour to discuss the subject of the day: the fact that street children are being blamed for everything, especially for things they did not do. The session is an animated one.

For any old theft or robbery in the neighbourhood where the children sleep they are suspected by the police and neighbours. Everyone has his or her personal story. Everyone has been wrongly accused and it hurts.

The counsellor asks whether they never steal. The kids and teenagers claim vehemently that they have never committed first degree theft – the theft of valuable items with the intent to enrich oneself.

This is attributed to "well-dressed" guys "with cars". What they do, for example, is pick up and keep what someone loses – it can be a wallet or a cell-phone.

Eventually, we talk about how one is instantly recognised and labelled as a street kid with dirty, ripped clothes and scruffy hair. Not all street children look like this, though. You would probably never suspect Tendai of living on the streets. The clothes this teenage girl wears are simple, but still are extremely neat and fashionable. Her hair is put up tastefully. She is self-confident and knows how to explain everything very well.

Tendai tells the others to take better care of themselves. It makes them less recognisable and prevents all kinds of prejudice, suspicions and bullying. At *Streets Ahead*, children can, for example, always come to wash their clothes. They learn that trimming their hair regularly and combing it daily will cost neither time nor money, and could be very effective.

Many artists tell me how they were moved by the *Orphans and Vulnerable Children* whom they meet through our activities. This amazes me every single time. On the one hand they are much closer to the children and teenagers with whom we work than I do. On the other hand they really seem shocked by the poverty and situations they witness. Personally, I am not touched that much. I do not feel pity, anyway. If I feel something, it is admiration for all these pleasant youngsters whom I meet in my line of work.

At two o' clock, I am home again and I pick up my youngest from school by two-thirty. Jane has a problem: her youngest son has terrible tooth aches. I promise to take time off work tomorrow to go to the dentist with him.

This will have to be in the morning, because during the afternoon I have to go to Mavambo with the *capoeiristas*. I just hope that I can make a deal with the dentist and pay him in US. I absolutely do not have time to change money in downtown Harare.

By three o' clock, I have a meeting with The Cleft's coordinator. This is a Zimbabwean organisation which links outdoor games to counselling of children. My organisation will sponsor them to supervise a number of activities for children at Mavambo. I will help them to document their activities. Moreover, they are interested in incorporating the artistic methods we develop in their programs.

By four-thirty I pick up the other kids at school and return to a busy garden with again a number of children. By this time I can appreciate it. My children never lack football pals.

By five-thirty, I go to the shop and return empty-handed half an hour later. The lines at the Spar's registers are inconceivably long. You cannot even move through the store, because of the number of people. This happens in the only stores who are allowed to be paid in US dollars and, because of this, are well-stocked. In non-Spar shops, the shelves are empty – and the hallways too. Oh well, no meat tonight then.

In the meantime it is six o' clock in the evening and the night watchman starts his rounds in the garden. I cook, we eat and afterwards I help Jan with a few school tasks. Tonight, I have nothing special to do. I drive our car into our garage, happy I did not have to drive a lot today. The mileage indicator shows 154.

I decide to watch some TV with the children for an hour first and then to start on the acrobatics module. I hope to achieve quite a lot when my children will have gone to sleep. But even before the eight o' clock Belgian news, I fall asleep in front of the TV.

Around nine-thirty, the children go to bed and wake me up. I crawl into my bed. It has been a pretty good day. My children were cheerful, my job was fun, I learnt something, worked with interesting people, met new people, the sun shone and I kept control of my fears. My fears will keep growing and piling up the older my children become, the older I become and the more Zimbabwe will collapse.

My greatest fear is to be violently robbed in this house.

Then there is the fear of being arrested and locked up because of illegal exchange of local currency – a vital survival strategy.

Fear of not being able to leave Zimbabwe if violent conflict occurs.

Fear that all my previous jobs did little to nothing to help the current Zimbabwe.

Fear of a car accident and no medical help arriving.

Fear, to be financially liable for the rest of my life for passengers in my car who get hurt or become permanently handicapped .

Fear of eventually not being able to organise a Belgian contract for Zimbabwe, of having become too old to get a meaningful job in Belgium or somewhere else.

Fear of failing my children – especially regarding quality education.

Fear for my children that they lack professional responsible role models.

Fear of having to watch my children leave to a distant country searching for quality tertiary education.

Fear of having to lose one of my children to something as simple as an appendicitis.

Fear of aids and cholera.

Fear of becoming "weird".

Fear of becoming socially dysfunctional or, of not fitting in any country anymore.

Fear of losing my bearings.

Fear because Luk still loves Zimbabwe and does not want to leave.

emailveerle@gmail.com

CHRISTMAS HOLIDAYS
DECEMBER 2008

I locked my office. Switched off the kiln and the electricity supply so nothing can happen in my absence, switched off the lights in our largest art classroom. The remaining teachers dropped in for a bit between eleven and twelve and several students, who are already leaving the country with their parents, are coming round to kiss and say goodbye, carrying departing gifts under their arms; a lot of girls are crying. I hold them tight, because I know that every year, the goodbye is forever. I really will not see them again in my life.
'Harare International School is the best there is, Miss Delchambre!' There you have it. Pleased I get into my car and speed towards home. Two-thirty, I have to plan quickly, because my flight is tomorrow!
The suitcases are already packed and I will not be able to see my husband again. He has been in the rural areas for over a week and because of the cholera epidemic, which is now raging through all provinces and cities, he has prolonged his travels.

'I've called the minister, we need reinforcements. It's unbelievable what we've been through today', he says emotionally over the phone. 'Can't you get me some journalists?'
'I wouldn't dare, honey, the secret service will find out in no time which white nose visited which province. Not smart. Leave it to someone else. You really are doing enough.'
Silence.
'We'll see each other in January, then', I reply. 'I hope that you will book a ticket soon, you're overworked and severely strained and the situation just got out of control. For seventeen years, this is how I experience November and December. It is serious and sad, but you can't work for more than ten hours a day. Please come to Harare soon.'
Arrangements are made with Eva, Daniel and Melody regarding the security of our little house, the holiday arrangements between Christmas and New Year and the care for our livestock: eight chickens, two dogs and three young goats. The Christmas presents and salaries are ready and safe. That night, I quickly check the two cottages alarm systems and, before night falls, I slowly walk past all the lonely spots in our garden.
I will miss the swaying greens, the birds that wake me at first light that shines on my face around six.
Have not been in Europe with Christmas for fifteen years!

I talk to some of Aad's Italian and Dutch colleagues, some friends and Chocolate Hans and agree to have dinner with them at my house. That will be fixed in no time.
'You should bring the kids. The pool is still clean!'
Quickly, I search through the literature and poetry piles, for the collected works of James Kelley. Now that death is so close to our lives and we are so close to Christmas, I reread his poem.
This last night in Harare.

The Harare Morgue: A Harvest.
The dead continue to arrive.
Chilled trays are brimful; bodies
like bunches of decaying fruit,
adults and infants piled together,
lie in heaped vegetable mounds.

Lockers full, the corridors were next,
cadavers tiered against the walls,
gurneys impressed for stacking flesh -
wherever it is cold and flat the bodies lie:
a warehouse of death, a silo of death.

No gas to run the cop cars,
No gas to burn the flesh and bones.

Those violently killed are being piled over;
patiently awaiting their just investigations
for years, they liquefy in their wintry sacks,
cocooned pools of fat, oil or carbon,
gone now into puddled muck.

Scythes of ignorance and neglect
cut the young ones down; AIDS victims
are bundled like thin, dry stalks,
hacked too soon from their roots,
sad sheaves stored head to toe.

No gas to run the cop cars,
No gas to burn the flesh and bones.
The indigent unclaimed are trapped
between walking upon and lying low
within the sweet consuming earth –
their also indigent kin unable to pay
the funeral ticket to worm deliverance.

*Forty-two were recently made fortunate,
gifted to the medical school,
with decent interment promised
for being slit, hacked, explored
down to every cavity, morgan and artery.*

*One hundred US dollars will buy
the Mbudzi graveyard burial–
three times the monthly wage–
so this dingy, municipal limbo
fills with its unfortunate harvest.*

*No gas to run the cop cars,
No gas to burn the flesh and bones.*

Poor James.
A kind teacher at our school.
He was not able to handle Zimbabwe for very long.
It cut right through his soul, this part of Africa.
I fold the poem back into the file and call the dogs.
Dinner time.
Two hours later, our little house is *sjokkeblokke* full, as we Flemish say here. There is an abundance of food, wine and children. A few mention the cholera, but it does not last long.
Just relax guys; we all work hard enough during the day!
A few late comers trickle in carrying large dishes filled with food.
I put some Latin-American music on below the Christmas lights and behold, the chairs are pushed aside and the crowd starts to dance.
At around half past one, I close the gate and the night is jet-black.
Aad is not here to comment on the firmament, even though I recognize a lot of stars.
Do they recognize us, tiny creatures, in this land of pain?

MARIJKE LEGERSTEE-ALCOCK
SCENTS OF AFRICA

NEW-YEAR'S EVE 2008 IN DOMBOSHAWA HARARE ZIMBABWE
It is never the same to me without raisin fritters and apple turnovers and cold nights with fireworks etc, but we still tried doing something "homely" and there always was one or more parties and we hopped from one party to another.
This year, I am on my own. I am Marijke Legerstee, daughter of Cornelis Legerstee and Lydia Schavemaker.
I am married to Terry Alcock, I have four stepchildren and, for about a year, we (Terry and I) are separated.
Terry lives in South-Africa and I still in my beloved Zimbabwe.

This New Year's Eve I decide at about five in the afternoon that I need to be on my own and to climb the hills near Domboshawa with my camera, wineglass and a bottle of wine as sole companions!!
Shupi, my domestic helper, lives in that area and I tell her that I will drive her home, no problem, that way she does not need to take the bus.

While driving away from home in a quiet and peaceful mood some things start happening. At the same time I hear an enormous bang (thunderstorm), there is an enormous lightning strike. Shupi and I yell full of fear, since we saw the lightning hitting the transformer with all kinds of scary sparks flying, and not a second later, the power is cut and simply does not return for two weeks. Quite cosy for all the parties that evening, thankfully, I have a generator both at the lodge AND at home. I am blessed, because candlelight every evening, not being able to cook and no water is a bore. Only the diesel consumption is rather expensive. So be it.
Meanwhile we have arrived at the lodge's main gate and I try turning left, but next I hear blaring sirens. Police on enormous motorbikes signal me to move my car to the side of the road, because our "Mastermind" will be driving through with the complete motorcade.
This wretched, horrible man lives, together with his wife, the *very First Lady*, around the corner from us; our "friendly" neighbours. In the whole country, there is no sugar to be had, but knocking on *his* front door in order to borrow a cup of sugar is quite unlikely.

Too bad, I would have liked to have a look in their pantry. Think there is probably enough sugar in there to supply a cup to everyone in the whole country! While he is driving past in his armoured black Mercedes with number plates ZIM 1, I cannot help myself from yelling.....! ....! and some other indecent utterances!

Shupi has heard me yelling these more than once and we look at each other, laugh and drive to her house through the pouring rain. The moment I drop her off, it stops raining and the sun comes out while I am driving on. Domboshawa does to me what it has been doing for over thirty years.

I cry from emotion and happiness, but this time, there are also tears, big tears, from sorrow: personal sadness and grief for Zimbabwe. The tears keep coming. I cannot stop, suddenly miss Terry and the kids and I start thinking about our 18 years together. The lodge we set up; the many, many beautiful journeys we made together with our fantastic circle of friends, family and Dutch visitors. And now here I was, driving on my own on New Year's Eve. Not that I am lonely, but the feeling of sadness is very intense and the sunset promises to be beautiful.

While I park my car and get out, I am stormed by a dozen children. One of them steps forward and announces he has cancer and is HIV positive; he is about eleven years old and his skin is covered in a rash. I greet him and look at him and all the other kids that look at me expectantly. Suddenly, I see a large packet of Bokomo muesli rusks lying on the back seat. I pick it up and give it to my sick friend. I will not forget their beaming faces quickly. They run away to open up the packet on a hillock enjoy with delight, waving at me excitedly.

It makes me so humble. I walk to the entrance and the same man issuing the tickets for years greets me affably and I know that he will be telling me shortly that his children are starving and what a bad man Mastermind is, etc. etc. I take the time to listen to him and confirm everything he says, meanwhile asking how much a ticket is. Twenty trillion Zimbabwe dollars, he says, but I can give one US Dollar, since that is the value!

My ticket friend is so kind. Then I start thinking: he has three kids at home who have almost nothing to eat, who do not go to school (the teachers are on strike, cannot blame them with a salary of USD 10 a month) and who have no power to watch TV. They probably live amidst the filth, since their garbage is not being collected, they have no running water at home and run a great risk of getting cholera. He is still that same sweet man I have known for twenty years.

I think it is incredible and start on my small hike to the top of the hill. After fifteen minutes I sit down on the rocks, sigh deeply and look around me. Nature's beauty is unparalleled! The setting sun takes on the shape of a big fire-red ball and I know that the whole sky will turn into the most beautiful colours red/purple/pink in half an hour.

I meditate for ten minutes, then I pour myself a glass of wine and I start playing a game with the clouds, or rather they play a game with me. Often when sitting here with family or friends we tried, all in our own way and our own reality, to recognise objects, animals or whatever in the continuous changing mass of clouds. Thus a cloud could be a beautiful poodle transforming in no time into a dachshund, or a king with a crown suddenly turning back into an elephant. My thoughts are distracted by this game and wander off to the beginning.

My first visit to Rhodesia in 1972.
At the time I was working for KLM at Schiphol, sharing a house in Amsterdam with three fun girls and travelling around the world during my days off. I was saving my vocational leave for a trip to Rhodesia to visit a certain Els. My plane landed in November 1972 and the moment I caught the first scents and took my first steps on African soil I was immediately head over heels in love, and this infatuation would become a deep love and adoration.
A few years later, I worked and lived during the war years in Rhodesia.
I travelled a lot for my job: Victoria Falls, Hwange and Kariba; deep into the bush, the *lowveld* and the beautiful Eastern Highlands, the mountains where I found and still find so much tranquillity and spirituality!
Already then I lost friends in the liberation struggle for independence.
Ian Smith versus so many. After a few years I left again for the Netherlands, missing my family, working at first for the Marriott Hotel at the Leidseplein. But decided that I wanted to join KLM again.
However, my homesickness for Zimbabwe was too severe and I returned to Zimbabwe for good in 1982.
The brilliant untouched game parks, all national parks, the extremely friendly population and all memories of friends and experiences are passing through my mind. Voices from below and the smell of fires being lit drag me away from my day dreaming and the sky is getting dark; time to drive home.

I feel at one with nature and again I am caught unaware by this feeling of "a little sadness", because so much has changed in the year 2000 in our prosperous country, where tourists used to flock. When I was back here in 1982, I worked for KLM again and had a great job which took me to Malawi for a few years where I met Terry.
A few years later, I decided to build a guest lodge on our premises and the doors opened in 1998. It was a great success from day one; peacefully set in a beautiful area of the northern suburbs of Harare, called Borrowdale.
Our country was in flourishing that year (1996): almost no unemployment, people were happy, there was enough to eat, everything was possible and there was a great atmosphere, shops were filled with local produce until the first farm invasions took place. In one day everything

changed and after nine long years, there is still only misery! Eighty per cent unemployment, maybe more, with an inflation that is going through the roof. Prices are changing on an almost hourly basis; quotes are only valid for the day and are now mostly in US Dollar!!!

Three to four million black and white Zimbabweans are leaving for Australia, New Zealand, Canada, South-Africa, America and England. The middle classes, the *fat cats*, remain of course, because they are getting fatter and richer, but people from the rural areas, and the day labourers and other workers are staying, not being able to afford to travel and leave the country. People like me stay because we have hope, because we have our work here and we love our country so much. Everyone who leaves loves this country as well but cannot manage financially to stay. Often, the deterioration in quality education for the children is decisive or they say 'we have seen the writing on the wall.' There are countless arguments for their departure, "it's their choice", however difficult it may be.

For some, there just is no choice!!!

Families are torn apart, friends lose each other. At the lodge, we have "farewell breakfasts, lunches or dinners" one after the other and the speeches are so emotional sometimes that I am walking around with a lump in my throat that I do not dare to say anything. That is how much I want to grab them and cry along with them.

I lose friends as well and my children go to Ireland, South-Africa, England, Scotland and life is changing so incredibly fast. Terry is out of a job in the tobacco business here and is presented with the opportunity of working and living in Mozambique; I stay behind to run the lodge!

Many families live this way; women go to England, are away from home for months on end and work in health care, thus earning stable Pounds. It is no healthy or pleasant existence! Meanwhile, we as friends remaining here have time for each other, we come together for coffee and a Dutch *'stroopwafel'* (if we are lucky) or a morsel of Dutch cheese and/or a glass of wine. With our Dutch and Belgian female friends we take turns to whine and have a good cry over the many frustrations; we help each other and we joke about it.

Somewhat supported, we carry on with our lives, after having exchanged where there was bread and milk today and where to buy chicken, telling each other: "We are well off!"

But there are of course moral questions, because horrible things are happening around us. During evenings with all sorts of people with some food and a whisky or wine, we talk a lot.

The tension during the elections in March was severe and of course Morgan and MDC won, but unfortunately, we were fooled again!

Discussions arise and I am finding it hard. Yes, I take care of 20 people and their families, but so much is happening behind the scenes and I know I

cannot engage in politics, since I am a guest in this country (or am I not?) And then, one cannot take a too fanatical position. At the same time, I often think why not??
I also pay taxes here, but am not allowed to vote.

Olivia, my other domestic, has lost as much as 20 kilograms in two months. After endless bickering I went with her to the doctor; she did not allow me to be present!!! Later, in the car, she tells me she has TB, which is possible since she is coughing all the time. She is on medication and since I am paying for them I ask her to see the pills. Absolutely nothing to do with TB, but anti-retroviral for HIV. Obviously, she does not talk about it, but now I am faced with a dilemma, because she wants to keep on working while barely being able to stand. So I try to explain that TB is very contagious with a lodge, guests and 20 other staff members; that maybe she should rest for a few months and that I will continue to pay her salary. But I still get a long face!
Sometimes you cannot win.
Yes, dear people, I come home after all these thoughts and am so happy to be in my own house. I pour myself a whisky, go to bed early because I would like to sit outside the next morning at sunrise in my lovely garden with the sound of the Heuglin's Robin, the sound of the silence and with a cup of coffee to feel the first rays of sun of the new year and letting the positive energy affect me.

Zimbabwe, a special country, loaded with energy, spirituality and enormously potential in many ways. From esotericism to the belief in the law of attraction.
We are here to make the difference; why are we still here after nine years of drama??
I love it, and we who are still living here are here for a reason. And despite days without electricity and lack of water and the horrible things taking place, we love our country and just by staying here, we can have a positive influence, hopefully.
Tomorrow, a new year begins; on the 20th January we have Barack Obama's inauguration; I am already looking forward to his speech. Will he rebuke Mastermind, somewhere veiled in his speech? We wait; we will also have talks in January 2009. It will be a year of big changes. The whole world is changing; it will be exciting.
My passion for Zimbabwe remains.
I believe in it.
Time will tell.

marijke.zim@gmail.com

WOMAN OF POWER

She was tiny
she was small
at the end
she knew
she had it all.

One day, lo,
she decided to break,
got wings
and joined
her sisters
across
the Lake.

Never
was the silence
so pure, so gold,
when the women
finally
finally
had been told.

The Jacaranda shreds
her sad purple veil
all mortals
remember
the one
who was
so frail.

October 2003

CHIDEMOYO MAFARARARIKWA'S POEM
14 YEARS – ART STUDENT

Line, Value
Texture, Form!
Shape, Colour!
Pattern, Movement!
Rhyme, Rhythm!
Contrast, Balance!
Unity!
Freedom of Expression,
Vibrations of Colour, Blend, Mix, Create
Capturing Light
Shading Darkness
Take it in
Clear your Mind,
Close your Eyes
Listen to your Heart,
Draw.
Paint.
Mould.
Sculpt!
This is art!

FAIRHOME AND FAIR TRADE

Passing eight roadblocks at thirty degrees and under a threatening purple blue-grey cover of clouds we are driving from Harare to Ngezi, near Chegutu. After twenty-five minutes of evading all the potholes, relieved, we leave the Sunshine City behind us. The landscape unfolds into the full green of the summer's rain season in the slow descent.
Harare lies on a plateau fifteen hundred meters high and the heat of the *highveld* strikes heavily the next thirty minutes. The grasslands and woodlands alternate, heavy in moist, warm smells and the trees are flaunting fiercely: the *msasa* and the *mfuti*, (or the Prince of Wales feathers), the *Bauhinia* in pink and white blossoms and here and there some low mountain Acacia on the granite rock-spectacle. In a prehistoric time, the rocks appear to be stacked on top of each other and these formations are thus simply called *"kopjes"*. Here and there, we discover the last groups of long arums in the grasslands. To the left and right of the now perfect road we see nature's transformation over the past years: the fields of abandoned farms are completely overgrown and changed back into what we call the bush: *Africa takes over!*

An hour's drive later, there are almost no paperbark Acacias in sight, but I allow myself to be explained what is eaten in this time of famine: the
fruits of the Waterberry of Mukute, the Baboon's Breakfast or the Mukwingwiziri, the Azanza (Snot Apple), the Key Apple, the Live Long Mushamba, the Mahobohobo, the Chocolate Berry, the Buffalo Thorn, the Wild Custard Apple, the Wild Medlar and the Donkey Berry.
The trip that easily takes an hour and a half, depending on the number of roadblocks and the curiosity or malice of the police, who are looking for weapons, drugs or just recently bribery, was not too bad today.
Chatting away, charming with compliments or just flirting are successful strategies.
'*Shamwari* morning! How is your day? Flashy car, hey! And a new uniform? Don't you look handsome?'
All of the licenses, which are stuck to my windshield, often turn out to be expired or bleached by the sun.
In that case, you blame the sun for everything. Mind, always stay extremely polite and, especially, make jokes. Paying a fine works faster on the highway than standing in line for a new permit, a permit that is only valid four months.

Stay calm, look the man right in the eyes. Act as a stupid blonde!
Next, the round, red reflectors, made out of a worthless self-adhesive plastic, seem to have disappeared from the bumper again! Keep yapping, woman, do not stop. Make something up.
I am allowed to continue driving, just for once.
The negotiations for driving a little too fast before or after a village are more difficult. The police cars, remarkably brand-new since a few months, are sometimes parked in the bush so you do not notice them. Entirely wrong, of course, because you want to increase your speed between the last and the next roadblock! Speeding is definitely wrong, it is true.
Usually, in these situations, I am on my way to my deceased father, I tell them, and the tears well up spontaneously. In a way, in this life, I tell the truth and nothing but the truth.
'Damn you, you dirty comedian', Chocolate Hans, my companion for the day, hisses. Since a few weeks, I do not drive alone anymore.

Today things go smoothly.
No checks, no need to open the boot.
The ritual is often ended by:
'Where are your daughters? We are still looking for a bride!'
'Let us talk about *lobola, shamwari!*' First discuss the dowry, buddy! We drive on, laughing and my project's sponsor protests.
'This can only happen to a woman, all these fines you manage to evade! Not fair!'
'Life is not fair. Look there!'
I break.
Three magnificent antelopes dance over the road, very gracefully and in floating harmony with each other.
'The fence will probably have been cut, by poachers', my companions thinks.
'We must remember to call the Pamuzinda Lodge guys later. Before we know it, Jeffrey will run across the road!'
Jeffrey the giraffe was adopted by the Pamuzinda managers, less than a kilometre from the orphanage. A lot of farmers, who also looked after game on their former properties, had to find a solution for their animals, sometimes very quickly, before they took their belongings and fled.
Pamuzinda Lodge has also got kudu, zebra, sable antelope, wildebeest and a baby giraffe. It seemed to adapt so wonderfully, that after a few months, he dared to mingle with the visitors, especially the male company, we noted, because we often stayed the night after our visit at the orphanage.

Ten kilometres off Ngezi and fifteen minutes away from Chegutu, underneath several old high palm trees and some low *msasa* trees, in the middle of the bush we reach the derelict house, now a home to twelve children and two day mothers. The Fairhome family is a home to three girls and

nine boys. The poor village community, through their little church, centre of a Sunday's social life, offers help to an ever-growing number of widows, and a group of children between five and eighteen.
All are orphans, half of them street kids. They were dumped in the bush during Harare's operation *"clean up"*.
My friend, Veronique, the former Belgian ambassador's wife took care during two and a half years of this special group of children, she did it in a professional way and with a big heart.

When she left there was no option for me but to continue her work. Every three weeks, I visit the kids, for three years now, or whenever it is possible.
The rust-brown chickens, of the "roadrunner" type poke around busily and in the open kitchen hut, next to the house where dinner is prepared. Several skinny dogs scratch away the flee population warily, shuffling in the white sand. The chicken coop is ready and I am relieved.
Apart from developing the garden next to the river, this was the second project. The farm has been abandoned a while ago by the new owners, the so-called war veterans. The silos that were used to dry tobacco leaves are about to collapse. The curing shed no longer have a roof, but function as classrooms for a few years now. Now the government schools are closed for a few months already, I try out a home study program with the two day mothers.

Hungry stomachs study hard and there has been no food for three weeks: the maize flour allowance or *mielie* meal and the *bulgur* that never arrived this month remain the conversation of the day. Working hard in the garden in between the rain showers is the only way to survive, next to sponsoring that I received three times from the Maastricht-Oost Rotary club. I use this budget sparingly.
Nevertheless, the children look happy: on Sunday, clothes are washed at the river, next, there is prayer in the shadow of long, white robes and finally, wood is quickly gathered to make the first cup of Tanganda tea for the day.
Juliet, Paidamoyo and Portia, eleven and eighteen years old, beautiful girls, eager to learn despite a learning disadvantage because of their situation, are already waving to us at the gate. They watch my small car plough through the mud.

Wellington, Peter, Aisha, Crispen, Ian-James, Farai, Accumed, day mother Louise and Crispen come out to greet us. Always shy at first, but the stories already bubble up while we offload the car.

Everything is meticulously put in the register: tea, sugar, salt, soap, seeds, fifty kilos of rice, some meat, corn flower, books and games collected by my students, clothes, paper, sketchbooks, colour pencils, acrylic paint to try out today, small erasers and thrown away study materials for a new project by my Baccalaureate students.

We discuss the reading program and together we build a bookshelf that will become a mini library. The bottom drawer is kept for the games and the first aid kit. So far, no sick ones, and no cholera! No more than fifteen minutes' drive from here a lot of people succumbed over the past weeks. Together, we talk about prevention, while the girls try out the new Singer with Louise, the day mother. At Pamuzinda Lodge, just nearby, they are welcome in the kitchen on Saturdays to learn how to cook. At the end of the afternoon, they get to take the lunch leftovers home and also get a coke as a reward.

The four eldest boys, who recently ran away, got a training as nature guide. With pride we called the project: *From Street kids to Nature Guides*.
I have no idea where they are staying or surviving now, but I miss them. Henry, Richard, Blessing and Ashley. They are probably between 19 and 23 years old right now. Proud and smart boys, survivors and probably too independent to listen to the day mothers, strong-spirited and headstrong. You could see it coming. I miss their roaring laughter and their jokes, but I do not feel pity. Aad, who came along with me often, taught them how to repair bicycles and to glue furniture. They made a choice and I am convinced that they think of Fairhome sometimes, somewhere. Whatever they have learned, they take with them in their lives. They are ready to take part in the national exams of the National Parks to get their Nature Guide certificate, but I think they are practicing their street kid skills again.
It is your life!

In an exercise to keep the boys writing now that the schools are closed, I ask the boys, who are between twelve and fourteen years old, jot down the story of the four eldest who left just like that.

"Some of our boys living at Fairhome, ran away. All their parents passed away. They were used to living by themselves and be free.
Henry was a very good boy, except that he was a thief. He was very good with us, the young boys and taught us many games. He stole chicken, cooked by our neighbour. He was beaten thoroughly by the owner of the chicken because he put the bones back into the pot. He ran away after that.
Richard pretended to be a quiet boy. He was very clever. He stole some of our blankets, clothes, books, plates and curtains. Then he hid them. He sold bicycle parts and spares that doctor Aad gave us, to some nearby friends.
He used the money for food and transport and he left us.
Blessing was a very good boy, very quiet. He was brown in complexion.

We thought he also ran away from us, but later we learnt his auntie came and fetched him. He attended form three in Selous Secondary School.
We hope he has a home again, like we have.
Ashley was also 18 years old when he arrived here. He is handsome and very dark in complexion. Before coming to live with us he used to be a street kid. He was very talkative and he liked drawing and reading novels very much. He ran away when all the other boys of his age ran away from this home. Maybe they were too old to come and live in a house. A house has a roof, so you cannot see the stars.
Maybe a street kid does not like a home. Maybe he needs a "street home". A home in the street in the town where he comes from, where he can come to wash or study and leave whenever he likes."

This affects me very much.
I begin to reread this part when we trudge back to the main road through the wet mud. We look back and see everyone waving still, standing at the rusty fence, in the late afternoon sun. With the new books, in several reading levels, they have a lot of work ahead of them for the next essay tasks!
'Damn it, Hans, end-of-the-month gathering in two weeks time. Perhaps we could discuss these issues. Maybe organise some more sponsorship?'
We zoom back and do not have to stop at any roadblock for a change.
We are blessed today, we thought. Also fairly satisfied about the afternoon with the kids. We have to stock up on rice for the next time, and a lot of it. The new food shortages concerning basic commodities are unpredictable.
So let's immediately jump into the two shops that are open on Sundays!

In Harare, we stop for a while at Bon Marché. We heard that they were stocking the shelves. Yeah, right. Rows and rows of lemonade, no bread today, no milk, no yoghurt, but heaps and heaps of South-African wine and the both of us measure out eight big steps filled with fourteen different kinds of biscuits, all of them imported. This despite the fact that our country used to produce its own flour and local biscuit.
No affordable rice to be found. Just a small detour past the Spar Ballantyne. I have not been there in eight days! We are flabbergasted. It is packed with people. Chicken meat is in stock again: a local frozen chicken Halal 8 US, while an imported one from Montevideo, Paraguay, only 3 US. A freezer full of turkeys that have escaped Thanksgiving, I swear, from Peru. Only, it costs 40 US.
Who wants cherries for 16 US a kilogram?
At the next shelf we are struck by the latest addition: Vitana, Panjere and Naan-e Roghani Biscuits from Teheran and Isphahan.
'Is this from that *The Gardener and the Death*, Hans?'
'*Justement*! Look there is more: Aidin Wafers, also from Iran. And Muddlers Bisquits from South-Africa and Cookie with Nuts, from Brasil.

Hot Chutneys, Ball's Sterk Blatjang, no less than seven kinds. And four kinds of Chili all the way from Bangkok. And further up: Picon from France, and there: Tagliatelli and Riscossos from Italy for eight to ten dollars. And Carapelli Delizia from Firenze, where your former boss lives now!'
We buy four local cactus fruits, healthy and tasty. Four US, sigh.
And two local mangoes, three US. Another sigh. The local fruit almost did not cost anything this time last year.
We get dizzy and we buy a bottle of white wine to round up this Sunday. We choose *"Nooitgedacht"*.
To accompany Hans' chocolates. Locally made!

MIA MOERS
HAPPINESS COMES UNEXPECTEDLY

My name is Mia Moers.
I have lived in Zimbabwe for over ten years now, at the moment living together with my three sons Araya (17), Naod (14) and Yared (11).
My husband, Debru Negash, who is Ethiopian by origin, works outside of Zimbabwe for almost three years, but fortunately visits us regularly.
I am the daughter of Jan Moers and Toos Soeterbroek.

My father has passed away, but was an avid calligraphist, a hobby which grew into a sort of second career after his "official" retirement.
My mother was a teacher up to her early retirement. However, she has so many hobbies that her days are still pretty much filled. It is mostly thanks to her that we all are great dog lovers.

A long time ago, I studied chemistry and geology in the Netherlands and I hold a doctorate in biogeochemistry. During the first years of my stay in Harare, I taught and did research at the University of Zimbabwe, mostly in the area of environmental geology.
For several years now, I teach at the Dutch School here in Harare and since 2002 I am also its Principal. This is a so-called NTC school, which means that our students attend one afternoon a week after their regular school hours, so that they can be taught Dutch language and culture.
My children go to the International School and I will be part of the science department from 1 August 2009. That is when the academic year starts. For the past half year, I am also a member of the Board of Directors. There are children of about sixty nationalities at this international school. This and the fact that it is an "International Baccalaureate (IB) World School" contributed in making my children true world citizens.

Life here in Zimbabwe is certainly interesting and very instructive too. There are so many things you take for granted in the Netherlands. When you come to a place such as Zimbabwe, you will notice that all your Dutch behaviour, habits and rules definitely do not have universal validity. On the contrary, people from elsewhere often find them strange, unnecessary or just plain preposterous.

Zimbabwe has taught me to be more flexible and realise that there are many different opportunities. Principles and fundamental behaviour have an entirely different connotation here. Often, they seem almost inappropriate and pragmatism is the only option. For example, there are several four-lane roads in Harare. Official, people drive on the left side, like in England, but on these roads, people drive wherever they want: left side, right side, very fast or very slow, with or without lights in the dark, everything is possible. My husband originally was outraged by this and tried to teach his fellow road users better manners, but he failed completely; they looked at him as if *he* was crazy. Like the saying goes: *When in Rome, do as the Romans do.*

Another issue is the wide-spread poverty. From a fundamental point of view, you would want to deal with the problem at its roots, but practically, as an individual, most of the time all you can do is give food, money, clothes, etc. The situation in the countryside is especially distressing.
The cleaner at the Dutch school recently told me that he sold the few cows he has for 25 Euro a piece in order to get *mielie meal* (the staple food in southern Africa) for his children. They live in the countryside and are in danger of dying from hunger. I can tell him a hundred times that a cow is worth much more than 25 Euro and that he should not sell them, but what does it help him if he cannot get more for them? The idea alone of not having enough food for your children makes me shiver.

It took a lot of effort to accept the fact that we have no running water for over a year and often have no electricity and telephone connection. Calls abroad are now completely impossible and Skype no longer works even though I have a broadband connection. Of course, I have little to complain about, because I can buy water from a man who comes by with a large tanker truck (very expensive) and I have a generator (also expensive).
So, I feel no pain, except in my wallet.

And then there are the groceries. Hyperinflation and the resulting decline unavailable items made me feel quite depressed a number of times. I never knew my "happiness" depended on the availability of Nutella and cornflakes.

And that is for the children, because I do not eat them myself. You cannot imagine how "happy" I currently am, now that life has been mostly dollarized; we can even buy Italian salami. Also for the kids, because I do not eat meat. And let's not forget Whiskas and Pedigree Pal (also not for me).

Sometimes, I wonder how I would define my "happiness" if I would be here without my children:
QUIETNESS; in this city, the traffic has decreased strongly in the past ten years, which means almost completely empty roads and no traffic jams. With a lack of electricity there is no loud music at the neighbours.
CLEAN AIR; as a result of several government measures and again due to lack of electricity there is very little industry left. And like I said, small cars.
LOTS OF SPACE; Zimbabwe is almost ten times the size of Holland and has less than twelve million inhabitants. Not what you would call densely populated. In my neighbourhood, most houses are on a property of four thousand square metres or more.

The ridiculous situation we find ourselves in, does lead to comical solutions. For example, when I want to pay my e-mail/internet bill, I can do it in kind: cows and goats, alive or dead, chopped up or not, it is completely acceptable. Old, but still functional electronics can also be used as payment. Or else you can use petrol or diesel coupons.

When you hear about the amount of problems in all aspects of life, it is almost a miracle that some services are still functioning. My youngest son recently injured his wrist. Here I was hoping that it would not be serious, because medical facilities are in danger of becoming a phenomenon of the past.
Three years ago, when the same son had a very visible fracture of his arm, I was up against a lot of medical incompetence. But armed with that experience, I was now able to find a qualified specialist and a good place to do X-rays. And of course there was no electricity and running water when we came to the several clinics, but the X-ray specialist was not easily alarmed and was able to localise an old, small, movable German X-ray machine and made it operational by means of a generator. And to be sure, she managed to produce a usable photo together with a handwritten report, because the computers did not work either. As a precaution, my dearest was put in a cast. And we were lucky, because the technician had been smart enough to catch the remaining water in buckets. I have to say that I am deeply impressed by their dedication and ingenuity.

For me, a normal weekday starts between five-thirty and six o'clock. In the summer it is already nice and light with a pleasant temperature. School starts at seven-thirty and the children have to do the daily routine of getting up – wash themselves – have breakfast before that time. Usually this does not go seamlessly, because they often go to bed too late.

Here, children have to be brought to school. It is not like in Holland where the kids go by themselves on bicycles or with the bus. There is no public transportation between school and home and cycling is far too dangerous: narrow roads without cycling lanes and drivers who do not watch out for cyclists.

In part due to HIV/AIDS, poverty and bad medical facilities the death rate is pretty high here. This is why, I think, people deal with death differently than they do in the Netherlands.

Here, it is more an acceptable fact, an unavoidable aspect of life. Thus: a cyclist more or less, too bad, it is a shame, but nothing can be done about it. Death is at the centre of our lives, every day.

In short, it is the parent's responsibility that the children arrive at school on time. Making the children prepare their own lunches (or clean up their rooms) is also not an option, seeing as there is staff that can do it for them. Fortunately, my eldest son has his driver's license and is burdened with a lot of tasks. As long as he thinks driving is cool and it is still a novelty, I gratefully make use of him: my personal driver and grocery boy.

The International school ends at a quarter past two, but after that all sorts of sporting activities and after-school activities take place. The school has fields and a gymnasium for all sorts of team and individual sports. For my creative and smart boys: more than enough sports! Around five in the afternoon they usually head back home. Time for dinner and homework.

In theory, it sounds as if I, with the children out of the house all day, can lie lazily on the couch all day, reading books, watching television. Unfortunately, reality is different. Doing groceries takes a ridiculous amount of time; often, it is a long drive (half an hour to the milk and cheese vendor).
Usually, half of what you need is not available, which means you have to look somewhere else or return another day. Several months ago, a part of the machine that separates the cream from the milk broke down. No whipped cream, *crème fraiche* or butter in the whole of Harare and this for almost two months. It is surprising that apparently there is only one copy of this type of machine in the capital city.

And then there are the queues at the cash registers; delays of half an hour are very normal. A good occasion to talk with several strangers and often you get useful information, for example where to buy wine at a reasonable price, or who imports French cheese nowadays.
Having arrived at the register, as a rule, the cashier never has change: American coins are non-existent and there are far too few American dollar bills in small denominations. This leaves you with the following options: 1. settle for a *"credit note"*, 2. ask the staff to look for small goods, such as

bread rolls, equalling your change, 3. ask the people behind you whether they have got change. Really inventive.

Another time consumer is paying bills, such as for water, electricity, telephone and local taxes. Not only are the queues long; everybody pays in cash (or used to pay with cheques), but you never know how much to pay, because bills are not being sent for many months now. However, it is clear: absence of either the service or a recent bill is absolutely not an excuse not to pay. I am expected to pay my non-existing water bill anyway. Apparently, there is a phone number that you can call to find out how much your bill is, but that has never gotten me anywhere.
Earlier this week, I went to enquire about my phone bill and whether or not it could be paid in American dollars. Nope. My bill was for the amount of five trillion Zimbabwean dollars, but if I had one American dollar, the official would be able to help me, because he just received his salary in Zim dollars. A so called fair trade. I gave him some extra, because I know for certain that this man earns far less than five dollars a month.
He's happy, I'm happy.

Cooking dinner also takes more time than it does in Holland. There are little reliable semi-manufactured products, which means that you will have to use the raw materials. Of course, it is healthy. I have a whole set of cookery books on the shelf, but almost every single recipe needs to be adjusted.
The rule is, you go to the store, see what is in supply and then find a matching recipe. If you turn things around, you get hopelessly frustrated. Fruit and vegetables are mostly seasonal here. At the moment, it is the time of (imported) grapes, peaches and plums. We feast on those, because we know it is over next month.

Right! And the remaining time is used for "real" work: preparing classes, teach, hold meetings, answer letters, talk to parents, attend committees, etc. etc.. I find it hard to always stay motivated in this imploding economy. You notice that people are forced to leave, because they have no means of supporting themselves, you witness how all sorts of well-functioning organisations and companies are brought to bankruptcy. It is even worse for the people who have no job anymore and are not able to leave. It is and will remain sad, all this suffering that seems so unnecessary.
Probably to counter this there is a lot of black humour and all sorts of dark jokes go around; we laugh a lot. It is clear, life keeps going on. Except, it is not always as easy to constantly adapt your priorities.
We are creatures of habit after all.

For these reasons, I assume, a lot of people are spiritual. The churches are full and "*mindfulness*" lectures and courses are much frequented. Everyone is looking for ways to cope with the constant changes and aggravations.
The meditation group, of which I am a member, is flourishing and meditation retreats are very popular. It seems that all this misery is good for something: a proper motivation to work on ourselves and find out who we really are.
A search for your true self, this is something we should be prepared to sacrifice for!

In the past years, I also have more appreciation for functioning democracies. A combination of malign and/or inadequate rulers and heedless and/or uninformed citizens can completely destroy a properly functioning system in an amazingly short time.

mia.moers@gmail.com

CORALS, CROCODILES AND QUEUES

I am up to my elbows in clay and, with a long wooden stick, I stir thirty kilos of clay powder and thirty litres of water in a large black drum. A matter of patience! Fortunately, it is only 33 degrees today, in the shade, so I can manage. The chickens and cocks come marching by and are followed at a safe distance by the three little goats. Carefully, they shuffle past and promptly skip back to the other side of our garden, where, as an exception, they are allowed to graze freely for a few hours. Markus, our domestic's grandson plays shepherd while waiting for the government schools to open again. They have been closed for three months now, no one knows what is going to happen, so Markus of four and a half years old not too unhappily specialises in shepherding our livestock.

Yesterday, I gave three women a job and let them sieve fifty kilograms of clay powder. This in itself is a day's job now that the local clay is no longer pure. Miniscule rocks create cracks when drying or baking pottery. It is a dead shame, because it destroys work you have been labouring on for days.
It cost me several works that came out of the first bisque firing or out of the second glazing firing broken, before I could analyse and figure it out what was the problem. I obtained these fifty kilos from a ceramicist who left the country in October. If you live in an area that deals with repeated power failures, you cannot run your kiln for eleven hours at a stretch. There goes your career as a ceramic artist!
The power failures are unpredictable, despite official "load shedding", I use my kiln mostly at night and hope for the best. Usually, it works, sometimes it goes wrong. When the price of a bag of 50 kilograms of clay suddenly became 500 US last November (price increase: from 40 to 500 US!), it meant the end for several of the last remaining ceramic artists.

The red and grey clay, up to recently the best in the whole of southern Africa, is brought in from the Gwaai River, past Bulawayo or from Mutare, Eastern Highlands. Both types of clay are soft and slightly elastic and in this wonderful rainy season, they can dry gradually, slowly and uncovered in their final shapes for days. The four Hakata bones I lay in a nearby corner, for luck. Sometimes it helps.
You often lose work between September and December, because you cannot win the battle against the heat. Protected underneath layers of plastic, the clay sometimes dries out in a matter of hours and spontane-

ously falls to pieces. I leave the question why I chose one of the hardest media to work with unanswered. It just feels nice when you work with ten fingers and the palms of your hands, you are close to the earth and in times of stress, clay works therapeutic and it heals! It is that simple.

Except, the process from powder to art is truly laborious and in these times of power cuts it is a Sysiphus labour. At a certain moment and after ten years of solo exhibition, there are no new, exciting crossroads in this country. Nevertheless, we carry on...

Ceramics is a passion that does not let you go!

Every day, for four days, stir for ten minutes with that three metre long stick until the mud bath in the barrel looks creamy and inviting.

The red-brown colour catches all the colourful rays of the sunlight which moves through the shiny dew of the palm trees.

It is now thirty three degrees in the shade after a heavy rainfall of an hour. The garden is bathing in silver and golden light, the bougainvillea is looking more radiant red than ever and the drops hang from all the green like a thousand diamond earrings.

The African spirits emerge from the damp soil.

'Eva, can you take over for the next ten minutes?'

A well trained arm promptly and expertly stirs through the clay with the wooden stick and whether it is boiling *mielie meal* that is stirred into porridge, or wheat into flour, nothing beats a singing African woman who takes her time and all of her concentration for her task. No job is beneath her dignity, no task is more important than another.

From the barrel, the clay mud is spread over Plaster of Paris for about three hours and then the wedging starts. The humid clay is wrapped up into packets that await the next trip packed in plastic and in dark cool rooms.

Roll kilometres of coils and you can start your coral's design. Three of them are waiting to have three centimetres added to them today. With my children's music in the background, the work goes fast.

I cannot start yet, my faithful help Eva realises.

'You better unpack your shopping!' she yells...

True.

The shopping by itself was a small nightmare today, after teaching.

Only a minor one.

Instead of leaving at five to seven, I drove off to school at five past seven. The final part of the road is for professionals who zoom past the potholes in slalom. I thought of doing the same, but, just before I reached the gate, I drove into a brand new pothole that was not there before the weekend.

Damn!

Twenty past seven, five minutes late (sometimes, the director stands at the gate at seven in the morning), the guards look at me.

'Guys, I am late for class, two tyres are flat and the rims look buggered!'
Forgot once again how the day is supposed to start.
Parbleu. I am reprimanded.
'Morning Patrice and how are you?'
Right.
You never start blabbering away like that; you are supposed to respect the rituals every time. In the end, they also have a calming effect. The hello, the question, the introduction to the start of a friendly conversation and, mostly, look each other in the eye smiling.
'Morning, Garikai. I am very fine, and how are you? Will you please, please help me with my car; I left it on the main road. Here are the keys!'
Garikai and his buddy happily take over and know that they will have earned something later. There is a garage further on, they know what to do.
Teaching went well, the Kandinsky project is almost done, my youngsters apply water paint using the most difficult techniques and the elder students work on an art appreciation essay.

I pay the guards, jump into the car and receive an unexpected text message from Daniel Badji, my Senegalese colleague: "Fuel at Lewisam, no queue." Everyone on their way there, with their coupons.
Lewisam is ten kilometres from school and en route to our house in Chisipite. When I arrive, there already is a queue, the most used word in our vocabulary nowadays, and I drive humbly behind the last car.
Ten years ago, I spent on average about two hours a week queuing in my car. Friends of mine collected the kids from school and I studied for an art history exam in the car, with a flask of tea or cold water.

Ten years later, I have Matisse, Chagall and the Pre-Raphaelites in my lap, Paolo Conte on the back seat and I consider a new art appreciation strategy. That is how you spend your time queuing for fuel.
During the liberation war, the Rhodesians built entire barbecue sets on their pickups in order to party all night and survive the wait. So no moaning today, we are well on our way. Moreover, we are on this side and not the other, the haves not the have nots, those who have no dollars, thus coupons and transportation. And a job. *Na also!*
Two friendly faces appear at the same time by the left and right window. This means: be careful. Still, this can mean they belong together. My window wipers are measured and they offer me a new pair for ten dollars.
'No thank you *Shamwari,* I changed mine two months ago.'
'Would you need any dog food, madam?'
Well, that is another matter. It is a stressful task to get dog food nowadays and just try mixing something edible for our mansion's loyal best friends at huckster prices. The imported stuff from South Africa is way too expensive.

'It is produced in Kariba and a lot cheaper than anything you find, Madam.'
'Let me give it a try.'
The final forty five minutes I gasp for air, because there is a pungent smell floating through my RVR. The dog chunks turn out to be crocodile food. Great. The Zimbos prove to be a creative people!
'Madam, some peanuts, do you need soap? Coke? A banana?'
'No thank you, see you guys soon!'

It is my turn. Forty-five full minutes later.
'How are you madam? Fine? You are the lucky little star today, we are closing the queue. The fuel is finished!'
Done! Behind me, I see a hopeless row of cars a kilometre long...
The yellow barriers are set behind my car.
Oof!
'I am so lucky! *Tatenda shamwari!*'
I am also allowed to fill jerry cans.
With the fuel and a fifty kilo crocodile I drive to Spar Ballantyne.
There, a hundred and fifty people are lining up in five different queues, month's end!
And, half an hour later, I am waiting in one of these queues.
Tired and not even with twenty-five percent of my grocery list. And ponder what the German word for windshield wiper is.
Yesss! *Wischblätter!*
Maybe I should have stocked them?

EMMANUEL RUBEN NEVES
JAPANESE SHOWERING

My name is Emmanuel Ruben Neves – for reasons that will be explained later, I am usually known as "Snowy". I currently live in Harare, Zimbabwe.
I was born in Harare, Zimbabwe (then Salisbury, Rhodesia, respectively) in 1957, which I suppose puts me in the dreaded "middle age" bracket. By profession I am a teacher.

DECEMBER 21, 2008:

Today began as what has become a "normal" day for my wife and I.
It's 4.30 AM and the sun is not even up yet. The sky in the east has started to acquire that charcoal blue/grey, harbinger of the impending dawn. I grab the buckets and go down to the swimming pool which has not been used as a pool for the last year and a half, but is now a reservoir for household water. While the City of Harare was in charge of supplying water, supplies were limited, but at least one could "plan" for those days when the water stopped trickling out the taps. Now that ZINWA (the Zimbabwe Water Authority) has taken over, the water has stopped altogether – for the last 18 months to be exact, which is probably a good thing as cholera has begun its insidious spread.
So here I am in my "Rhodesian bungalow"[2], situated in a suburb with the unlikely name, for the middle of Africa, of *The Grange*. The area certainly does not reflect the English definition of a "grange" in England, but, no doubt, when the original farmland was being carved up for residential blocks, nostalgia for the home country played a factor in the mind of the original colonial land owner when the area came to be named. Of course no attention was paid to what the area may have been called in the Shona [3] vernacular, possibly because very few, if any, people were living in the

---

[2] – a three bedroomed house, with a cottage attached. The type of building can be found throughout Zimbabwe's urban centres and probably result from there being only one or two accepted architects in the colonial era. These houses all follow a similar pattern, with their most annoying features being kitchens that were designed by men that could not cook and who had no reason to ever suppose that they would have to go into the kitchen, having, no doubt, a meek and submissive wife, or the ubiquitous "cookie" (on almost slave labour wages) to provide the expected daily fare. They are comfortable though, reasonably spacious and with most built on at least an "acre" of land, relatively large gardens, which often have a swimming pool and/or tennis court squeezed in.
[3] Shona is the language of the indigenous inhabitants of the area

originally thickly wooded area. Most of the Shona lived on the edge of the *High Veld*[4] at the time of white settlement (c. 1896).

But here I am with my buckets, gathering water from the pool in the same fashion as someone in *kumusha*[5] would collect it from the river. Out in the courtyard, between the main house and the cottage, a fire is going in the Weber[6] so that the water can be heated as ZESA, the Zimbabwe Electricity Supply Authority, is staging yet another power cut, or "load shed" or whatever they want to call it. The water is heated and Lynn, my wife and I, have a "Japanese Shower" from the buckets, using kitchen jugs to scoop the water onto our bodies. The exotic nature of the "Japanese Shower" has long since lost its novelty and its appeal – having heated the water on an open fire, one needs the wash as one has begun to smell like a kipper. But at least we can face the day confident in the knowledge that we are clean. As for drinking water, a friend with a borehole brings water in 25 litre containers, which we decant into the bath in the guest bathroom. I was going round to collect the water myself this morning, but as I hit a pot-hole[7] last night, shredding two tyres, my car is unserviceable and thus I shall rely on the good will of my friend Dave. Tyres are available, provided that one pays in American dollars. In fact, with American dollars, South African Rand, Botswana Pula etc. one can acquire anything, usually at three times the price charged for the product in South Africa. So, am I happy? The answer is an unequivocal "yes". Perhaps the joy comes from the ability to "make a plan", to overcome the adversity that one faces on a daily basis. A person living in say London will never understand the joy, the sense of achievement that comes from filling one's tank with fuel, getting fresh bread, milk and eggs. Since the advent of the US dollar stores, commodity supplies have greatly improved, and the joy of "making the plan" has been replaced by the more consumerist joy of choice and availability.

Kariba and Nyanga are both close enough to enable a weekend escape from the stress of Harare living. The sheer joy of 5 nights on Kariba houseboat, fishing and drinking beer, enjoying the wild animals, has to be

---

[4] The *High Veld* is an area of high altitude (1500m) in Zimbabwe, which was originally thickly wooded, which the European settlers recognized as excellent land for growing tobacco amongst other things, and which was largely ignored by the Shona as viable farmland because of the inability of traditional farming methods to deal with heavily wooded areas. Most Shona settlements were located on the edge of the *High Veld*, where soils were more marginal, but which were easier to farm; Great Zimbabwe being the most outstanding example.

[5] The Shona term denoting the Communal Lands, areas of rural settlement, created from the original "native reverses of the colonial period"

[6] A kettle barbeque

[7] Harare's streets are littered with potholes, as the City Council, which is now run by an illegal "Commission" has not repaired the roads in years. In fact there is a joke that asks how one can tell a drunk driver in Harare – he is the one that drives straight

experienced to be believed. Nyanga, whilst producing similar levels of joy, does so for very different environmental reasons.

When there, one could be forgiven for thinking one had been transported to Scotland – the rugged hills, the heather and of course frequent rain and cold ensure such a reaction. This no doubt explains why that arch-colonialist, Cecil Rhodes, built a country retreat there – it might also have had something to do with the seclusion that suited his ambivalent sexual preferences. It is strange that the national park that surrounds his estate is still called the "Rhodes Nyanga National Park", what with all the post-independence name changes that took place. In fact this anomaly is projected into the lives of ordinary Zimbabweans in the country's property laws. Perusal of any title deed, ancient or recent alike will reflect that one still lives in Southern Rhodesia and in my case Salisbury. Apparently the legal costs relating to changing the status of property rights in Zimbabwe to more correctly reflect the present political dispensation is prohibitive – so free Zimbabweans continue to live in Southern Rhodesia!

Nyanga has been a constant source of delight for me. As the Senior Tutor at a local College (at which I taught for 27 years), it was my privilege to take many groups of my students to the mountains so that they too could experience the wonder of the place. The students themselves on these camps provided a great source of inspiration to me as a teacher, as did the students at the College itself. In relation to the camps there is one incident that stands out in my mind that reflects the fun, the tribulations and the overall satisfaction of those "Sixth Form Camps". The incident at the time was treated with the mixture of levity and concern that it, in my opinion, deserved, even if it did involve an alleged "suicide attempt". But unfortunately, the parents of one of the students involved contacted my Director, a most admirable man by the name of Abdullah Suleiman, who required me to write a formal report on the matter.

The background to the incident involved a brief love affair that had taken place between two students (called for the purposes of this article George and Nicole) shortly before the camp. Nicole revealed to me on the camp that she feared that she might be pregnant – the affair was over by this stage. Nicole had informed George of the situation but was very firm in pointing out that she placed him under no obligation as concerns the pregnancy. She further informed him, quite clearly, that the affair between them was definitely over.

From his actions and his statements George obviously felt to the contrary and that they were still very much an item. He in fact, had a long discussion with me on the matter in which he professed "undying love" for Nicole. I tried to tell him that it was pointless pursuing the matter in view of the fact that Nicole was at that time showing a decided interest in another student. This obviously caused George some distress, as he did not find it easy to accept the rejection, given the circumstances.

A further element must be introduced here to explain the "suicide attempt". For some time before the camp George had been vociferous in stating to his peers that he had discovered a new religion of which he was the only follower. The god of this religion of his was a water demon which he called *Ashen Suga* – he wore an image of this demon around his neck, purchased some months before in an occult shop in Wiltshire, U.K.. Whilst on the camp he would very publicly worship *Ashen Suga* by rushing off to the Nyagombe River (near the campsite) at odd hours and swim fully clothed, returning to the campsite soaking wet and always stating that the demon had been speaking to him.

On the day when the alleged suicide took place, the students and I had spent the day at a local hotel playing various board games because of the miserable weather. We had been due to go hiking that day, but the rain and cold put paid to that. Whilst at the hotel, George made many attempts to speak to Nicole but she refused to speak to him. It was not pleasant to witness this, but I then believed and still do, that 18 year olds should be allowed to solve their own problems as far as possible. On the return to the campsite George immediately left the camp telling me that he was going down to the river. Thinking he was off to another worshipping session I thought little of it. He returned half an hour later, soaking wet as usual. He was rambling in his speech, but quite frankly, it was very much an exhibition. He announced that he had thrown himself in the Nyagombe River with the intention of killing himself: he was certain to ensure that Nicole was in earshot of all this. He went on to relate to the, by now incredulous, group that after he had thrown himself into the river, he sank to the bottom where he waited to drown. The water demon then appeared to him, kissed him and whispered: 'Live George'. A water reed floating on the surface then "emanated" a golden light; he reached for it and it pulled him to safety.

It must be pointed out the river into which George threw himself is nowhere more than a metre deep, and as it is considered safe by the National Parks for young children to swim in, George was in no danger. George also played in the College First Water Polo Team, so his swimming abilities were never in question.

Thus the entire incident was not a suicide attempt at all but an attention seeking stunt to make Nicole guilty. I was later accused by George's parents that I had been gossiping about the incident: George's antics on camp concerning *Ashen Suga* were so public that everyone there began to talk about it, especially as his belief and methods of worship were so bizarre. As it turned out Nicole was not pregnant and George continued for a few more weeks to worship his trusty demon, until he realised that it was no longer the attention grabber that it had been initially.

Teaching in this country, and particularly in the College where I was based was such a life enriching, stimulating, rewarding and enlightening experience that it made living in Zimbabwe all the more worthwhile. My own school life was equally rewarding. In fact it was in my Form 2 year that my French teacher, an ogre by the name of Tom Learmont, gave me the nickname *Snowy*, no doubt in an effort to forever link me to Tintin's dog – pointing out that the dog's name was in fact *Milou* if one read the books in the original French merely earned me "two cuts" for insolence and a now permanent nick-name!

Life has indeed been good, in spite of the initial "whining" of this article. I always find that if I take time to count my blessings, things always appear to improve. I have a particular weekly delight of Hashing to look forward to. Every Monday evening at 5.30 PM, a band of runners, walkers, and dog minders set off to find a trail set by the hare designated for the week. The Harare Hash House Harriers belong to an international group of "drinkers with a running problem". The concept originated in Kuala Lumpa in 1938 amongst British forces stationed there who decided that while it was a good idea to increase levels of fitness with a war threatening, it was also wise not to risk dehydration induced by the exercise – thus they recruited the owner of their favourite bar, The Hash House to supply beer at various vantage points. Essentially an expat organisation, the Harare Hash has its origins in the efforts of Sue Swain, the founding member and original "Grand Mistress" of the Harare Hash House Harriers. What Sue found in Harare, in January 1984, freshly off a flight from Nairobi, in terms of Hashing was not encouraging. She was drawn to a group of runners that jogged weekly by their home on the University of Zimbabwe campus. The fact that the group ran a road circuit (Hashers love running in mud), didn't have beer bellies and looked very fit did not bode well. When asked about the Hash, one runner thought she was referring to his dinner the night before.

The next stop was the Australian High Commission, where she surely would find someone who knew about the Hash. Looking highly suspicious, the security guards refused her entry and made her sit in the reception area. After several hours wait a portly looking gentleman called Andy Bearpark emerged carrying a pair of running shoes – he had heard about the Hash but was not sure if one existed in Harare, and that he was not a Hasher: his life was about to change.

Flyers were distributed to all Sports Clubs in Harare on 13 March 1984. Sue set the trail, marking it with shredded paper and returned to the

Sports Pavilion on the University Campus to find a large crowd milling around. The Hare yelled the traditional "on-on" and Harare's inaugural run was off, over the campus lawn, down a drain and through a hole in the security fence.

The trail led left: the pack, composed in large part by that group of fit, non-beer guzzling road runners went right mumbling how slow the pace was and what strange people the Hashers were. Eventually the pack returned to the Pavilion to celebrate, in true Hash fashion, the completion of their athletic endeavours with copious amounts of cold lager. As the sun set in a typical shower of reds and crimsons, the beer was quaffed, new friends were made and the Harare Hash House Harriers was born.

JANUARY 11, 2009:

I began this article with my groaning about water and electricity – I have since been blessed by having the means to acquire a generator and have a borehole installed. I really appreciate the long hot showers now, and will never take them for granted. I have left the College where I spent 26 years of my life living the dream of what I considered to be effective education. In my teacher training days my favourite text was "Teaching as a subversive activity". I cannot recall the author. My entire teaching career was based on the principles found in that book, and I am proud to say it still is. I teach from home now. One dream ended and I have begun a new one.

BASIL ON THE OPERATING TABLE

What an artist and an epidemiologist are not good for. We will accept every little challenge that is not too far out.
Accompanied by a phenomenal view over the *mopane* and *msasa* trees, the weeping wattles and an old coral tree, richly scattered over the hills and without any other home in sight, we drink our first glass of wine. At Assia and Bengt's, in Glen Lorne, ten minutes from my home in Chisipite.
It is past five and while Assia's boys are playing on the ground next to us, we await the sunset. They are putting together a poem using the magnetised words from "Naughty Poetry", from Exclusive Bookshop Cape Town. At this moment and in this life where we can shake off the stress that is laying over us like a coarse; itchy blanket, we laugh and enjoy the view. There is only this. Just the two of us; no one has to be brave, smart or ingenious. We were like this all day.

We talk about the latest "Mindfulness" course by Lama Rob Nairn, the spiritual leader in, the search of peace and inner balance in this all too painful existence. The pain of not being able to handle and put into perspective everything around us. That we are not so young anymore, or is it about caring too much? The depressing apathetic behaviour of the people around us, the despair and the hopelessness of the local situation we cannot change.
The day is done; everything that is unpleasant has mellowed and flew away like dead autumn leaves.
We talk about my children and her children, how well they are doing, how proud we are and how they cope as young world citizens. And that the concept of home is bigger than the country that is stamped in their passport.

DIFFERENT, that is how they call themselves and what they feel like, the *Third Culture Kids*, with Europe in a back pocket, Zimbabwe and Cape Town in the other. We look through my pictures of the last solo exhibition. We talk about the last flight between Nairobi and Amsterdam. All of us passengers were punished with an insecticide spray in the plane, just before take-off. And whether or not we actually deserve this, coming from Harare.

'Look at this photo, I enjoyed that evening', Assia says.
'Do you remember, that speech of Boudewijn, the ambassador? A thirty minute professional talk on the colour "red" because your show was called *Red, a ceramic exhibit on passion*? What a lovely man!'
Corals with pearls and Japanese dishes. I have lost count of what has gone into the world. With every parting, something dies inside of me, that is how painful it is to say goodbye to a loved one.
The waiting is for Aad.
He is going to operate on Basil, the dog. If he, in his days, was able to operate on everything that grew on people, Assia thought, than surely the Labrador's cancerous growth could be handled, right?
The costs of a night's admission, diagnosis, and especially the anaesthesia for this ancient friend would certainly raise to 400 US! The fees for top of the line animal care are incredible. Thus, an alternative is a human doctor and a small risk. In both cases, Basil might die and in one case Bengt and Assia are saving 400 US$ minus a few beers!
Whilst waiting we spent the time by reviewing all possible first names we can find.
The local staff here has wonderful Biblical names by the way: Shepherd, Virtue, Elijah, Moses, Joseph, Charity, Chastity and all the apostles' names. Shona names: Munyaradzi, Rumbidzai, Rudo, Gwinayi, Tonderai, Tendai, Dzidzi and English names: Lovemore or Loveless, Firstborn, Lastborn, Sixpense, Melody, Precious, Wisdom, even Punishment and Hatred, or like the twins of our mechanic: Clutch and Plate, and let us not forget the bastardised English names such as Onias (from Onerous) and Cremance (for Clemens).

Meanwhile, Assia and Bengt's gardener Speaker and doctor Aad have arrived. The latter, happy but tired, white around the nose, drinks a beer first. However, Speaker, not all white around the nose, but polite and helpful is about to play his part in the daily soap of this existence.
Mayor, the female domestic, scrubs the wonderful wooden garden table clean and looks at us with a roguish smile. Eyes like burning coals this girl has!
The operating table is dressed with a black bin bag, *et voila!* We act like we have been working as nurses all our happy little lives. Without mouth caps, or uniforms or operating theatre. We will invent our own theatre.
Doctor Aad gets up. I can see he is exhausted.
It has been a day. Aad's secretary had to leave for Kambuzuma all of a sudden. Another child in the family passed away of cholera there. A little boy of five years old. Aad gave Anna a ride home. The poor parents could do nothing else but chop up a kitchen cupboard to make a simple casket.
That goes right through the heart. Even after 27 years of working as a doctor in Africa. And years in the tropics count double. That explains the first beer.

Assia and Aad lured Basil with half a valium in a piece of meat. This calms him down quickly and together with Speaker they lay him on the table. *High* with a vacant stare he whimpers for only a second while the ketamine takes effect. Aad starts to work on the growth on his leg. This might be a sensitive spot when Basil is going to try to start walking again.
We have to hold him tightly while the thick hair growth is removed.
A lot of cutting needs to be done and we quietly continue discussing the day.
Assia talks to her beloved dog encouragingly.
'Perhaps you should give him some more of that stuff, Aad?' I suggest.
'Can't he have a bit more anaesthetic?'
'Stay out of it, please. Do you know the term overdose?', the on-call surgeon answers. Wow, little respect is shown to the assisting nursing staff, but okay, forty minutes later, with some extra anaesthetic from the syringe and minor blood loss and an entire suturing procedure later, we are all very relieved. A big growth is taken out, and the paw, adorned with beautiful stitch marks is bandaged up.

Aad is the one who is suffering the most, he is recovering from a broken collar bone himself and I can tell he is in pain now. Nevertheless, we stay cheerful, put Basil in a big basket filled with blankets. Speaker keeps watch and Mayor swiftly disinfects the table and we call out for the Assia's sons.
Well, this calls for a good bottle.
A wonderful plate of couscous prepared with love by my Belgian-Algerian friend and half an hour later, Basil gets up, or at least he is trying. The rigid bandage and a light-headed mind are not really helpful in this phase, so the darling staggers back and falls into sleep in the blankets. Speaker and the boys drag the basket (with contents) to the outside patio that borders the bedrooms.
It is not yet eight o'clock and we exchange some recipes. The men are back to watching Aljazeera. Zap to BBC, Sky and back to Aljazeera. Why not celebrate Obama's inauguration while we are at it. We listen, touched, to be honest.
"Yes, we can!"
Well, we can do it too!
We talk about homemade *pâté* and cheeses, the *harissa* soup, variations of bread making now that we are able to get fresh milk again, and the popular *potjekos*.

There you go:
A few simple recipes for when the world crisis forces you to get used to traditional vegetables and wild herbs. We have been doing so for ages. Fried grasshoppers, flying ants and *mopane worms* I will leave for the next book.

PUMPKIN LEAVES, WONDERFUL VEGETABLE DISH.

Softer than spinach *a la crème.*
You can plant pumpkin everywhere and best of all on your compost heap.
Pumpkin leaves are eaten all over the world, the soft yellow flowers too.
A little labour intensive perhaps, but also very relaxing.
Fill a basket with young pumpkin leaves and look for an onion and tomato. The young pumpkin leaves are very hairy. You can rip off the leaves in one move, but you have to be patient. It is worse than cleaning Belgian chicory!

Steam the freshly cut leaves in a little water.
In another pot, stew the onion and a finely chopped tomato, without the skin. Add up to three cloves of garlic. Stew in butter if available and, even better, in some olive oil, preferably imported by your best friend.
Add the steamed pumpkin leaves to the baked onion-tomato sauce, stir, add fresh black pepper and you are done.
A spoon of cream can be added, but it is bad for your health.
This recipe goes well with rice, pasta or oven-baked potatoes.

FRIED PUMPKIN FLOWERS.

You can pick soft-yellow flowers in the rainy season when they are still small, those tiny calyces with white and yellow lines, and a five-fold, yellow pistil.
Rinse about thirty of the youngest flowers under drinking water. Make a batter out of flower, water, an egg, half a cup of beer and throw in some fresh herbs, whatever is growing: parsley, basil, mixed Provencal herbs, fresh black pepper, some salt and a spoonful of *sambal* or any other chili that you have chopped yourself lately.
Fry it, just for a bit, in sunflower oil, or in whatever oil that is available, make it hot. Fish it out of your frying pan when it looks crispy.
A special starter.

ORANGE AND PUMPKIN SOUP, TURKISH-ZIMBABWEAN MODIFIED VERSION.

Depending on the number of visitors clean a quarter or half a pumpkin and dice it.
Finely chop 4 onions, a generous amount of fresh garlic. Slowly stew everything in gradually heated olive oil.
If available, add: 300 grams of shredded bacon.
Add: 3 table spoons of turmeric, 4 curry leaves, 4 vegetable stock cubes, 3 star aniseeds. The last one is a luxury, not a must.
A spoon of soft Indian curry powder and a tea spoon of (fresh) rosemary.
Let it all simmer, remove the star aniseed before blending the soup.
To make a change, add hot stock or two cups of freshly squeezed orange juice.
Finish with 4 spoons of finely chopped English or Turkish (large) parsley.

ORANGE LENTIL SOUP FOR 12.

Chop four large onions and sauté them preferably in olive oil.
Add homemade chicken stock or 5 chicken stock cubes.
Throw in 1 kg of orange lentils (green, white or brown) and four litres of boiling water, lots of garlic, salt and freshly ground pepper.
Prepare a mixture of the following ingredients separately: a spoonful of cumin, coriander and yellow root or turmeric. Six bay leaves, sweet basil, a touch of cinnamon, a small red pepper, 2 teaspoons of *sambal* or chili, and half a tea spoon of curry powder.
Mix everything with two table spoons of freshly squeezed lemon or lime juice and 6 shredded freshly picked curry leaves.
Add this mixture to the pan when the lentils are boiling.

Peel 8 large tomatoes, sieve them and add them in the soup.
Add to this one, two or three fresh celery stalks, a handful of sun-dried tomatoes, and perhaps 4 red peppers, finely chopped, and preferably added near the end. Let everything simmer until soft.

If available: Add 3 chicken filets cut in strips to the hot soup at the end.
Put 6 baguettes spread with garlic butter in the oven. Serve the soup with a handful of freshly cut parsley and lemon thyme. (In Zimbabwe this can be replaced by steamed, freshly cut *covo, chomolliah,* or wild Zimbabwean spinach, or *rape*, a traditional vegetable, or local *tzunga*, tasting in between young sorrel or purslane).

Call your friends!

HARISSA SUDANESE SOUP, HARARE VERSION: *HARIRA*.

1500 grams of lam or beef stew, or mutton
4 large chopped onions, preferably red onions
150 grams of freshly cut coriander and 3 table spoons of coriander powder
100 grams of fresh parsley
4 beef stock cubes
Coarse sea salt and fresh black pepper
Saffron and freshly cut ginger *a volonté*
20 ml of olive oil and 20 ml sun flower oil
7 large, mature and pealed flesh tomatoes
A box of genuine Arabic tomato puree, or concentrate.
200 grams of sugar beans, 150 grams of black eyed beans, 100 grams of large white Spanish Favella beans, 40 grams of chickpeas and 50 grams of kidney beans. Make sure that all the beans are soaked in water over night and pre boiled.
Any quantity or mixture of the above is fine, really. Just add whatever you feel is nice!
If possible: Add 500 grams of fat free minced meat rolled into balls, if not:
2 large eggplant, finely chopped into cubes
6 small, orange, yellow, red and green peppers cut into strips
Separately cut 10 small, fine baby marrows in strips and steam them
1 fresh hot chili pepper, without seeds, ground in the pestle
3 eggs, whisked
150 grams of vermicelli, the smallest kind
2 grated lemons and lemon zest, cut in strips, preferably dried in the sun before preparation
Sauté the onions, fry the meat, including all herbs, spices, stock cubes and sieved tomatoes.
Add 2 litres of water and cook everything in a large pressure cooker.
Let it cool down and if necessary add more stock.
Add the grated lemon zest and lemon strips in the last 5 minutes; do not forget to add the baby courgettes and possibly some fresh garlic.
If necessary add one to three spoons of fresh Arabic tomato puree.
Serve fresh lemon next to the bowl of soup.
Mix in the three whisked eggs just before you serve the soup.
Serve with rosemary or parsley/garlic bread and if available fresh figs or dates.
More than enough for a large crowd!

What do we do without electricity?
If you want that distinct wood and smoky flavour, this recipe can be prepared outside if no electricity is available. The *"potjekos"* version or "all your food in one pot", is a tradition of the first settlers.
The women used to cook beside the ox carts in black iron, round three legged pots. You can find these here in all sizes, ranging from 5 to 50 litres. At home, we have three sizes, an ideal solution and alternative to power and gas failure.
The difference is that you sit next to an outside fire and the cooking takes longer due to the soft and long simmering but at the same time, you can entertain your first guests.
The most firm vegetables are layered in first. Fresh herbs and spices come in last. Just make sure that the pot is kept close for as long as possible. Beans can be replaced with butternut or potatoes and if you do not want meat, use any kind of fish, dried or fresh. These are of course first fried, taken out and added later on top of the layers of vegetables near the end and stewed quickly.
Enjoy!

POEM BY IAN JAMES

I am Ian James, 12 years old.
I have my hen.

She likes the *mielie* meal
she likes the *mielie* meal cobs
and eats
picks
picks
picks
and eats.

My hen and me are the best of friends
my hen likes fighting
and she likes food.
She is white
she is all over white.

I love my hen

My hen lays eggs
for us at Fairhome
my hen lays five eggs for Fairhome.

I love my hen
she is beautiful!

WOMAN

And didn't you
suffer, my woman, because
you walked and walked
and no man would stop
and offer to carry
the water
on your head.

And didn't you
implore the spirits
my woman
for rain
and rain
green richness
and rain
and no man
would help you
prepare
those fields
your cries
in vain.

And didn't you
suffer, my woman
the milk dry in your breast
the boy too weak to eat
the baby too thin to scream
and no man came
to take the children
to offer you
to rest.

And didn't you
Suffer, my woman
The lines deeper on your face
Your eyes sad
but your presence
full of grace.

No man
To tell you
your beauty is
beyond understanding
beyond
loving
and
longing

No man
deserves you.
No man
should
touch
those hands
those feet.

You are
one
of
the many
African queens.

BIG HOUSE – SMALL HOUSE
HARARE 1976

Standing in the doorway
of the Big House
a bunch of Flame Lilies in her hand
waiting for the sun to set
thinking of her children
far away and unaware

the loneliness settling in
the deep despair closing in on her
the sharp pain of fear
growing in her heart

the dinner laid on the table
the darkness set
Orion bright and clear and far
the stars witnessing her husbands' steps

She realised once more
He would not come home
not tonight,
not again.
He would sit and dine
at Small House
having children on his lap
as young as his youngest grandson.

Where to go from here?
Taken for granted
exiled in Africa
too late to flee
too sad to remain
too old to be chosen again.
Arranging the flowers
silently opening her best French wine.

ESTHER STEIJN
A NEW START

My name is Esther Steijn, daughter of Bert and Evelijne.
I am a graduate of the Institute for Business Administration and Economics in Utrecht – bachelor of Business Economics – and 15 years ago I followed my then boyfriend to Zimbabwe, where he started a rose farm. Here, Allard and I got married and got two children, Maxime and Christiaan (now twelve and nine years old.)

Today, I went to support my children during a swimming competition at Lilfordia School, a boarding school forty kilometres outside of Harare. They went with the school bus, fitting for a school team, and mum followed with her own car.
Nicely cruising over the bumpy road, playing some music in the car and enjoying the African landscape: a grocer who has carrots today and who is promoting his wares by hanging them in a tree beside the road, as if they were Christmas decorations.
A man who is transporting his elderly father in a wheelbarrow, because he is probably unable to walk himself.
The fragrant and fresh trees that are blossoming now and which amazed me when I arrived in Zimbabwe fifteen years ago: the purple Jacaranda trees, the wonderfully fiery Flamboyants and the tropical Frangipani.
The policeman who halted me during a routine "roadblock", asking me how I am doing.
'I'm fine', and how is he doing today?
'I'm ok, thank you.'
When I tell him that I am on my way to a swimming competition for my children, he wishes me good luck and allows me to drive on.
We gently wave each other goodbye.

During the competition, everyone is encouraging each other's children and the atmosphere is cheerful. All the parents have brought their own food and flasks filled with drinks, because we all know that we will be there for a few hours. The delicacies are shared amongst each other. The school even put up the usual coffee table with homemade pastry for the visitors – a custom, which, in these times of unobtainable ingredients, has been abolished by many schools.
The children are proud of their achievements and, neatly dressed in their uniform sports outfits, they say goodbye to the team of the organising

school and thank them for their hospitality. On the way home we turn the volume up and sing along with Mika and chat about their day and, interested, they ask about mine.

It may seem strange for an outsider who hears so many bad things about Zimbabwe that we are happy here with our life. Really, we are no ostriches and, in our own way, try to assist the Zimbabweans, who suffer under the current rule. On the other hand, you cannot allow your fun to be taken away by the country's situation and I live according to the principle that I want to enjoy all the positive things around me every day. And these exist in abundance.

The table that Allard and I gave each other as a present for our fortieth birthdays this year is ready next week. The local carpenter has made a tabletop of the railway sleepers we found in our garden when we started renovating. Nice and rustic, that is, with lots of holes and cracks and nice and large so we can enjoy it in the garden together with our friends. In two weeks time, the table will get inaugurated during my birthday dinner. All the guests will bring their own version of lasagne. I am taking care of the salads and the drinks and this way, together, we can enjoy an evening that does not involve slaving in the kitchen, but focuses on the essence: being together.

Meanwhile, I am busy planning monthly gatherings for a diverse group of women. I organised four informative mornings about various subjects, such as "Parenting for Prevention"(how, as parents, you can prevent your children from becoming addicts), "Personal Goal Setting"(a manual for discovering your goals in work and life), "Wellness"(analysing yourself by means of reflection, meditation) and "Saving Starfish"(a collection of sources who give us factual information about threats to man and animal in the current Zimbabwean society and how we can help). For the next year, there are, amongst others, some more light-hearted subjects planned, such as setting up an ecological vegetable garden, photography, a morning about sex toys and lingerie (I am curious how this goes down with the traditional English ladies) and a guided tour in landscape gardening visiting a number of country houses.

I am also thinking about the concept of an open house in Harare for cancer patients, their family and their friends. It is a concept about which I am very passionate and which does not exist here yet. There is a need for it, as there are more and more cases of cancer in this country, both among the white and black population.
Would it be due to the stress of the past years?
Is it due to the changing food situation?

I am unable to find the underlying cause, but I can offer my help to those who are confronted with this disease.

I travel around the region frequently for my part-time job as a representative for a local artist who makes African art in Sterling silver. The high quality of his work asks for an equally unique environment in which his products can be displayed. The atmosphere of safari lodges fits well in this picture. That is why my job takes me to Africa's most beautiful spots. I enjoy escaping from the day-to-day life of housekeeping and mothering during these work visits.

However, after nine years of working for someone else's beautiful products, I would love to use my abilities for my own goal and, slowly but surely, I work towards realising a professionally passion in Zimbabwe.

The right people love to share their experiences and honest opinions with me and apart from my fear of failure nothing gets in my way.

Just goes to show – life starts at 40!

Wherever in the world.

END OF THE MONTH DRINKS AND MORE RAIN!

For years on end now, a Dutch friend, Goof and I organise a happening that is called *the End of the Month drinks*. A happy hour. We organise the same at school, but only with colleagues and their families. You can bet, both initiatives are successful!

We tried out "our" End of the Month drinks night according to different formulas over the past twelve years: get together with all the Dutch and Belgian people in a bar in a suburb, sometimes it would be in town, sometimes at a lodge and then again at one of our homes.
Bridges were built between Belgians and the Dutch and between Walloons and Flemish. *Der kleine Unterschied* does not matter here. It was about being able to socialise for an evening, in one's own language, or in English. After all, a lot of us have partners who speak a different language. Networking was another benefit. The older Belgians, who fled from the Congo or Rwanda and who are retired here, found some new compatriots in this way. People way beyond the retirement age were able to find some extra work, because their technical or traditional knowledge is still highly appreciated. This comes in handy for those local Belgians who have a pension which has shrunk to the value of one loaf of bread a month!

For some time now, we are calling the initiative "Friends of the Belgians and the Dutch". I have no need for the restricted, nationalistic spirit in this state of Zimbabwe. Everyone who wants to relax can join and we do not work with introduction systems like they do in Dutch student fraternities that use the motto: "You're in, I'm not". In these times, everyone is part of the group, no matter what type of origin. Local friends, foreigners, friends of friends, and so on. Harare is the global village, let's unite!
Expats and diplomats came, enjoyed the company on these nights and left Zimbabwe several years later. A settled core group of local Dutch and Belgians continued the tradition.

The location we visit the most lately is Pangolin Lodge at Marijke Alcock's. It is in a pleasant wood log cabin near the edge of the city, in a wonderfully self designed garden.
Over the years, Christmas parties were held here, national holidays were celebrated and world championship football matches were shown on the

big screen. We sat together and unlike in Europe, we learnt, in a natural way, to deal with people you would otherwise never talk to, get together with, or befriend.

The most recent formula is that we try to change the location every month and casually improvise a get together at somebody's home. Everyone brings something to nibble, or prepares a pan of soup, or homemade snacks. Everybody contributes wine and beer. By adding movie nights, we avoid the subjects of politics or phone costs, absence of electricity or the latest prices. This keeps us mentally "sane". A bunch of seasoned Dutch guests get a kick out of talking about the political situation for hours on end. Unfortunately, I have the feeling that often, we cannot fathom the actual mindset of the rulers and how the decisions in politics are being made. All this for the simple reason that so many essential considerations, double agendas and historical traditional values are different on a fundamental level. Perhaps they just deserve respect instead of judgement. Matters which we will never hear about nor understand due to our Eurocentric way of thinking, even after nearly thirty years Africa. We know a lot about nothing and judge all too easily in a Western way.

Just meekly accept the difference, is what I have been doing these past years.

The rainy season has started.

We listen with satisfaction to the sweet pouring rain. Sometimes, it rains for ten hours on end. This is followed by a pleasant spell of heavy, humid air. The beauty of every sunrise and sunset remains a returning topic of conversation every day. The sound of the receding rain on our roof tiles on the round rooms soothes and eases the enervating sound of whirring generators in the suburb.

Meanwhile during this season, the garden, in a matter of three weeks, happily transforms into a jungle of so many tones of green, too many to keep up with and an interesting topic to start the next art class with.

'Guys, how many shades of green do you think we would be able to paint on a giant colour wheel? And why?'

The phone rings and disturbs my musings.

What? The phone, the "landline" is ringing? After four days of being out of order?

A Belgian newcomer, Bruno.

'You ARE going to organise a movie night end of January, right? Please do! It was so nice and I have met so many new people!'

'In that case, Bruno, let us use the January End of the Month drinks as a New Year's celebration. We'll do the movie in February, okay?

But first, I have to find a venue quickly. We could ask Olga and Luc or Hans. He lives a bit further out, but does have a beautiful view. Oh well, it is not of the utmost importance, because it will be dark as anything by seven-thirty anyway. Yes, yes, with English subtitles, I know. Or French, if it is an English production? I know darling! Okay, ça va. See you. *Baisers!*'

I put down the receiver and at that moment there is a big bang in the neighbourhood.
Oh, great. The transformer, a total loss.
Not that again.
No more electricity and I do not know for how long.
This means no movie at my place next week.
Let's think.
What do we have to offer?
Simon was received well November, last year.
Alles is liefde? It is time to put away that Saint Nicholas DVD.
And *Joyeux Noël*.
Before I drive out to school, I have to make a quick decision and discuss it with Veerle and Olga, for that movie night at the end of February.
Planning two months in advance never hurts.
Zwartboek?
Paris, je t'aime?
Sea biscuit?
The painted veil?
Entre les murs?
Flandres?
Abdellatif Kechiche's *La graine et le mulet*?
That reminds me of the couscous I left on the shelf of the Spar: 15 US for the smallest box. All the way from Algeria.

Before I can decide, the phone rings again.
'Patrice, I am sorry', Rosemary says.
'I can't come with you to Fairhome this weekend. My little niece of four years old just passed away. Yes, cholera, yes, in Chitungwiza township. Yes, I am leaving now to see the family.'
Voilà. I have returned to reality, ice cold and hard as nails.
It gives me the creeps.
It could have been avoided!
Rosemary Kamangwana, my Shona counterpart in the Fairhome project, has lost four relatives already. She warns me for the cholera situation in Ngezi, where "my" street kids live on the abandoned farm.
'No worries Rose. I will drive there tomorrow, Saturday. No, I will take my gardener Daniel with me, promised, I am not driving alone anymore these days. As long as my car takes me through the mud, it is not a four wheel drive. Go well.'

All the imported South-African food is finished. I do not want to, nor have the energy, to seek out all the shady places in the industrial area to compare the prices of imported wares. I find fifty kilos of rice and twenty kilos of *mielie* meal in the container hidden deep in the green of the garden!
That is something, at least for the staff and Fairhome. The very evening, I drive for more food and drinks for the street kids to the neighbourhood Spar. To my great consternation, all the shelves are stocked.
It frightens me that they are fully stocked.
I am not used to it!
'All the shelves are full. But there is nothing to buy', someone next to me says. An elderly, shrivelled European woman, with half a loaf of white bread in a dirty, old plastic bag. There is nothing to buy. True. The prices are outrageous.
I quickly buy some basics for the kids.
And think of Munyaradzi, the deceased girl. I have seen her several times: smart, happy, sharp. Eyes like fiery coals. Not shy!
Oh, how she did not deserve this.
Munyaradzi, rest in peace.
Cry the beloved country!

THE NIGHT OF THE CHOLERA

Your fears
face
facts.
Your
face
fell
silent.
Your
husband
sat down.
Your girl
is
no
longer.

ITAI DERERE
MY LIFE AS A SHONA ARTIST

My name is Itai Derere and I am an artist, a stone sculptor.
My father is now 64 years old and is living in the rural area of Mhondoro in the Mashonaland-West. In principle he is no longer eligible to work, but to my surprise, he is still quite active – he has to be – and can work as a young man of 35 years old.

I have a strong mother, still alive and taking care of my father who is often in pain because of kidney stones. I come from an extended family. In all we were nine. I am the first born of my father's second wife. I lost one brother because of HIV Aids.

Today I live with Lina, my girlfriend, and our daughter Violet, who started her grade one – that is the first year of primary school – in 2009. In Mabvuku, a high density township about ten km from Harare city, I am now trying to go against the wind of poverty, if not against the ruling landlords of Zimbabwe. As I am speaking now, we are forced to scrap for food, every day. Waking up in the morning, it's always going against the wind, to see how lucky I am trying to manage to find a small something to eat, using the little money I get from selling the stone sculptures I am carving.

It has been a long time we have had no water running from the tap and still there is none. What you hear in the early mornings is the sound of people going to the wells to fetch some water. Early, I say, because there will be a long queue on the shallow unprotected well. Indeed nowhere else you can get some water. Can you imagine how the sewer can be if there is not enough water to run it. For sure it will definitely block, because few of us have money to buy toilet paper. Imagine again a carton box used in the same toilet instead of toilet paper, without enough water to flush it. Because of the blockage most of the pipes are broken and the sewage is gushing out, transforming most of the roads in open sewage canals. This causes the spreading of cholera as well. It also has turned out to spoil our daily breath of fresh air. I usually travel from Mabvuku to Greendale and back and you can tell just by the smell of air that you are near Mabvuku. Thinking I was the only one, you can hear it also the same observation from other people sharing the same commuter omnibus.

Talking about Greendale, it is one of the nice low density living areas in Harare. I was offered a work space there by some German friends who liked my art. Greendale became my shelter, my food, my inspiration and my hope for the Zimbabwe of nowadays. But let's stop dreaming.
Although the shelves in the stores are no longer empty; the price tags are now in US Dollars. Where do we get the US Dollars? Where do we, impoverished artists of Zimbabwe, go from here?? It seems to me that those with money own the shops and can import from abroad to charge those without money.

Something happened a few days ago. My sister phoned, that one of my younger brothers from my mother's side passed away. We had to go to the Alaska Mine near Chinoyi in the northern part of Zimbabwe to collect his body. This mine was once working but is now a ghost town. All the expenses we had to make were in US Dollars. I hired a nearly broken car, because it was cheap and belonging to a close friend, but it was in fact not road worthy. The owner, my friend, was the driver in case he had to look after it in case of a possible breakdown! Safely arrived at the mine the same night, we took off past midnight. There it was a big shock to hear that in fact my brother died in Zambia. He had "jumped" the border without any papers in the hope to find work in Zambia. Alas, over there he died of malaria. There was no option but to go and try the impossible to get him home. On our way to the border town Chirundu, we had to pay some bribery to the police to get through with our half broken car without papers.

On arrival we slept on empty stomachs because we had to budget the few dollars I still had to use them to carry the body of the deceased. It was difficult on the border the following morning. At about lunchtime we had to give the Health Officer petrol to help us cross with the car to Zambia. On arriving at the hospital, they told us to go back and bring the authority people from Zambia Police to be present for identifying the body of our relative. On our way back it was the same procedure at the border together with the Health Inspection. As soon as we managed to cross the two borders, we went back home. Those two days on the road we had nothing to eat, but a cup of fruit juice Mazoe and boiled maize because maize stays long in the stomach.
We had to bury my relative in the morning, because he was already in a bad state of decomposing. Because we came back the same day very late at night, there was no food available to feed even ten out of the fifty people that attended the funeral.

That same morning somebody came to our house, reporting that one of my sculptor-colleagues, Nicodemus Mamvura, just passed away. A sad

happening again, because the famous artists in the Mamvura family, they are all going, passing one after the other one.
There was nothing at my relative's place to cover his burial, so we had to gather some money to buy something to eat for the guests. The women went from door to door in the neighbourhood, collecting *mielie*, salt, cooking oil, vegetables and sugar to run the kitchen.
We buried him the same way as we buried my young brother.

Mike Nyakuromba, one of the oldest artists of our group and a close friend, died today in the morning and we had to be called to see that his body could be transported to the mortuary awaiting the burial. He had been ill for a long time and he had no money to get to a decent hospital. There was nothing to be done, because there was nothing left but to die.

You cannot even put your money in the bank, because they steal it, or you lose it on inflation every day. With all that, you have to lead a life, is it possible, if I can ask?
My daughter needs a school!
My little Violet, my everything, deserves proper education!
What can you do if no one is operating the schools, all teachers gone to Johannesburg for greener pastures to try other ways of living, rather than dying of hunger in Zimbabwe.
I was in a hot meeting with the parents-teachers association this last week, trying to find a solution about how we can pay teachers for their services to our children, if they had to teach. We had to come to terms where they had to bring down the levy price they had proposed and came to an agreement of 65 US Dollar per term.
The question is, how do I get this money and where?
As an artist on stone sculptures. I might.
What about other ordinary people without a job? I can work on a piece, ask for a price to foreign friends if they like the piece and can risk to ship it and sell it in Europe to earn something for us back home to live on.
Just a bit of what I am is an artist.
In my art I am in between the real world and the spiritual world, between shadow and light. The stone has to speak to me, before I start working on it. I only stop working when there is no communication anymore between me and the stone. Mostly it takes a long time before finishing a sculpture. Sometimes I am working on more than one stone.
But everywhere in Germany where my sculptures were exhibited, there was a lot of interest and selling.
Alas, most of the gain was not for me, because I sold my pieces for a not such a high price to the people who organised the exhibition!!

You may have seen one of my works and be eager to reach me and see more, you can e-mail me on nyamaitai@yahoo.com

VICTORIA FALLS: MOSI-O-TUNYA
THE SMOKE THAT THUNDERS!

And never will the raging stop
fog will hang eternally.
The smoke-screen of droplets,
the chains of foam
cut
deeper than ever
thanks to the rains
where
every rainmaker
dances
'round the holy circle
screamin,
the Zambesi stream digs
the longer
the deeper
new history
into the gullies.
The water is savage
the battle forever
the Victoria falls
will
sing
forever.

PADDY HOBLEY
RETURNING HOME

My name is Paddy Hobley. I am a teacher of various subjects, mainly English, from pre-school to university level. I am also a writer. I was born in Harare, Zimbabwe (then Salisbury, Southern Rhodesia) in 1952, the eldest of five children who are now scattered around the world. Our mother is Pat, whose paternal grandparents trekked from South Africa through Botswana to settle with their 12 children on a farm in the south-west corner of Zimbabwe, early in the 20th century. At the age of eighty-three, Pat demonstrates her rugged pioneering stock by still working full-time, as a conveyancer.

My British-born father, Bill, joined the British South Africa Police after service in Burma and India in the Second World War and never returned to Britain or saw his family again. He brought to his police career his special brand of Stiff Upper Lip British Military notions of Duty before All and uncompromising morality and honour.

My mining engineer husband, Mark Pacey, was also born in Britain and came to Zimbabwe in the early 1980's. He is so temperamentally and technically suited to the "make a plan", trouble-shooting, lateral-thinking, self-sufficient spirit of mining in Africa that he cannot contemplate returning to the tame and restricted life in Britain.

Mark and I have three sons: Steven, who is 16, William who will be 20 shortly, and David, who would have been 22.

I have this persistent childhood memory, a picture that sums up "home" for me.

The eating part of the picnic is over. The greasy plates are stacked, attracting flies. The fire is smouldering into white ash. Adults loll on blankets in the scanty shade, talking quietly, their beers sucking up warmth. I wander off behind a pile of granite rocks, balancing their way into the sky.

The sun beats hot through the thin cotton of my frock. I have to pull my shoulders back to lift the hot cloth from my skin. The dusty, smoky air of October is thick, parching my throat as I draw it in. Invisible cicadas shimmer the sound of the heat haze all around me.

Behind the lingering smell of our fire hang the scents of baked earth, bleached grass, powder-dry cattle dung.
Just in front of my small grubby feet I find an arena of sandy soil between clumps of last season's blond grass. I squat down to examine its treasures. The perfect funnel of an ant-lion lair yawns but the little brown ants scurry about their own business, avoiding the trap. Ovals of dead *msasa* leaves in shades of warm brown form a drift against a small tree root with the hard, spiky spirals of *msasa* pod, some grey-beige leaves with sun bursts of little black dots on them, fragments of twig and bark. The chestnut lozenge of a seed has two little holes drilled into its heart. A glossy, black *Matabele* ant marches past, as long as my big toe. Across the top left hand corner of this little world a beetle struggles with a perfectly-formed ball of dung at least five times its own size, standing on its back legs to lean into the ball and heave it forward a millimetre or two, then scrambling on top of it and rolling it another little turn by the falling off the front. I wonder how it will know when it gets where it is going? A tiny breeze passes overhead, clattering the leaves together briefly, trembling the little disks of shadow. A bird sounds a clear note in the next clearing.

Our basic assumptions about how landscape ought to look tend to be formed by the place where we spent the first few years of our life – and this landscape operates as a symbol for so much more than the physical place alone. When I have been away from Zimbabwe for about six months I start to be ambushed by glimpses of this child-sized scene. In the past I have glanced out across the snows of Minnesota or the mountain-and seascapes of Cape Town and known home sickness, summed up in this square foot of sandy soil. The dramatic beauty of Scotland, the warmth of new and old friendships there, the availability of every sort of material comfort and dignity, the even-handed, human-rights awareness – all of these were impressive, attractive, beguiling, but they did not make Scotland home.

Leaving Home

Our Christmas of 2007 was devoted to the type of family debate that middle class Zimbabweans know so well: Should we stay? Should we go? If we go, where should we go? What will be best for the children? What will we lose? What will we gain? What about our old age?
David, home for Christmas, argued vigorously that the prospects for William and Steven were so limited in Zimbabwe that they should join him in Scotland and begin to move towards training, qualifications and employability as soon as possible and that, furthermore, Mark and I needed to start building a plan for our old age that did not rest on the shaky future available in Zimbabwe.

In March 2008 the younger boys and I left Mark behind to keep the home base going and arrived in Scotland, as David had been urging. We set up house in a steep-roofed stone cottage an hour's drive north of Glasgow, with views across Loch Long to the mountains of Cowal and to the mouth of the River Clyde opening out to the Atlantic. From here we anxiously followed the news of the elections back home in Zimbabwe, at first with some optimism and then with growing horror. We joined the rest of the outside world in believing nothing but the gloom and doom picture served up by the media.

Meanwhile we had a life to build. I took a job cleaning in a gracious National Trust house. We battled our way through the complications of new relationships with the authorities, bank accounts, utilities, transport, frequently feeling like raw bumpkins bumbling clumsily in the sophisticated First World. We began to find our way about, to make tentative headway into a new community, to develop new favourite foods and pastimes. The boys joined a Sailing Club, started job hunting and gave some thought to starting college in September.

Now that we were on David's territory we revelled in all that he had achieved in the year he had been in Scotland, were entertained in his flat in Glasgow, driven about in his car to be shown the places he had grown to love passionately. We were introduced to his new friends, we were flown in a seaplane of his employers, Loch Lomond Seaplanes, and were impressed at the extent to which he had found his niche and grown with this little company to joyful manhood in his expanding work responsibilities and the delights of a social life with colleagues, eating and drinking and extreme sporting on water and in the air.

On the 12th of May we went to Finlas Mountain, overlooking Loch Lomond, on a glorious evening in the late spring. David and William climbed the mountain with an old friend from Zimbabwe and a new friend, a Canadian seaplane pilot, to go paragliding. A few hours later, when the cold night had bitten deep, David died on that mountainside from injuries sustained in an accident, despite the best efforts of the scores of paramedics rushed to the scene. As I cradled his broken body and began to understand that he was dying my thoughts turned to Zimbabwe, to Mark alone and unsuspecting there. And it seemed obvious, once the worst had happened, that we should rush back home, to be together, to go into a family huddle in our house and to begin our healing process.
Mark joined us for two weeks. We got through the necessary aftermath: the official enquiry, mourners gathering from all over the world, the cremation, placing David's ashes at the foot of an ancient ash tree on the banks of Loch Lomond where the seaplanes dock.

But it was six long months before the boys and I returned home, months in which we tried to be sensible, to uphold the programme that David had championed so vigorously – of launching William and Steven on a new life and making the most of the progress we had already made. Many people, both within and outside Zimbabwe, urged us to stick it out in Scotland, arguing that the political and economic crises in Zimbabwe was only deepening, that the arguments about the limitations of the opportunities for the boys were even stronger now than they had been at Christmas.

But eventually we knew that all three of us had to return home.

Returning Home

I am home, back where my body and mind respond instinctively to so many brazen and subtle hints that this is where I belong. Back where I can begin to unpack my grief in a safe place.

I know that the majority of my fellow Zimbabweans are suffering: physically, mentally, emotionally, under unprecedented economic hardships and human rights abuses that cry out for redress. But just for the moment I have come home to recover, to draw strength and comfort from all that is nurturing in the country. I cannot yet enter with any zest into the conversations about the facts and figures of deprivation, the current crop of political and economic outrages, the potholes, the lack of water and electricity and phone supply, the scarcity of basic food stuffs and ludicrous cost when you find them. I am too busy soaking up the familiarity of people and places.
I am still revelling in the essential greetings between all people including total strangers, encountering each other for the first time that day (translated from the far longer formal Shona greeting):
'How are you?'
'I am fine. How are you?'
'I'm fine.'
– and a feeling that the exchanges are not just formulaic.
I am seeing creative solutions to scarcities and privations, a good-humoured practicality, an atmosphere of *bon homie* amongst fellow sufferers in queues. Still, incredibly, far more loud, raucous laughter than I ever heard in Scotland outside of a late evening pub. Yes! Yes!

I know there are many exceptions, many appalling things happening – but allow me some time of pleasure in those things that give my home its special flavour. And of course there are the personal parts of being home like being back in our sprawling family house (even if it is looking scruffy, dusty, neglected) surrounded by acres of much loved garden (parched,

depressed looking and somewhat flattened by rampant poultry) but all of it redolent with memories, sweet and bitter-sweet.
And friends – who know my whole history, who know my parents, my siblings, school, university, jobs, triumphs, failures, marital and parenting ups and downs as well as I know theirs, who do not need long background explanations. Friends who are longing to hold me while I weep over David's death and will be there when I need quiet talk and when I need to drink red wine and laugh and will still be there when I need to weep again.

Yesterday there was the storm I have been longing for amongst the Scottish autumn mists – the storm I had tried to describe to people in Scotland without success – the build up of towering, glowering thunder heads split by whiplashes of lightening, rumbling with thunder, wind swirling and lashing the trees and then the first drops of rain drawing that smell out of the dry dust that I cannot describe and find I have not even remembered properly when it comes upon me again. And finally the down pour, sheets of water, little lakes spreading within minutes to be thirstily absorbed by a winter-dry earth.
I am now sitting on a balcony at a place I last visited with David, looking over jumbled piles of granite boulder the size of double-decker buses or skyscrapers and beyond to distant hazy mountains (most of which I can name individually) and up into the limitless blue sky. I am on a level with the tops of the *msasa* trees, some of which still have a touch of their new spring foliage in reds and oranges. A steady breeze from the east rakes and silvers the leaves. I can hear frogs chirruping, celebrating the new-found moisture, cicadas buzzing the rising heat, birds calling to and fro (birds that I can often identify).
I have been down and found an arena of sandy soil between clumps of last season's blond grass. I have squatted down to examine its treasures. The perfect funnel of an ant-lion lair yawned but the little brown ants scurrying about their own business and avoided the trap. Ovals of dead *msasa* leaves in shades of warm brown had formed a drift against a small tree root with hard, spiky spirals of *msasa* pod and some grey-beige leaves with sun bursts of little black dots on them.
Fragments of twig and bark.
The chestnut lozenge of a seed with two little holes drilled into its heart. I haven't seen the *Matabele* ant yet but I do know that I am home.

POEM FOR HILDE, A FAR-OFF FRIEND

I miss you.
I miss you.
my far-off Flemish friend
my morsel hunted game
my dashing doe

Why
are you not here
on my journey
through the sleepy Shona village
where the heat
bites
across the rocks
and pieces broken
pottery
pieces
melt and grow
together
again.
The yellow helms
they cut your foot.

And I
I wanted to cook the dry maize
with you
underneath the old stem
of a very large sunflower.

I wanted
to share the grains with you
the salt on our hands
and to watch the horizon
the fire
in the baobab
and quiet!

A lizard
would lick the rocks
at your feet
until the last light
kisses
the blue-purple-green hills

I would
wait with you
until you
finally
can
be silent,
without my hand
on
your mouth.

WILMA HOEFNAGELS
HALF DUTCH, HALF ZIMBABWEAN

My name is Wilma Hoefnagels, daughter of Willem Hoefnagels and Miet Haazen. I grew up in Asten, in a pure, Dutch farmer's family. A small, mixed business: about some ten cows, twelve pigs and a bit of land on which my mother, very progressive in those times, cultivated asparagus.

Everyone in the family had to work hard in order to keep the family running. Before school hours, my sister had to milk the cows, my brother had to clean the stables in the weekend. That is how everyone had their daily and weekly chores.
For me, the youngest in this large family, "work" started at about age four with raking the lane to the front and back doors. Let's just say that was the start of a long career. Growing up with a lot of female role models. Mother and four sisters, but also two brothers. Mom ran the business with a strong character as if it was the most natural thing in the world. I am not at all surprised I ended up in Zimbabwe, running my own business.

Today, I wake up in a total war. A genuine territorial battle between Tommy and a grey stray cat. Like the lions in Hwange National Park, Tommy, my cat, has been busy marking his territory, because we moved two months ago. Apparently, that did not go too well. After a long fight, hair is flying everywhere, Tommy jumps on my bed hoping for some protection. He is the big loser and this time it is serious. His tail is seriously injured. As a farmer's daughter, I am inclined to think it will heal by itself, it usually does. After studying the wounds, I reconsider. I decide a vet really is necessary. The vet is clear: the tail needs to be shaven under anaesthesia in order to assess the damage; he is not sure whether he can keep the tail. I pay the bill and Tommy is in the animal hospital.
On my way to work, I am hugely embarrassed. How can you do that? Bring a cat to the doctor and paying a fortune for it? How am I going to explain this to my staff? Am I going to explain it? Most people here cannot even afford a doctor for themselves or their relatives.
I am ashamed, but at the same time, I know that this is yet again an example of a difference I have to live with. After about 13 years in Zimbabwe, I know how things are and I have pretty much adjusted. Still, surprises surface again and again, and it is hard to decide what to do with them. I chose the easiest way: I do not say anything about it.

As an expatriate, your life is always split in two: in Zimbabwe, you are half Dutch, in the Netherlands, you are half Zimbabwean. It is certainly not the case that the one is better than the other. I love Holland, but for now, my home is Zimbabwe, because I also love Zimbabwe. Despite hyperinflation and huge problems in the country this feels like home.

When I arrive at the workplace after my visit to the vet, work is well on its way. I have a workshop where we rebuild trucks into so-called *overland trucks*: busses with extra space for camping gear and luggage and with a high road clearance so bad roads will not be a problem. We arrange several trips in southern Africa with nine *overland trucks*. It is a real challenge. All vehicles demand a lot of maintenance: repairs, paint-jobs, keeping camping gear clean, etc. My workshop manager, Joe, coordinates everything and in the low season when there are no trips, the truck staff – drivers, chefs and travel guides – come to help with repairs. A mixed company of Zimbabweans.

Together, we try to turn the travel experience gained into crafty, practical solutions. This demands imagination, especially in a country where you lose a lot of time finding materials and parts and with arranging all the documents like permits. Eventually, it always works out. Even when considering the phones, that may or may not work, electricity, that comes and goes and especially no running water.

There is no normal course of events, no daily drag. If you think you have got everything under control for the outgoing trip, suddenly, somewhere, a new rule or law surfaces for which you would have had to apply in five-fold four months ago, including certified copies of about a dozen documents.

I came here by accident, at least, that is how it feels. As a travel guide, I visited a lot of places in the world. I started out in Mexico and Guatemala and eventually I worked in Africa, realising that with transport of my own a nice company would have a chance of survival. Continuous travelling around with tourists is nice, but you cannot keep it up your whole life. With the purchase of the first vehicle there was a need for a space to work, preferably in southern Africa, with a central position and good infrastructure. This description exactly fitted Zimbabwe.

The atmosphere in the country played a large part in the decision. Zimbabwe is a wonderful country, really indescribably beautiful, but it is the people who make the country what it is. I particularly refer to the ordinary citizens of the country. I know of no country with nicer people.

For this reason, I fell in love with the country the first day I arrived in Zimbabwe. I took Zimbabwe into my heart immediately, no neighbouring country could invoke this feeling. Now the country is in a big economic recession, no one can understand why I still do not want to leave. It is not the wealth, or the infrastructure that makes or breaks a country, it is its inhabitants that make up the atmosphere. Especially now, it satisfies me greatly to at least have several employees who earn a decent wage with which they can maintain a large family.

This leads me to the greatest challenge I face here: how to do this in a man's world. My company truly is a "male" company: at the moment, I employ only men and we do a man's job. In fact, I just run a large garage with big vehicles. Coming home with clean hands after work is an accomplishment. Especially when you realise that we have no water. The tap in the workshop has always been dry.

When I arrive at the garage today, everyone is working busily. Joe is engaged welding a rack we can hang underneath a truck so that there is space for gas cylinders and camping seats. Let's first go through the planning with him. He knows the city like the back of his hand and always knows a place where we can repair or buy things. Throughout the years, he has become my right hand man. He started out as a completely inexperienced driver and thanks to his attitude and dedication he is now workshop manager and is regarded as one of the bosses by the rest of the staff. I could not do without him, but all the other guys need him too: for them it is so much easier to talk about their problems or questions with him. No matter how hard I try to break through, a female boss, and white, forms a barrier. So be it. We discuss the priorities: which trucks need to be ready first, when do they leave and what staff to deploy. Then we discuss the list of necessities, of which we both know that I have to spend the entire day in the car to gather everything. During the meeting, Farai, my most experienced driver suddenly appears. We have not seen him for a month and the moment he enters I get the fright of my life. In one month he turned from a massive guy into a skinny, scrawny man. Sure, he is still tall, but that is all that is left of him. I could cry.

He tells me he had malaria and suffers from stomach acid, which is why he cannot eat, but he is recovering. He was close to tears himself too.

We all know what this is about, but we are still in a situation where people prefer not to pronounce the infamous word, even though Farai knows how open I am about things.

After his departure, Joe and I totally agree: Farai cannot do any more trips. First of all, he is too weak and we both conclude that we should be happy if he is able to hold on for a few more months. When AIDS strikes here, it strikes hard and the end is near. He will be my third employee who will die of this disease. It is shocking to see how quickly the disease can strike.

His lifestyle is presenting the bill: six children with six different women and always a "big house" and a "small house", as it is called here: a lover besides his wife. I decide to buy a big box of condoms to put in the workshop, so that everyone who thinks they need it can take them.

It does feel a little bit as if "it's too late to lock the stable" and whether it will help remains uncertain. Surreptitiously, I think about Tommy again: that lucky one is just lying on the operating table today.

Joe and I discuss the employee situation and decide we need new drivers. We both know how hard it is, because the requirements are high, if not impossible. It is quite something that is expected from a driver who has to deal with mostly white tourists from different countries. The most difficult thing is to find people who can handle this "normally". Those who can sit round the camp-fire and chat, but at the same time are able to say – *no* – to the customers and make demands. That is not easy for the average Zimbabwean, who is used to blindly follow white people's orders. Of course they also need to be able to drive safely and have some technical knowledge so that minor technical defects can be repaired on site. Sometimes, the roads are so bad that everything literally shakes loose and may break. We also require at least some intelligence regarding bookkeeping and math. We travel to different countries during the trips and deal with different kinds of currencies and knowing its value requires a lot of skills. Exchanging money in each country, preferably not too much and not too little, thinking about where to fill the fuel tank, because price differences between countries can be huge, knowing what to do at border crossings, and so on. It seems impossible, but up until now we have been able to find good people. Usually we send them on a training trip first together with an experienced driver; the best training.

Joe continues working on the truck and I throw myself on the emails. Communication is the most important aspect of getting jobs in and coordinating them. The more work the better, not only for me, but it keeps my staff employed. This is vital in a country with a huge unemployment rate. Fortunately, the phones have been working for a week now, wonderful. I can easily reach people and what is more: I can be reached.
How happy can you be with just a working phone, especially after not having one for eight months?
Today, Mo also calls: he works for the church and through the churches he is working on a project to provide people in the rural areas with food. He is mostly working on the logistics at this time and wants to use at least one of our trucks for transport. Together we make a plan, next week we start.

An entirely new thing for us and at the same time one of our drivers has some work for some period.
Kelvin also calls. He conducts a trip with international students and wants to know which button he needs to press to get money from the ATM: savings account or cheque account. A simple problem this time. Sometimes I have to deal with the most extraordinary things. A cook who did

not realise that eight dollar is worth a bit more than eight Rands. Yes, especially exchange rates can escape notice of an inexperienced traveller. Of course, we try to assess the value on the basis of our own currency. Just like we convert back to Euros, they try to convert back into Zimbabwe dollars. Or: one rand is an x-amount of million Zimbabwe dollars. It is just insane.

Or there is the cook who did not realise that the Europeans expect a bit of a higher standard from the food they are served. We do not eat the same thing three times a day: *sadza* (maize meal porridge) with a sauce. And we do not always go for the cheapest brand, but demand more in terms of flavour and quality of the food we eat.

On the other hand, our travellers can completely surprise my employees. Sometimes the staff cannot stop laughing about the things those Europeans do or think. For instance, they are all asked whether they live in a hut, whether they have water and electricity and whether their children go to school and can read and write. Of course they do, even the questions create total surprise. It also irritates them when the customers tell them they have not seen the real Africa until they have at least seen different villages with huts, preferably with tribes running around half naked. We know that the real Africa like they expect it does not exist. Here too there is development and everyone just wears clothes so at least they will not die of the cold. In the end, we all laugh about the amount of *naïveté* and I am proud of "my" boys.

Brian is busy cleaning all the camping mattresses. We have about 250. During the trips he is the camping assistant. I almost literally picked him up from the street. I was asked to take up a board function of a local pool society. We play competitions in Harare. Always in dim-lighted bars in one of the high-density areas every weekend. In Holland, you would call them *townships*.

In doing this, we believe we can keep a number of prospectless kids from the streets, teach them fair play and pick up some experience by giving them responsibilities. After a few months, I thought I could give one of them a chance and thus Brian came under my employ. Absolutely no experience with any kind of work, 21 years old, really too shy and seen nothing of the world yet.

Come and work in the workshop first, see his attitude and let him hear stories from his colleagues. Next, I bought him a passport and sent him on a trip for no less than three months to Zambia and Malawi. A little bit of fear and some trembling, because he was very naive. The driver who went with him received special instructions: keep an eye on Brian and make sure he does not get into trouble. I feel like a mother hen who has to take care of little boys. His job on the trip is simple; I do not worry about that: help out with cooking, doing the dishes, put up and break down tents, pack stuff, etc.

To my great surprise, he came back as a completely different man with a lot of experience. Unprompted, he started to tell stories about what he had experienced, but better yet: he saw prospects in his own life. His new big plan: follow a cooking course so that next season he could perhaps go as a cook. After he had hung out at home for years, he came to the workshop after two weeks of staying home, because he was bored. I am glad with it and the customers are too, because the beds have been cleaner than ever before. His family is happy as well: part of his salary goes to his parents and he buys food for his granny in the countryside from his bonuses and tips. It feels good to know that I offer at least a few people some prospects. A job in the Netherlands would be easy, working from nine to five and then go home, have money on the bank every month.
But this feels right.
The reward is there in a different way.
I pick up Tommy at four o'clock. He is drowsy, but his tails has been saved. He will be his old self again with the help of a shot of antibiotics. Suddenly, I think about inquiring about the costs of AIDS inhibitors and whether they help. Who knows.

wilmatembo@hotmail.com

MEASLES AND SCHOOLS

As long as it rains there will be cholera.
As long as the vaccination programs are not organised, a next vulnerable group will be affected. Malnourished children will not survive something simple as measles. That is what I think about these weeks during my daily trip to school. All those schools that will not open. All those poor teachers!
Sometimes, I am relieved when I drive onto our wonderful campus. I can shut everything out in a beautiful mini kingdom, among our 435 students. In a wonderful, great art room with all the facilities I can only dream of and with an imposingly big kiln.
Our school is the second smallest and one of the youngest in Africa, but it belongs to the top among the International Schools. It has fully equipped computer science units and a library containing no more than 30,000 books and research material.
The school was founded in a small villa in 1992 and is now fully accredited by ECIS (European Council of International Schools) and NEASC (New England Association of Schools and Colleges). The accreditation process is a detailed "assessment" of programs, staff, policies and facilities done by a team of experts. After every five years of accreditation, the specialists scrutinise the school again. Our HIS, Harare International School, withstood the severe procedure and there are only five International Schools in Africa who have earned this official ranking.
With the offer of *International Baccalaureate* to 60 different nationalities comes intensive career and guidance counselling. We have a separate unit of remedial teaching specialists at our disposal, as well as an *English as a second language* program. Drama, music and fine arts are highly thought of and that is why I love this school.
I have stopped to defend myself, like many of my colleagues, to fight against the easy gossip, the stupid rumours and the exaggeration of the public in our large village of Harare.
We know what we stand for and what we offer and, most of all, how we want to guide our students on a multi-cultural level, in a quickly changing multi-ethnic world. Soon to be our global future! All of us are painfully aware of the high fees. One is really fortunate if the employer pays the fees (U.N., Embassies, Red Cross, NGO's, etc.), for others it is a big investment.
Some parents live very modestly in order to finance one of the best school educations you can find, one that by having a world vision, teaches analytical and critical thinking and in which the child is central.

There is a reason why the corner stones of our philosophy in our *mission statement* are: "promoting international understanding by universal education and world culture exchange through student driven learning, research and creativity".

Before the start of every school year, we work in sub-groups on the adaptation and execution of the set objectives. We strive to educate our students as inquirers, thinkers, communicators, risk-takers, as knowledgeable personalities, principled and with moral reasoning, caring, open-minded, well-balanced, reflective, responsible, self-directed with personal goals. Our school community actively works on positiveness. Understanding and appreciation of Zimbabwe's beauty and its people have grown to become two important guiding objectives.

In my ten years at Harare International School, I have seen all my colleagues work hard on this and I particularly appreciate those with a local passport!

I got my introduction ten years ago from an impressive vice-principal and through a lot of reading material at the signing of my contract and one concise statement: "Respect from the pupils will have to be gained and earned by you and not demanded by force as in many school systems". And this is still how we work: earning respect by working and not forcing respect according to hopelessly antiquated norms and strategies.

A lot of our children and their parent have travelled in many countries and the parents themselves often have different nationalities. Hence, the term: TCK, *a Third Culture Kid*. The homely environment is of vital importance. Our extensive campus is really fancy and it could have been more modest. The garden is lush and planned out with an entire range of indigenous trees and shrubs and guinea fowls and peacocks that parade around as if they are in charge!

The "social hangout" until five or six o'clock is just fine, because there is little interesting to do for our youths in this capital. New plans are made, in working groups, for hours after homework support. For many seventeen and eighteen year old youngsters school is a "home" after school hours and 30% of our students have a local background. I love to talk to them, sitting on a bench under the only European chestnut tree we have. Often, both their working parents have though jobs in an entirely different and remote African country or on another continent. The girls mostly love the talk about their major and minor issues and worries in life. And about what is home and future and which cultures are actually better.

In class, each of them has the choice: students can call me Patrice or Miss Patrice or Miss Delchambre. No one in this school gives them a similar option. It is explained to them what "we within our school community" mean with respect and manners, through a self-developed "mission statement" at the start of the academic school year.

New students enrol in early December, about a week before the Christmas holidays. In January 2009 during the first week and also in the middle of the school year, I got another four new students from other local private schools. It takes some time and effort. They often misunderstand the meaning "free and liberal" as applied in our school. It does not mean "free and easy". Nothing could be further from the truth. All our students, particularly our IB students, work really hard to get their diploma.

Barack Obama is also a TCK, a *Third Culture Kid*, who loves to illustrate our global world's changing nature. The classic profile of a TCK is someone with a global perspective, who can easily adapt socially and who is intellectually flexible. He or she can think "outside the box" quickly and skilfully and appreciates varying modes of thought and reconcile them. For some, the search for identity is a challenge, but at the same time the development ensures a strong awareness of one's own personality. (Sense of self: this is who I am, no matter where I am).

Thus: "No drama Obama".

Obama has chosen several fellow TCK's for his government. That is inspiring and interesting. For those who like to read more about it, see Obama's *Third Culture Team* by Ruth E. van Reken:

www.thedailybeast.com/blogs-and-stories/2008-11-26/obamas-third-culture-team//p./

Time to feed the dogs, the chickens and the goats.

It is Sunday.
The cocks crow and Melody brings me four mini-eggs laid by our Bantum Bumps. These are equally divided.
A flock of sunbirds drink the nectar from the blossoms, wet with rain.
I measure the Valkenburg nut tree I got from a fellow Rotarian, Jan. Almost half a metre now. It did not grow between half October and early of December. Thanks to the lush and rich rains, the leaves suddenly shoot and I can measure five millimetres a day at the end of January!
I walk, stop and count all the palms and other trees I ever planted. And now, after eight years I can walk underneath them.
I always was the shortest in class.
And am yet again.

KUNDISAI MTERO
WORD, VISION, SONG, SPIRIT

My name is Kundisai Mtero.
Kundisai in one of our vernacular languages means "to conquer". I guess one would say "Victoria" in English!
I come from a family of four children, one brother and two sisters, me being the youngest. Originally we were five.
My brother is called Zivai (Knowledge); my sister is called Shungu (Determination). Another sister Natsai (Proper) sadly passed away in 1986. She was only 27!

I was born on the 31st of December 1958 and was one of a pair of identical twins but again sadly we lost my twin sister in 1959. She was indirectly a victim of the apartheid era of that time. Fungisai, as she was named, was born with a very serious heart condition and needed urgent medical attention and possible surgery. Being a black baby, no doctor was prepared to perform the necessary surgery to save her life and she struggled for eleven months and gradually succumbed to the heart ailment.
My parents were devastated. Apparently we were so identical, only my mother could tell us apart. Because of my gregarious and extrovert personality, it is often said by my family that I make up for the two of us!
My father, who sadly passed away in 1996, was the strongest influence in my life. His father came originally from Zambia (which lays North West of Zimbabwe) and migrated to, at that time, Rhodesia, met my grandmother and he was taken into her village and ultimately this became his home. So, my roots are most definitely Zambian and I constantly remind my siblings that we have to make a trip to Zambia to research on our family tree thoroughly even though my father did explain the history to us. This history reveals our paternal origin to be from the Mumbwa district in Zambia, of the Ila tribe and our real family name to be "Shabuwe".
My father was an extraordinary man, a great educationalist and a disciplinarian; liberal but firm. He worked as a civil servant in the field of Education during the Rhodesian era and continued to do so when Zimbabwe became independent in 1980. He was appointed the first black Permanent Secretary for the Ministry of Education and Culture.
Sadly he suffered from a stroke and was forced into early retirement due to ill health. He never fully recovered until his death in February 1996.

I was very close to him and undoubtedly his death left a huge void in my life. Often I feel that when he died a part of me went with him.

My mother is still very alive and at her age of 77, still very active. She too worked for over 30 years in the Civil Service during the Rhodesian era, and became the first black female graduate in Adult Education and Community Development at the University of Rhodesia. She also retired in the late 1990's to tend to my father but continued and still continues to be very involved in community and social projects, with an emphasis on women's self help projects, and gender equality. She sits on several boards, both private and parastatal and works with children in various orphanages, in particular the Mbuya Nehanda orphanage just outside Harare. To me, she remains "the woman of substance" with a fierce zest for life!

My core profession is optometry and I run my own private practice in the heart of town, called "Three Zeds Optical, Private Limited", named after my three sons: Zuwa (Sunshine), Zivai (Knowledge) and Zano (Words of wisdom). Having attended school in Rhodesia up to 'O' level stage, my parents sent me at the age of 16, to the United Kingdom to complete my 'A' levels at a private all-girls boarding school in North Devon, England.

I cannot begin to imagine the tremendous sacrifices they made to make that possible at the time!

After completing my 'A' levels, I undertook my Optometry degree at the City University in London, and finally came back home, to independent Zimbabwe in 1983 as the country's first black optometrist.

I am a single mother of three sons, as I mentioned above: Zuwa, Zivai and Zano and even though I am a divorcee I cannot describe the joy they have brought and continue to bring into my life!

My home is in an area called Glen Lorne in the northern suburbs of Harare and even though we have not had water for a year now, as I write, I still look forward to my drive home daily from work to enjoy the tranquillity its location offers.

My core passion is music. My parents identified this in me at a very young age and encouraged to develop in it as an extra curriculum activity at school. The boarding school I attended from a very early age was run by German nuns of the Dominican order. They too saw my interest and were instrumental in my musical development. I learnt how to read music, play piano and ultimately taught myself to play the guitar. And even now at my age I am determined to learn to play the saxophone.

Other than the fact that I think the saxophone is a beautiful instrument, I feel it is too "male dominated" and I have often admired the few female sax players who have majestically broken that gender myth of it being perceived as a male instrument!

My father was a music lover too, oh so very much, but his musical ear was never so good. Even though he loved to sing I remember always flinching at the notes he would hit vocally. That is the typical enigma of people who are "tone deaf"; they never know that they are!

My mother, on the contrary, has a beautiful and sweet singing voice and it is to her that I owe my love and passion for singing. She often sang to us as children, whether on a long journey by road, or just before we went to sleep, she would sing us lullabies. During school holidays, we often had concerts at our home where my late sister (also a pianist with a beautiful voice) and I would perform, together with my brother who would play the guitar. My other sister was always the backing vocalist and the "stage manager". Oh, we had fun!

To this end in February 1999, I founded and formed an all female *a capella* quintet called "African Voice" of which I am the musical director. *A capella* means singing without any musical accompaniment and I truly believe that our voices are our instruments.

I enjoy arranging and directing the songs we sing from a wide repertoire of early/classical gospel, soul, jazz, blues, spirituals, African Traditional Reggae and contemporary songs from the wide musical arena.

As I am a Rotarian, we hold a big charity concert annually to raise funds for some of our many projects or to donate to the Rotary Foundation for the good cause. We do, however, also perform at private functions like weddings, corporate dinners, etc. We meet once a week after hours, to rehearse, connect and to bond! And because I love working with young people, I teach and direct both the Junior and Senior Boys' Choirs at St. Georges College, an all boys High School, where my sons attend school. I love male voices so I enjoy every minute of it. So yes, I have a full life: my optometry practice, being a mother, African Voice, Rotary and Choir Director of St. Georges and I thrive on it! I find particularly the musical aspect of my life very therapeutic.

These to me are the things that make my life whole, that help me to focus on the positive things in life and not dwell on the negativity in this beautiful country Zimbabwe, which I call my home.

It is for this reason that despite the fact that we may all feel uncertain and unsure of what the future holds for us here, what I am certain and sure of is that it is here that I want to be, for it is here where my heart is, it is here where my soul is fed and it is here where my spirit will always fly until it is rested.

Cry, my beloved Zimbabwe.
koo@zol.co.zw

SLEEP?

You live
this African life
only one,
in any case
the lived life
claws
twice over
into your haggard skin.

This life
every day
with the red bougainvillea
the purple jacaranda
the red African Tulip Tree
the Sabi star
the heat of the morning wind
the heaviness
of the evening flowers
the sensual
nightly sounds
a thousand crickets
the barking of a dog
and women
drag themselves
again
to the well.

The scent
of wood fire
crinkles
silently
into your room.
Why are you
allowed
another two hours' sleep?

PAMELLA SITHOLE
PAMELLA, A MOTHER WITH THREE BOYS

My name is Pamella Sithole.
I am the daughter of Rogers Mukandawire and of Jessy Sithole.
I was born on the 25th of April 1975 and I am Zimbabwean, born in the second capital city Bulawayo.

My father is Zimbabwean by birth but his granny parents come from Malawi. My mother, Jessy is also Zimbabwean but her parents are from Zambia. My parents met in Bulawayo and got married there. They were blessed with one baby girl. That is myself!

After three years of marriage they divorced however, and my mum moved to Harare. She took me to her own mother in the rural areas who would look after me so that my mum could earn some money.
My mother met a new man, Joseph Sibanda, a divorcee himself and they fell in love. In 1981 they got married.
I was six years at the time and they both decided it was time for me to be taken away from my grandmother. I needed to attend Grade one!
From Grade one to Grade seven I attended school at Chipembere Primary. I then attended Mukai High School, but unfortunately only up to Grade four because my parents could no longer afford education. School fees became too high, uniforms and shoes unaffordable!

When I left school, I met this guy, Vusumuzi Laher. We fell in love, got married and that was in 1994. On January 31st 1995 we were blessed with our first baby boy, and called him Vusumuzi Junior.
I was a full time housewife and my husband, at the time 23 years old was a soccer player in the Zimbabwe National Team. In 1996 he was invited to play for a South African team, Cape Town Spurs, now Cape Town Ajax, so we moved over there!
We stayed in Cape Town for two years. My husband performed very well. But then Satan came in his way, his ankle got broken whilst playing in the field against another team. The doctors tried their best to fix the ankle but they failed and his career ended then and there. We had to come home to Zimbabwe, both unemployed.

Vusumuzi started a small company, producing wooden cabins.
In 2000 we were blessed with another baby boy, his name is Mussah!

The business was thriving but in 2002 things started changing. The material one needed to purchase was now becoming very expensive. People did not buy from us as they used to and the whole company started collapsing! Life was getting tough!
We started having problems between the two of us, as my husband was now drinking. He drank too much alcohol and then he started fighting with me, shouting at me and harassing me.
That time I became unhappy and felt abused. We were living at his grandparent's place. You can imagine how it is to stay with in-laws! There was nobody helping me, nobody assisting me, except for my own mother. I decided to move out, together with Vusumuzi. We went and started renting a two roomed house.

In 2005 we were blessed again with a third baby boy and we named him Panashe or Khaled. It is a Muslim name. Now life was becoming very tough. I decided to look for a job and my mum talked to the owner of Dazzle Hair Design. The owner decided to give me a chance.
I felt very lucky because I can handle African hair and I am able to do plaiting. I started working as a shampooer, the lady who washes everybody's hair. After washing I give the clients a gentle head massage. My husband's company got broke and at present he is jobless. He is trying his best to find employment but as things got very difficult in Zimbabwe, he has not been lucky at all. He is just staying at home now.

The place where I work, at Dazzle Hair Design in Chisipite, is nice. The problem is that I only earn 50 US a month. The transport is already one dollar per trip! The next problem is that we are no longer employed full time as the business has become low. Everything is falling!

At this very moment, my three boys, all very bright, cannot attend any school. They were enrolled in a Governmental school but there are no teachers left at present! I plan to take them to Phoenix, a small private school in Hatfield. Alas, the fees are 300 US per child which I cannot afford! What to do?

Imagine my life! Imagine me now staying at home with my three boys who have no education, no school, whilst they are really supposed to attend a school! Food is so expensive now, very expensive.
At the moment I can only feed them porridge in the morning and *sadza*, our *mielie meal* staple food, in the evening for supper.

Every day I cry and pray to God.
Maybe things will change.

The life we are living as young mothers is very painful. Sometimes we just drink water and go to sleep then, because there is nothing in the house to eat and no more tea with sugar to drink.
Most of the days, in between my job in Dazzle, I am looking for piece jobs, like sweeping, washing, ironings at other people's houses. This is needed to do, often after working hours, in order to feed my family.

May the Lord hear our prayers.

11 AND 12 FEBRUARY 2009

This is a really marvellous, historic moment in Zimbabwe just like 1980!
The cab drivers hoot all day long!
People are hardly working or not working at all at the Msasa industrial area, today.
There are exceptions.
Hans' chubby ladies pack 8000 Belgian pralines in 2000 cute Valentine's boxes. An order for Air Zimbabwe, for the coming weekend. They are quietly working, listening to the inauguration of our new Prime Minister on the radio.

The vegetable sellers roar with laughter. Everyone is smiling in the morning sun. Never did I see so much depression disappear in the final moonbeams of this one night, the night to 11 February, in the last ten years.
The road is glistening in the early light after the rain and people are waving excitedly at me, a lone driver in the morning on the way to school.

Today it is going to happen!
Is it going to happen today?
Today, hope rises above despair.
Today, relief rises above heavy breathing.
Today, courage wins from fear.
Today, a country lives in hope.
Let it live in hope for a while!

At school, all the faces of the Shona and Ndebele colleagues are beaming. It is no longer "wait and see", no longer "nothing will change".
Instead, everyone is shouting: *'Something will change.'*
The kitchen staff is shouting: *'Yes we can!'*

Hail Mary, full of grace, how was it again?
Holy Mary, full of grace, pray for us sinners?
Give us six more graceful months.
Did all my fellow Rotarians light candles tonight at the Church of Our Lady?

The security guards at the gate look spotless: they have got their uniforms ironed; their cheeks shine with Vaseline, proudly saluting: *'Madam, this will be the new Zimbabwe!'*
'See now?'
Let us see...
There is hope in these frightful days.

At night on 11 February, the never changing classic Zanu PF face reads the ZTV evening news, that we gathered during the day, with a surprisingly happy face.
Tsvangirai has been sworn in.
We have a new Prime Minister.
It is a *Marriage of Inconvenience*, the BBC reporter says much later, but some fixed marriages work, right? But what about the long run?

Today, the 12th of February cheerful music blasts in the car. I am on the way home and on the way to champagne with a few people, who take the opportunity to celebrate this first step.
I have not switched to a ZBC music channel in years.
I guess I will stop on the side of the road for a bit.
Listen to a voice that unites all the millions of Zimbabwean voices outside of Zimbabwe:

'I am on my way home
Mama, won't you hold on?
Everything is going to be fine.

I am on my way home
Baby will you hold on?
I am on my way home
Everything will be okay.

Mama, won't you hold on?
Darling, won't you hold on?
I am on my way...'

GRAHAM DUNBAR BOGDAN ACUTT
TO STAY OR NOT

My name is Graham Dunbar Bogdan Acutt, I am single or at least separated. I am the son of a well known 1970's Zimbabwean painter, Lilla Renata Janik and of Dan Patrick Acutt, a prominent and retired business executive. Both parents, divorced, live in South Africa, my mother in Cape Town and my father in Knysna. I am the last of once a large clan living in Zimbabwe.

I sit on my patio alone. It's early in the morning, a very early 5.30 and midsummer, the usual time I wake to prepare for the day ahead. The world only needs me in two hours time but I require the interlude to prepare myself for the onslaught I know that awaits me today and every day now it seems.
I live on a prominent hill, my little thatched roof cottage squeezed perfectly between the indigenous trees of a *miombo* forest that lies like a dropped blanket over the land. From my elevated position I can see to the horizon in the east through a valley that is bound by gentle rolling hills running away parallel to my vision. The valley below filled with a large dam and just beyond it, untendered land that seems to be a temporary home for race horses that gallop around in large open paddocks. In the far distance I can just determine enormous large granite swellings that hide the true horizon and will turn from their current dull blackness to grey, almost silver by midday and then a burnished pink at sunset. So prominent are these in this part of the country, they have taken on a mystical significance with the local people, a place where spirits still reside.

The dawn sky is clear for once this past week, clear of brooding clouds, a convergence of weather that brings the annual rain in angry dark thunderstorms. It's a relief to see the sun peek over the horizon as I have missed it in my recent early morning meditations. Missed the way it arrives at a different point everyday reminding me that I am part of a much bigger place, the universe, a necessary realisation to keep everything in perspective. The dawn was its inevitable dramatic explosive African event, a blood red eastern horizon, quickly fading to pinks, turning the sky from its star marked blackness through to grey and now a clear light blue.
I am not really alone, the birds have joined me, flitting through the branches in the variegated tree canopy overhead, their myriad songs

rising above the general stillness of the land as it prepares itself for another day.

It's a prolific life, hopping from branch to branch, establishing territories, or attracting mates in a chorus of bird song, red wings, metallic purple bodies, yellow chests, colour everywhere, the first dance at sunrise, the first chance to express being alive.

I need this time of peace to more than just prepare myself but also to reflect on the chaos that seems to surround me, a country in complete free fall, its fathers no longer seeming to care about its children, and a sense of anarchy pervading every thought, action and emotion. Any semblance of normality is constrained by tumultuous events that can only be described as unbelievable. The whole picture bringing into question why I am here and can I stay here.

I was not born here but in South Africa. My father, a Rhodesian, met my mother, a South African, at University of Cape Town, he a business student, she a nurse at Groote Schuur. A mixed heritage runs strong through my veins and not typical of us whites living in Africa. My father, a mixture of English and Afrikaans, his great grandfather one of the first white settlers to this country at the end of the 19th Century. My mother is of Catholic Polish and Austrian Jewish ancestry, both of her parents escaping the devastation of post war Europe, my grandfather losing his beloved country to the Soviets and my grandmother's family of ten lost completely to the horror of a concentration camp.

I delight in my recollections of my childhood, one both blessed and marred by beauty and war, love and sadness, joy and bitterness. We lived in the then Rhodesia, a country of exquisite beauty but tainted and damaged by a passionate liberation struggle. The irony of it all was much of the beauty was hidden to us, kept away by the dangers of the war that were most intense in those very areas that we wanted to visit. Instead we remained in the relative safety of the cities and towns and lived a most blessed and privileged life. Salisbury as it was then called was a clean neat city, with large suburbs, its roads lined with jacarandas and flamboyants, exotic trees that would annually burst into colour carpeting the roads thickly with bright blossoms of pure lavender and bright red. We went to school in uniform, riding bicycles in groups, delaying our arrival by looking for any distraction, aggravating the soldier ants of a termite mound, climbing trees to inspect a new dove's nest or damming a small river and making small boats out of seed pods to chase them along their course.

Schooling was of the British type, much discipline, intensive study and compulsory sport that occupied us for most afternoons and spilled into the Saturdays with sport fixtures against other schools, a different one every week. We played rugby, hockey, tennis, water polo and cricket with the early part of the year marked with athletics and the end of the year with swimming, all very competitive and designed to keep our minds active, our bodies fit and a youth out of trouble, away from society's illnesses, and part of a system that was established to shield us from the world.

Our homes were nestled on one acre properties, some larger, virtually all with swimming pools and well manicured tree filled gardens. We had domestic servants, a cook, a gardener, and more than often a maid who also acted as a nanny. They lived on the premises in small outhouses, tendering to every one of our needs becoming as much a part of our families as relatives but there was an unspoken understanding that they had their place.

We were a pariah state, rejected by the world for our system of separateness, a political and socio-economic system that kept the two tribes, white and black apart, distinctly marked by the haves and have nots.

I reflect on how naïve the whites were at the time, thinking they could challenge the world, the will of the majority, in their attempts to maintain supremacy and control of land that was not entirely theirs. To try impose a new culture and a new way of thinking on a land and its people who had patiently waited and hoped to be included in the riches and bounty of their own entitlement.

As a child I never really understood nor experienced the war only touching it when I watched in trepidation as my father prepared for his "call up", a compulsory time every year he had to spend in the bush as a soldier, or watched the eight o'clock news to hear who had been killed in that day's fighting. As much as my family was liberal we as children were influenced by the propaganda of an authority trying to convince us of the righteousness of its ways. It never seemed possible that things should be different and travelling to my grandparent's tobacco farm some 100 kilometres from Salisbury, with a gun between the car's front seats seemed normal, just as being taught as twelve year old on the farm how to shoot a wide range of weapons for self defence. I did resent the war but only from a petulant child's point of view. Having a typical child's curiosity it was almost painful not being able to explore the farm and its much uncultivated virgin bush with its scattered grey granite kopjes.

I fantasized about trips in which I would carry my trusted shotgun on hunting and fishing expeditions into that unknown land, camping out and living off the land. But this was forbidden and too dangerous.

Being excluded from the world came with a cost that I never really understood until I was much older. We were cut off from everything that made us feel part of what was happening, and as a result the culture of us whites became inward focused to the point where there was an air of superiority. The world left us behind in the latest trends, whether it was business thinking, technology, or something as simple as fashion and entertainment.

This was brought into stark reality when we would go to South Africa on an annual holiday, the only country prepared to accept us whites. The contrast of this modern state to a child was often too much to handle but nevertheless as equally exciting. It was an opportunity to eat an incredible range of sweets, savour exotic seafood, spend time romping through large shopping malls with so much on offer and have competitions counting how many different makes of cars there were. It was thrilling to drive down a six lane highway with flyovers and hear music on fancy radios that would only later reach home in three month's time.

My mother's family which usually hosted us on these trips brought into focus for me as a child that there was much more to the world than just the life in Rhodesia. Their deep continental culture and heritage manifested in everyday of their lives held me entranced. It was so refreshing to spend hours playing chess with a very patient grandfather or listening to my grandmother on the piano, my mother on the cello and aunt on the violin playing Bach. There was a certain joy to celebrating for once a spiritual Christmas and Easter in the customs of a mixture of Polish and Austrian influence that made one feel part of something much bigger and older. This "other" way created a yearning to discover my other roots, my heritage that was founded in Europe that seemed so richer and more fulfilling. Returning back home was always difficult, it seemed a step back in time, a place of less culture.

Rhodesia became Zimbabwe, a conclusion that was inevitable.
For most of the people it brought hope, for others it was despair and I watched as I lost a lot of my friends as their families fearing the worse fled the country. For those that stayed, it was an opportunity to fill in the shoes of those who had left and take opportunities that for so long had been denied of us. The new black government was benevolent to us whites, pragmatically so, we still had the only skills and were still very much in possession of much of the nation's commercial assets.
So we were left to our own devices, an unspoken agreement that would only be honoured if either party was benefiting the other and the nation as a whole.
I was fourteen years old at the time and for me it was an opportunity to fulfil the long denied dreams of exploring my country. The farm beckoned and I impatiently waited all week for the weekend when I knew I would go to the farm. With a packed bag for two nights and a shot gun in the bush, I would set off early in the morning with the farm's "gun boy", Henry, and his pack of scrawny, tick and flea infested hunting dogs.
I remember now with fondness these trips and how they taught me much about the land, its people and Africa. The two of us would disappear into the bush with only the dogs as company and though initially there was not much conversation we fast became "friends", sharing in the thrill of

tracking a bush pig for hours and the adrenalin rush of the final chase, dogs baying, and the blast of a shot gun. The nights sitting by a small fire cooking freshly caught fish from a nearby river, under stars that were so prolific, chatting in reverent whispered tones about the day's events, listening to the tree frogs, crickets, the screech of a barn owl and the distant cough of a leopard. I would listen to Henry's gentle voice as he explained in pigeon English his perspective of the world and delight in his stories of the goings on in the farm's compound where the worker's live. He had an almost apathetic fatalistic view to the world, humbly accepting his lot and yet at the same time hoping for a better future, if not for him but for his children. He had faith that it would all come right in the end and if he could not do anything about it, the bwana, my grandfather, the man who controlled his life, would sort it out for him. On these trips, I felt as though Africa coursed through me, that I was part of it and this was my home and destiny.

It was a far cry from my life in town. I was now at a private senior school, a Catholic one for boys and we had new friends, black ones. The cultures never really mixed but we learnt to rely on and trust each other on the playing field, copy each other's study notes and defend each other against the school's authority. We became friends at school but outside we retreated to opposite sides of the fence. With the slow opening up of Zimbabwe to the world, our narrow minded perspectives started to broaden and the lure of the outside world beckoned. By the time I finished school most of my class had left the country, both black and white, to distant continents, either to University or to other temptations. Today, there are only two of us left from that class. I left to university in Cape Town and the delights of that cosmopolitan environment of that magnificent institution and equally beautiful city.

It was there, that I began to feel my African roots weaken in a city that was a far cry from the rolling grass and tree covered land of the farm, from the gentle voices and laughter of the blacks at home.

Cape Town has never appeared to me as part of the continent, and as much as it tries even today to remind you that it is, it always fails to convince. With each successive year of my degree completed, Zimbabwe's call as home weakened, replaced by Cape Town and the lure of the European continent. The farm had long ago been sold, my friends scattered to the world, the European influence of my mother's side of the family strengthening my resolve not to return to "true" Africa.

The ugliness of South Africa's *apartheid* further confirmed my resolve to seek a life elsewhere and with typical youthful naivety shut Africa out of my soul. But it was not to be, a failed degree pulled me back to Zimbabwe, unable to stay in South Africa as it would have meant compulsory call up into its military service to defend and protect apartheid and a disappointed father closed all financial resources for an escape to Europe.

Devastated I returned to Zimbabwe, a country that had changed little from whence I left it. My disdain at the parochial environment both culturally and socioeconomically, was buried as I focused on my career with just rewards being promoted to positions in companies at an early age and exposed to responsibilities that would have been unheard of in first world countries. As the years rolled by, dreams of a now very distant Europe faded, dulled by the priorities and commitments of a professional career. It was a comfortable life filled with the usual middle class routines, familiar faces and sites, problems easily dealt with, people with cultures that one understood and therefore could motivate, discipline, manipulate and manage.

Marriage was inevitable, to a woman, Bryony, the mother of my two beautiful children, a boy and a girl, Daniel and Savannah, now 14 and 12 years old. I am now director and part shareholder of my own young start up company having survived some appalling business decisions over the past twenty years, some my fault, others that I had no control over as is typical in this part of the world. I never explored Europe until recently, it never seems to amaze me that I had ample opportunity to go there, enough money and plenty of time but I never did. It was very easy then to use the excuse that I was too busy but in hindsight I realise it was fear, fear of the confirmation that I should be there and my life in Zimbabwe was not true to my soul. A failed marriage opened the doors to a beautiful person in Italy and it was with trepidation that I stepped aboard a plane to confront that fear. It was a complete shock to my system being in Europe, not least aided by the emotions I felt for my lover, Antonella, who had so completely and perfectly captivated my heart. There was a deep sense of being at home, of belonging, revealing in the freedom of expression, the joy of cosmopolitan attitudes, the prolific stimulation of heritage, history and culture. And with easily generated resentment and disdain I looked south to my home in Africa knowing I had to leave what should be my home here in Europe.

Regrets of choices, self inflicted or unavoidable that have resulted in me now living in a country that is once again the pariah of the world. It's a full circle, reflecting that all things are controlled by nature and her cyclical influences, one that in this case, has taken over 30 years to manifest itself. The country, the one that I have made my home is in free fall, spiralling out of control, the people, dying of cholera, less than 20% of them formally employed, a local currency that has totally collapsed with absolutely no value, an infrastructure that supplies intermittent service, sporadic electricity and no municipal water. Government schools and hospitals closed because the staff can't afford the transport costs to get to work, productive land and other resources lying idle, communities and their institutions social or economic, barren.

We were the bread basket of the region and had the highest literacy rate in Africa, it's all gone now and possibly never to return in the way it was. Once again my friends have left or are planning to.

I had to return, here is my life invested, emotional and financial. I watch my children, frolicking in Africa, their feet bare and muddied by African soil. I see on their faces their delight, curiosity and wonder as they interface with a world that in its self is pure and true. The children understand the meaning of life and how fragile it is, that it is up to them to make the most of the opportunities provided them. They have seen the harsh realities in nature, an antelope killed by lion, a guinea fowl snatched into the air by an eagle, their own indigenous black brethren forced into poverty and misery by its own government. I watch them benefit from a superb private education, playing the sports so well that they love. My dreams that they experience the joys and beauty of my childhood are being fulfilled and I know that when they come of age they will leave Africa, hopefully to Europe another of my dreams.

I will arrive at work today and wait patiently while the 12 hour night security guard opens our gates for me. He will, as he always does, stand proudly to attention, his ankles together, his chest puffed out, arms ramrod straight at his side, head held high as I pass him by in my car. I will as I always do, I walk up to him and greet him with a: *'Mangwanani, Marara Sei.'*
'Good morning, how are you?' Despite the appalling state of his uniform, his boots in tatters, his shirt faded by too numerous a hand wash, his trousers torn, a face exhausted by a lack of sleep, I find a beaming smile and bright eyes. An expression of both sadness and despair, but also hope that things will get better. I see the Henry of my youth.

graham@tcc.co.zw

NEVER AT HOME

You Ndebele queen
did you collect
the clay
from the river banks
did you find
any gold while panning
twelve hours a day?
You Ndebele queen
you bore twins
you buried twins.

Your husband came for Easter.
Your husband came for Christmas,
he came to beat
he came to beat and eat.
He came to eat.
Stale his breath
your savings gone
he left for Jo'burg again.

You Ndebele queen
you carried on
in silence.
Planting
ploughing
feeding
dying
no feelings left.

HOMESICK FOR AFRICA

Always will
I
long
for the pink *granadilla*
the mango's yellow delight
the Flame Lily
at Christmas
and the sweet
sunset's pride.

SHEILA BELL
SHANGAAN SHEILA

CHARACTERS IN THIS CHAPTER
Paolo – my husband – *l'extraodinaire*
Patrice – good friend
Marina – has been living in Zimbabwe for the past 14 years
Olive – friend and neighbour from Uganda
Sandy – sister and pal
Harry – the Campari mixer
Nabil – friend from Yemen
Yemenite Chickens – so called because where given to us by Nabil!
Alex – our trusted gardener.
My name is Sheila Bell and I am Zimbabwean from the Shangaan group, which is a small minority in Zimbabwe. Most people when they read about Zimbabwe are aware of the Shona and Ndebele, but minority groups such as the Shangaan and Tonga are hardly spoken about. You will not be surprised to know that Zimbabweans themselves are unaware of these ethnic groups, which have a larger presence in Mozambique and South Africa. As children we loved listening to my father, Francis as we grew up. There is my mother Hilda, and my two sisters Helen and Sandy. I am the proud mother of Tashana, 23 and Matteo, 12.
We are thrilled that Tashana is back home after studying abroad for the last five years. Her brother more so. He attends the Harare International School where Patrice is his art teacher!

I met my husband Paolo in Zimbabwe. He arrived here in 1987 and unfortunately for me, his first love was Zimbabwe. After a number of years we left Zimbabwe, only to return in 1997, so when the opportunity came up for us to come back home in 2007, there was no doubt in our minds that we should follow destiny's call, even though we were sailing against the wind. After living for several years in Italy, then Latin America (Bolivia, Peru, Argentina, Chile and Brazil) and in Africa (Kenya, Djibouti, Somalia, Egypt, Somalia and Mozambique) we felt ready for this Zimbabwean experience.
Before moving, I made a call to Marina in Harare. Their family has endured a lot over the years, but she told me they would only leave if the situation got unbearable. My conclusion after this was: 'If they could cope, so could we.'
Out came the suitcases!!

It is very difficult to explain to you the situation here because the picture presented by the foreign media and that of the local government are not the same.
My experience and reality is different. The fact on my return home that people of all classes are still friendly, makes me realize how Africa is different. There are things I appreciate here, like "eye contact" while talking to people. This direct communication, maybe for the fact of being a woman, was difficult in other places such as Somalia and Egypt.
Seeing people smiling, looking one another in the eyes and greeting each other, as well as strangers in a shop, on a bus, in a train 'Good morning', 'Good afternoon' and 'Good evening', things that in Europe no longer exist gives me hope for the future even though this is not the perfect situation!
The spirit of existence in strong family bonds, the beautiful blue sky 360 days of the year, the reception you get from ordinary people, these are immediate and intense and are all things (I believe?) to make people hopeful for a better future.
The foreign media has a view of the situation and daily life in Zimbabwe as an abnormal, out of body experience. Something rare and out of this world that is seldom experienced, and that does not have many keen volunteers for the job. However for those of us that are here, it is a challenge to do the daily tasks that most take for granted, but so far we have managed.
The aim of my story is to give you a more realistic view of the life as a Zimbabwean today during these trying times.
Yes the aim is also to highlight our story as Zimbabweans but not for pity but rather as a story of certain things that do happen here.
Each story I will tell is different but all with the same aim; of finding basic commodities and essential items for everyday life and living a normal life.

As a Zimbabwean I have learnt one thing, we are unbelievably resilient and I am extremely proud to mention this fact. My day begins early I wake up and get my family on their way to commencing their busy days. Then after they have set off, I begin the tasks for the day. I am a mother, wife, driver, and the main procurer for my family and the extended ones (all in all 15 people), of all the necessary daily essentials like food, water, fuel etc. My husband jokes that he is going to "put a ban" on my driving because of the number of kilometres I do daily on my rounds in search of anything useful that I can find. I will be honest there have been times when finding even bread is an impossible venture. (Now, the situation, as you can imagine, has still not yet changed however if you are willing to pay a small fortune you can find most of the basic commodities sans luxuries.)
Later in the day, I have to figure out how to get "Zim" cash for groceries! I head out to my bank and discover that the well over 100 metres queue has been there since 7 AM this morning! The latest update from the bank is that we are only allowed to withdraw the equivalent of US$ 5.00, enough to buy two loaves of bread, but by the time I've done queuing in the bank,

the bread queue at the bakery close by has dispersed because the bread has finished! So, now I have the cash I have to think on how to quickly spend the "Zim" dollars before they literally devalue in my hands. I have to come up with an alternative plan. Living here we all know how to "make a plan" as the expression goes. If plan A doesn't work then get on to plan B and so on.
So, now I can either:
  a. use the cash to buy airtime for my mobile phone
  b. pay the electricity bill
  c. buy 2 kg of flour to bake bread at home in case we have electricity.

Whichever "plan" I decide on today means there will be the other two to accomplish tomorrow. These are the simple day to day issues that in a normal situation could easily be taken care of, but it is also true that this gives us the courage and strength to carry on. You are constantly on the move and aware of it.

It was all Paolo's idea to take the Yemenite Chickens from Nabil, who was leaving the country. Smiling, Alex brings in two freshly laid eggs from the garden. If you have never tasted a Yemenite egg, I can tell you it is the best thing ever! And finding things such as eggs is no easy task in Harare.
If you do find them, they are usually being sold along the road side in the mid-day sun and sometimes you can just see the crack the baby chick has made in order to get out of it in an incubator! So that is why we favour our Yemenite chickens. Of course having those means I have to abandon what once was a beautiful and flourishing flower and vegetable garden because these free range Yemenite Chickens eat everything they come across! But we would hate to see them kept in a chicken run because we already have the rabbits there that are constantly breeding. Total today: forty-three.
The door bell rings and it is Olive at the door, carrying her beautiful hand-painted bowl filled with salad from her garden (that is where I sometimes get my fresh veggies!). Next are Sandy and Harry bringing the Kebabs. There is a Jimmy Dludlu video playing on the wide screen on the terrace outside our house, while Paolo puts the finishing touches to the sound from the projector, then together we arrange the benches, chairs and tables so that everyone has a good view of the screen from their angle. Slowly more cars arrive. In comes Patrice carrying a fantastic array of homemade Sushi! Yum! She and Aad go and check on Mimi, the goat they have given to Paolo for his 50th birthday. Apparently its brilliant and noisy condition is approved by everybody!

There is a moment of confusion as greetings take place, and food is taken into the kitchen, arranged, then brought onto the dining room table. Tonight is outdoor cinema night!! This is a way of socializing with family and friends after a long and sometimes hard day. The film we have chosen tonight is *Crash* that tells the story of people from different cultures and backgrounds and how through a common link, their lives meet.

In a way our lives in Zimbabwe are similar in that we are all in the same situation, but we try often to get together and give each other a hand, if necessary to make our lives better.

One of these ways of looking after one another, besides socializing and directing one another to where commodities can be found, is the joy of cooking and exchanging recipes.

I would like to offer you mine!

Here is a very simple and delicious Sicilian recipe that I often prepare for friends. Enjoy...

BROCCOLI AND ANCHOVY PASTA

INGREDIENTS:
1kg broccoli
40g anchovy fillets (under oil) chopped
3 garlic cloves (cleaned and halved)
1/2 cup bread crumbs (toasted)
4 tbspn olive oil
1 small red chilli pepper (broken into small pieces) salt to taste
500g pasta (Orecchiette)

– Cut the broccoli so that you have the small stems (mouth size).
– Boil the broccoli in a pot for 10 minutes. When broccoli is cooked, remove from the pot but do not throw away the water. Remove from stove and leave in the pot.
– In a pan, put olive oil and leave to heat.
– When oil is hot, add the halved garlic and chilli pepper. Fry for about 2 minutes until garlic is golden.
– Then add the anchovies and 2 tablespoons of anchovy oil to add flavour and cook for a further 10 minutes. Stirring occasionally.
– Add the broccoli and cook for another 5 minutes.
– When broccoli is cooked, remove from stove and sprinkle toasted bread crumbs.
– Bring the broccoli water to boil. You might need to add extra water, sufficient to cook the pasta.
– When the pasta is cooked, sieve water and mix with broccoli sauce.
BUON APPETITO!

FIFTEEN HOURS ON THE BUS

The old black man
sits
with yellowed teeth
yellow maize
in his hands
yellowed nails
yellow-white circles
his sweet old eyes
next to me
in the dirty yellow bus

does the dirty yellow bus go
to the end of the land
Where is then
the end
in this yellow light?

Dirty yellow the bus
faded yellow the sky
strange yellow the soy
dirty yellow the tobacco

the bus
the man
and I
yet
we count
the nine
empty hours
in
the heat
yellow

Soon
we smell
the same
we share
a cigar
and laugh
sleepily

waiting
for the yellow
morning
at dawn
after a strange
sleepless night
the sleepy man
the slow bus
and I.

THOMAS AND BRUNO
IT'S A SMALL WORLD IN ZIMBABWE

We are Thomas and Bruno, two thirty-year-old Belgians who, at the time of writing, live as development workers in Zimbabwe for nine months now. The following is a fictional diary based on real facts, which illustrates how people are trying to overcome the daily obstacles in Zimbabwean life. The type of anecdotes is completely true and typical, but on some occasions we have changed time or names in order to improve readability.

DAY 1
Freshly arrived.
Warm, but not stifling. Besides, Harare is at 1500 metres.
Looking around curiously, in this country of which we have heard so much.
At the airport, we try to exchange American dollars into Zim dollars. These are exchanged at the official rate of 1 USD = 30,000 Zim dollars. When we check what we could buy which such an amount at the coffee shop, next door, we see a cup of coffee for 90 on the menu. Probably 90,000. Hmm, three dollars for a coffee, we assume, not particularly cheap, but affordable. However, the waiter calls us back.
No, no, that cup of coffee costs now 90 MILLION. To make it easy they leave out all the zeros on the menu. Some quick calculation then we find it difficult to believe the outcome: a cup of coffee costs 300 USD, or about € 240. We will wait with exchanging at such a rate. The waiter looks around discretely and whispers that it is better to exchange somewhere at the black market rate.

Even though we have no local currency, we do quickly visit a Spar store. It looks a little East European: three rows of one brand of washing powder, two rows of powdered milk and the rest completely empty. Even the fresh vegetables are missing, apart from a case of onions. Pork trotters are the only meat. We want to find comfort in some beer and take two one litre bottles to the register, but they absolutely refuse to take our American dollars. It is strictly forbidden. We see no one who discretely offers to change our money and we do not dare to ask for it.
Oh well, let's go home empty handed.
If this is how it starts...
1 cup of coffee, 90 million.

DAY 2
A Belgian colleague lends us some Zim dollars and informs us about the exchange rate that day. Armed with this knowledge, we go out on the street and discretely ask around. Eventually, we do find a guy near the bus station who agrees to trade, but at a lower rate than our colleague told us. We accept anyway and exchange € 50 for 5 billion Zim. He leaves for a while and comes back with a plastic bag. This is filled to the brim with money and we trust that it is about right, because counting it on the street is impossible. When we stack it up at home, it is 54 centimetres high.

Even though a large number of Harare's inhabitants carry one, and often, two mobile phones, it is no picnic getting your hands on a SIM card. It soon becomes clear that these are almost solely available on the black market and at the steep price of € 75. For this adventure, a Zimbabwean colleague takes me under his wing and out on the street. After three hours of driving back and forth between several stores where the cards are offered furtively and a questionable deal on the street, I am the owner of a Zimbabwean prepaid mobile number.

Sometime later, my neighbour Edward tells me that he knows the GSM operator's president and "through her, you can get a subscription for a lot less money". Bruno is enthusiastic and asks Edward to take care of it.

DAY 3
The week after we have arrived, Harare's most important festival takes place: The Harare Festival of the Arts – HIFA! Everyone eagerly looks forward to it, because Zimbabwe's cultural life is very limited. This week is jam-packed of concerts, theatre performances and other shows. We meet Rahim, who works together with Veerle. He is a multi-faceted artist who makes a living with temporary jobs. There is a connection and we start talking about his life as a gay man in Zimbabwe. Homosexuality is forbidden here and a large stigma surrounds it.

DAY 4
After four days, it really becomes clear: every sort of human contact strictly starts with a variation on 'Hello, how are you doing?'
And I mean every contact!
Asking the time, at the register, when you are exchanging money on the black market, and of course also when saying hello to acquaintances who even extensively ask about the situation at work and at home and whether there is electricity and running water.

In that respect, we are blessed. Electricity and water are almost always available, which does not apply to everyone. Apparently, the next street up is connected to a different network, because at night you can hear the roar of the generators there. Another explanation that street is without light and water is that the leader of the opposition lives there.

DAY 5
Inflation. Everyone talks about it, the newspapers are filled with it, but no one could explain to me how, what, why. But I am able to feel the inflation in only five days Zimbabwe! That pile of money of a few days ago is now worth almost half of what it was worth. We need to change tactics and exchange the money bit by bit. And spend it immediately!

DAY 7
Farai, a Zimbabwean colleague, a fun 27-year old woman visits us at home unexpectedly. I feel quickly at ease in her company. Is this the beginning of a friendship?

DAY 12
Our only white neighbours live two houses away from ours, an elderly Zimbabwean couple, Ken and his wife Val. We get talking. Ken used to be Zimbabwe's second largest wheat producer and owned five farms and two ranches, where they used to hunt. Since 2000, the Zimbabwean government has disowned many white farmers. Of the 3,000 to 4,000 farmers that were left now only about 300 remain. Even that number is quickly decreasing. Ken explains to us that one by one his farms were taken away. He is very bitter about it and often uses the word "they". "They" took it away, "they" are driving the country into misery, and "they" just do everything out of envy and jealousy. Sometimes it is not entirely clear who he means, the government, the Zimbabwean, all the black people in Africa? I try not to go into it that deep. His last farm was occupied only three months ago and it did not happen gently. He patrolled with guns in his hands and fear in his heart for nights on end. In the end, he barely escaped. My pity decreases when he tells me that he flew away with his private plane. I guess he is not doing that bad. At the moment, he hopes for compensation, perhaps not under Mugabe, but under a different, more moderate government. It is difficult to know what to say to him. This man has lived and laboured here his entire life and knows the country and its politics much better. However, a lot of what he is saying goes against my convictions.
I think it is unjust that before 2000 a handful farmers owned more than 75% of the best farmlands. Now, most if it is fallow and Zimbabwe's entire farm production has collapsed.

DAY 15
It is the end of May and on this side of the equator the days are short because of the winter season. When we get home at night around 18:00 it is dark and there is no electricity. For the first time, we experience how

many people in Harare live night after night. The difference is, we are not prepared for it: no candles! On the other hand, we realise that, due to the fact that we have a gas stove, we will always be able to cook, electricity or no electricity! Our experience is short-lived, half an hour later the light turns back on.

DAY 20
Due to the high rate in which we go through our supply of movies and shows (long live the external hard drive!), we decide to find another thing to do on Sunday night and go to the cinema with Farai, our colleague. Apparently, the films come to Harare about a year after their release date, even if they are offered on DVD at the local video store. It still remains a charming occasion, the hall is one of those old-fashioned cinemas with a curtain that opens and enough space for your long legs.

We meet Constance, who lives three houses from ours and who offers her services as a household help. We have a think about it. We know, in Europe it appears as bourgeois and decadent. As if you are too lazy to do your own dishes or as if you think it is beneath you. On the other hand, we miss the modern household appliances that make life easier. Besides, domestic work is looked at differently here. You provide someone with work and in doing so, with income, often to an entire family. In the end, we decide to have Constance working for us one day a week. I ask how much she wants for it. Four billion, she says. That is about five Euros. It makes me feel weird. Someone who comes to work for you four days a month and will not even get a Belgian hourly wage. We offer her eight Euros a month, piece of cake for us, but more than double the wage of a full-time teacher here. I promise myself that I will treat her with much respect.

That night, we have organised a games evening. We play Risk until deep in the night, with lots of conversations and laughter. Our supply of beer is completely gone now, but seeing as they brought a few bottles each, it does not make us feel bad.

DAY 51
The elections and the foreign media attention result in several new international sanctions. The German supplier of the paper that is used to make bank notes is not permitted to supply to Zimbabwe any more. The exchange rate for cash money no longer rises and even drops a little bit, because cash is becoming scarce. However, the inflation keeps going on and the prices at the store are constantly *adjusted upwards*. The effect for the ordinary citizen without a local cheque account: everything has become prohibitive in a few days. Thus, a small bottle of 500 ml olive oil is the equivalent of € 125. Four rolls of toilet paper are sold for € 150. As is often the case in Zimbabwe, there is a way to circumvent this. The trick is

to have a bank account, because, apart from exchanging cash, there is such a thing as a "virtual" exchange. Instead of getting Zim dollars in cash for your American dollars, they place Zim dollars on your account. This system works using a different exchange rate which, these days, is higher than the cash rate. If you can pay by bank card or write a cheque, suddenly the prices at the store are not as high any more, far from it. Have a nice lunch for € 1, drinks included, that is nice. If you have an account, that is. We have none, but our network expands daily and, in these difficult times, we can ask our friends and acquaintances who do have an account for help!

DAY 60
Games evenings have become a tradition too, sometimes alternated with a movie night. During discussions, Rahim and others uphold a very critical attitude towards the regime and the current situation. Even though they are certainly intelligent and well educated youths, they have difficulty to find work at all. However, there are few complaints, in contrast to many of our other Zimbabwean friends. It is an omen that they are gradually bringing along less and less beer. They cannot afford it any longer.

DAY 75
There is no water coming out of the tap since yesterday evening. We have had half a day without water before, but 24 hours without a drop is a situation we are not familiar with. Our Sunday movie trip has become a tradition, often with our colleague, Farai. We get along well and afterwards we chat a lot with some drinks. By hanging out with Farai, bit by bit, I get familiar with the Shona culture. I like to explain my analysis of work situations which I do not fully understand. She thinks it is amazing how far off the underlying reason I am!

DAY 76
Still no water. Apparently, the water has been cut off in the entire city and its suburbs for three days. The responsible public service has no money to buy chemicals to purify the water. It is unimaginable how much you can miss water. Not washing is not too bad in the end, but we get really frustrated from a 1001 things: cooking rice? No. Wash off the juice of a nice orange? No. Flush the toilet? No, and after a few days, the smell is disgusting!
There is almost no drinking water available in the shops anymore, because everything is bought up.

DAY 77
While I get ready in the morning, still without water, I look out the kitchen window by chance. There is real rush to our yard. A neighbour who has a water well has thrown his garden hose over the wall, so that Ken and Val,

the white Zimbabwean couple can fill their pots and buckets. Everyone rushes towards it and people are running up and down with everything that might be able to hold water: bottles, tins, yes, I even see an old baby bath that is being filled up. After I have filled my tins and some bottles, I look for more containers. Who knows when we will get water again; let's just fill up everything we can. My eye drifts towards our dust bin. A quick rinse and it will at least ensure we can flush our toilets again. It was actually one of the nicest mornings here: a very happy atmosphere at the queue, lots of laughter and jokes.

'Soon, we will have to wash ourselves out here', the voluptuous neighbour says.

'Yes, I will certainly come and watch', the seventy-year-old neighbour says roguishly.

DAY 92

I am startled when I open the door for Constance. It looks like she has an Easter egg in her mouth. Her right cheek is all swollen up.

'Inflamed tooth', she mumbles. I am not sure what to say.

'You should not come to work if it hurts too much, you know.' She shakes her head, no, no, she will be alright.

'Do you need help for the dentist?' I ask.

'No, no, I will go tomorrow.' No hint at all that she could use some money.

DAY 101

After mutual deliberation, we decide to double Constance's salary. She is very punctual and precise. We just feel bad that the wages are so low in Zimbabwe. Even though it used to be true that many things were cheaper than in Europe, it is changing rapidly and everything becomes more expensive now.

DAY 134

We have been living in Harare for four months now and I am surprised how quickly someone gets used to routines. Even in an entirely different culture, in a completely new country with other customs and another language, you develop a daily routine in no time. Could this be a sign that I am "getting used" to Zimbabwe?

DAY 150

One of my greatest pleasures is my means of transport here: my bike. A Yamaha 200cc, bought from a Frenchman who left. It is such a great way of starting the day, cruising underneath a blue sky past the traffic jams. Until you break down. A flat tyre because of a huge nail. I check out a few garages using public transport. No one fixes bikes, and if they do, at outrageous prices. Discouraged, I want to go home. While I wait for a van, Ken, our neighbour, passes by and picks me up. During the trip, I tell him of my bike problems. That afternoon, I go to work on foot. When I come back, surprise! Ken is working busily, fixing my bike. We have to make a plan, because we do not have all the necessary tools, but use that typical and practical common sense that seems to be universal. We succeed in changing the tyre. When I want to thank him, I am close to tears. Often even the hardest things here are a lot of work and everything just keeps on getting more complicated. And now having this problem, suddenly, out of the blue someone else helps me fix it! Ken does not know how to react to this much emotion. Later that night, I put a *thank-you card* under his window, with some Belgian chocolate.

DAY 184
Big news: a few stores are allowed to sell in dollars. To do so, they first have to buy a license from the government (20,000 USD and 15% of their turnover, it is said), but after that, they can officially sell their goods in foreign currency and thus, import goods more easily. Result: the shops are stocked again, but apparently it is hard to lose the price-raising reflex: some prices keep on getting higher. Good for us, those who have access to American dollars, but the average Zimbabwean cannot buy anything in the stores anymore.
We hear rumours that in high-density Harare neighbourhood cases of cholera have been diagnosed.

DAY 203
The past weeks it has become clear that there is cholera in the country. First in some high density neighbourhoods, now in nine out of ten provinces.

Statistics from Government and NGOs disagree, but in any case, a lot of people die of this easy treatable disease. However, health care in Zimbabwe is almost non-existent: closed hospitals, shortage of basic medicines, no money for doctors and nurses. To us, cholera is like a ghost you cannot see, but you can feel it is there. This morning at the office, Farai told me that an employee of a partner organisation in Harare died of the disease. That really comes close and a quiet fear gets under one's skin.
When you think that 15 years ago, one could find the best doctors of southern Africa here, in a exemplary social services system, you can understand the frustrations of the Zimbabweans. An utter disgrace.

Farai turns out to have a daughter! In the six months we often meet, she has never once talked about her daughter. Weird, isn't it? This is a classic example of my newest theory, which states that the Shona do everything to make you feel comfortable, do not get angry often, nod even though they think *no*. In other words: Shona avoid confrontation. Perhaps a cultural trait they have inherited from the British. According to this

theory, Farai would never tell me about her daughter on her own, out of fear to shock me, because she, as a single mother, did not live up to a standard social model.
Of course, it is just a theory, but this is how I try to understand my surroundings, bit by bit.

DAY 210
Constance does not beat about the bush this morning. When I give here the monthly 20 Euro, she says that she can hardly buy anything for this amount.
'It is not even enough for a month of cooking oil, let alone something to cook.' Actually, I think it is great that she bluntly asks. I give here 50 Euro and she shakes my hand to thank me, touching her right elbow with her left hand, a sign of respect and gratitude.

DAY 280
The prices have become a bit more reasonable, because the people can now compare them and shop at the cheapest store. A couple of months ago this was impossible. The prices changed several times a day and you never knew whether they had that product elsewhere, so, as soon as something was available, you would stockpile it. That is why we once went without sugar for three weeks, nothing to find. When it was finally available, we stocked it and now we have twenty kilos of sugar in the cupboard. One thing less to worry about. But now, everything is available in bulk.

Christmas is coming and you can notice it, there are decorations and even a Santa who entertains the children in the hallways, ringing his bell. And thus, life goes on. Is it better or worse here than in Europe? In some aspects certainly worse. But socially, there is a lot of solidarity here. Everyone helps everyone with everything. The worse it gets, the more people help. But that often means a debt and you do sometimes notice people asking for a favour in return. Here in Harare, live and let live often means *Help and be helped*.
There is a theory, the "small world theory", that states that, on average, only seven people are needed to link two people anywhere in the world.
You yourself "know" President Obama, through my acquaintance in Tanzania, who has a friend in Kenya, who used to be in love with the daughter of a carpet seller, who worked in Obama's grandmother's village. This theory is really suitable during our life in Harare, Zimbabwe, which begins to look like a village in which everybody knows everyone after a few months.

There is also a computer game, The Sims, that involved building a functional city, with roads, parks, houses and industry. However, sometimes there were natural disasters, earthquakes and the like that destroyed your work. This is a feeling we often have, that you have to create an entire network of links in order to make your life in Harare pleasant of even liveable.

Life here sometimes reminds me of that curious Chinese curse: "May you live in interesting times."

www.brunodeceuk.blogspot.com – brunodeceuk@gmail.com
www.thomaspouppez.blogspot.com – thomas.pouppez@gmail.com

HAKATA, OR THE FULL MOON STONES

Three thirty
the neurotic rooster
screeches
shredding
the African secrets
apart.

Fireflies vanished
light fairies of the night.
Bats vanished
in the shadow of
a distant full moon
the green frog concert silenced.

Waking with four friends
waiting for the whitest cloud
slipping
in front of the moon.

Four ivory moon stones
I will toss
for four women's stories
Chirume
Tokwadzimu
Nokwara
Kwami.

Five thirty
the African grass sings
the morning dawn
stretches
orange.
We lay
our weary heads
to rest.

BENGT POST
ZIMBABWE: NIRVANA FOR THE NIHILIST

Everything is music. Not only the beautiful sounds of my friends and colleagues "Rebel Woman" Chiwoniso, Adam Chisvo and many other local musicians, but also the persistent howl of the neighbours' malnourished dog, the heart-rending chants at the funeral of our maid Loveletter, who suddenly passed away, only forty years old; the synchronised hoots of two wood owls calling to each other across the garden, the desperate wail of the inconsolable young mother who just lost her child, still a baby, to cholera; the hypnotising reverberation of the *mbira* – our national instrument – the deafening sound of an overhead thunderstorm (to add insult to the injuries of Aids, drought and famine, more people die from lightning strikes in Zimbabwe than anywhere else in the world). Zimbabwe is a constant assault on the senses. Every day it takes your breath away.

My name is Bengt Post, 48 years old, married to Assia Bouzidi and the father of Sander Salah Madiba (11) and Daan Saad Thulani (9). Resident of Harare, the Sunshine City, since 1996.

It is March 4th, 1995. My brilliant friend and colleague Bernard Chidzero Jr. is celebrating his birthday in his apartment in Brussels. Four days late – his birthday is February 29th, shame – but he is celebrating it together with a good friend, Assia, who has her birthday on March 4th.

Bernard and I know each other from high school in Geneva and fate or whatever brought us back together twelve years later when we both joined the same strategic consultancy firm, he in Brussels, me in my native Amsterdam. When we lived in Geneva, Bernard's dad was the head of the United Nations Conference on Trade and Development (UNCTAD). The analphabetic son of a Malawian farm worker (many of Zimbabwe's farm workers originate from Malawi and Mozambique), he was "discovered" by an English Missionary when he was around twelve years old. Six years later, he was studying at Oxford University, and later obtained a PhD from McGill University in Canada.

When the University of Rhodesia withdrew its offer to appoint him the first black professor because he had married a white woman from Quebec, he joined the United Nations until he was asked to join the first independent cabinet in Zimbabwe in 1980. He would occupy various ministerial posts for the next fourteen years and was highly respected by friends and foes alike. It almost lead to the post of Secretary General of the United Nations, a race he lost, only just, to Boutros Boutros Ghali. He never recovered from the blow and his deteriorating health forced him to retire in 1994. Dr. Chidzero died in 2002 in the Avenues Clinic of dehydration, they had forgotten to replace his drip. Life and death, heads or tails; in a country in crisis, the line is disconcertingly thin.

So it's March 4th, 1995. Zimbabwe is written in the stars. In Bernard's living room, I can't help but stare at Assia, who is there with her boyfriend; his dad was the head of the European Delegation in Zimbabwe just after independence. And just to add to the constellation, a few months earlier Assia for some still unexplained reason made a bet with Bernard that she would one day live in Zimbabwe. Yeah, right. Bernard bet a ridiculous amount, which he agreed to pay out over 25 years, in monthly installments.

Assia and I had not met before. We struck up a conversation and were still chatting when the party was dying down. A few months later she moved in with me in Huizen, near Amsterdam. Huizen is a notoriously conservative town, with a high percentage of semi-fanatical Dutch-Reformed churchgoers, not the ideal environment for an Arabic woman who hardly speaks a word of Dutch. Assia was born in Algeria. Her father, Salah, was active in the resistance, along with two of his brothers. It cost their father his five shops in Skikda (Albertville), which were all burnt down to the ground by the French army. Salah met Assia's Belgian/Hungarian-Jewish mother Anny on a business trip to Brussels. He worked for the Government in Algiers as the head of the Intellectual Property Department until he succumbed to lung cancer, only 38 years old. Assia had just turned seven. Her mother decided to move back to Brussels with the three children and this is where Assia and I met twenty years later.

I had lived in Brussels for nearly five years as a child in the sixties, in Waterloo (only four years old when I met mine) and St. Genesius Rode. My father worked in the same street in the centre of Brussels where Assia was living when we met. Later in his career my dad worked in the tobacco industry. He made it to Zimbabwe well before I did, in the early eighties, and remembers being astonished by the wealth of the tobacco farmers, whose wives, in his no doubt somewhat reformatted memory, drove around in pink Cadillacs like colonial Lady Penelopes. That is the other side of Zimbabwe, surprisingly downplayed by the international media during our sustained crisis of the last ten years.

In 2000, exactly twenty years into independence, Bernard and I helped organise the only special congress ever to be held by the Commercial

Farmers Union, bastion of the country's white commercial farmers. During the many preparatory strategy and scenario planning sessions, the participants reluctantly acknowledged that too many white farmers had continued with their lives and farms as if nothing had changed in 1980 and behaved as if they were still running the country. What goes around comes around: it's one of nature's incontrovertible laws. But then again, 'Thou Shalt Not Steal' is one of the Ten Commandments.

A few years ago a party had been organised by a group of deputy ambassadors at Imba Matombo, a luxury hotel across the street from our house. Friends of mine provided the music that evening and were shocked to find that they were all but ignored by the diplomatic partygoers. Food and drink were scarce, at least for those providing the entertainment. This type of discrimination remains, unbelievably, widespread. Many times I cringe at cocktail parties when black people are, in their absence, disparaged by native Europeans without the slightest trace of embarrassment or self-consciousness. And often by those who feel very strongly that in their country of origin, foreigners must integrate into their culture, if they are to be allowed in at all! But I digress.

In 1995 Bernard and I had both spent almost five years with a management consultancy company and were both itching for a new challenge. Bernard already had plans to establish an investment company in Zimbabwe. I told him I was ready for a change and it didn't take us long to agree to make the move together.

I didn't know Africa at all – made a bus trip in Morocco when I was eleven – but Sub-Saharan Africa was a place I only knew from tv: famine in Ethiopia, (the end of) Apartheid in South Africa, genocide in Rwanda, a cannibalistic emperor in the Central African Republic, a cold war that most Africans were totally unaware of being fought in Angola, Mozambique, Zaire, ... How could I not want to go?

Bernard and his Dutch wife Dorien assured me that Zimbabwe was different and that, although by no means immune to Africa's problems, it offered spectacular landscapes, wild animals, a beautiful climate, friendly people, no stress, the Victoria Falls, the mighty Zambezi, a great education system, good health care, excellent infrastructure, a thriving agricultural sector, strong economic growth.

So I quit my well-paid job, sold my house, packed a container and booked a one-way ticket to Zimbabwe for Assia and myself. Impulsive? Nah. You only live once, if you're lucky.

We landed on April 7th, 1996. The rainy season had just ended, every imaginable shade of green was basking in the gentle April sun. Bernard and I immediately got to work. During the Queen's birthday celebrations at the Ambassador's residence on April 30th, I met the son of a Dutch farmer who had come to Zimbabwe in the fifties, as had many other graduates from Holland's tropical agriculture schools after Indonesia became independent, and whose 600-hectare farm was in the process of being liquidated. A year later we bought the farm, together with three Swiss partners. And believe it or not, thirteen years later we still own the farm. I never thought I would be part of a disappearing breed, but then again, perhaps I have been such all my life.

It didn't take us long to realise that there was a large market for development consultancy services in Zimbabwe and that the skills we acquired in Europe could be easily transferred to this public sector market. So we decided to focus on aid and development organisations such as USAID, the World Bank and other sponsors of the poverty industry, of western hegemony, call it what you like. In any case, it worked. We were beginning to make some money and when Estela Gil-Alberdi, a former fellow student, colleague and good friend, moved to Maputo, Mozambique, where her husband Andrew had landed a job, we decided to establish an office there. A year later, we did the same in Lusaka, Zambia.

It must be said, making money in the poverty industry is one of the highlights of free-market thinking. If you really want to make a killing – pardon the ill-chosen pun – you should go work in the food aid business, not the WFP, although they also pay quite well (and tax-free of course), but trade (not aid!), that's where the money is, lots of money. Hordes of people get very rich on food aid, mostly subsidised surplus production from the West. Hey, somebody's got to do it!
Sure, but there is something surreal about discussing strategies on how to reach the poorest of the poor at a conference in a five-star hotel in Victoria Falls, sipping G&T's to the sounds of a local *marimba* band. Still, business was booming.

Until the shit hit the fan. Despite our reliable recommendations and riveting reports, Zimbabwe slid into a massive crisis, and the international community stopped sending money. All of a sudden we were dependent on our two satellite offices for our income, with 75% of our staff in Zimbabwe! Ouch. Three offices create lots of overheads and we slowly came to the realisation that despite all our hard work, our clients tended to be a lot better off than us, when we are taking all the financial risk, while they lived like kings at the expense of the taxpayer: one of the many paradoxes of the poverty industry.

Here's another: Try luring someone into the private sector in Mozambique. They are all much better off working for the very donors that are supposed to help build that private sector. In the development world, we believe 'Give a man a fish and he'll eat for a day – Teach a man to fish and he'll eat for a lifetime'. But what happens when the teacher has a monopoly on fishing rods? Okay, enough paradoxes.

Bernard and I have both been playing music since we were children.
He is a drummer, I am a keyboardist. We ended up in a "Rhodie" band with some friends and call ourselves *the Herb Boys*, Zimbabwe's alternative to *the Spice Girls*, only better-looking. Bernard stopped after a year. I continued for a while and then joined another band, *Bush Guru*, started by my friend Gary Redding. Gradually, through Gary and another friend and singer, Charles Summerfield, I got to know the Zimbabwe music scene and the many great musicians we are blessed with.

In 2003 I decided to take a six-month sabbatical to record a cd with *Bush Guru*. The recording was not a big success, but I was enjoying this music thing and getting less and less excited about the poverty industry. So in 2004 I started my gradual and so far not massively successful transition from business to music entrepreneur. I quit the company and decided to buy a farm in Mozambique, near Chimoio, just across the border, together with two partners. What was I thinking? The farm was 350 kilometers from my house – I left Monday mornings at 5:30 and drove back home at the end of the week. At the time, many Zimbabwean farmers moved to Chimoio to grow tobacco for the big US buying companies. Anyway, I ran the place for a year, assisted by a Zimbabwean who had his farm taken, and gratefully accepted an offer from a UK trust to buy the place.

Back to square one. In the meantime, Bernard had signed a fantastic contract with the International Finance Corporation, part of the World Bank group. So now both founders were gone. We more or less gave away the company to the ladies who ran the two satellite offices. And got ready for a new adventure.

Mine started in February 2005. During that month my drummer friend Steve "Sparx" and I organised a meeting with two of Zimbabwe's best-known singers, Chiwoniso Maraire and Busi Ncube, *mbira* master Adam Chisvo and Charles Summerfield. We made a plan to bring together eight musicians from different bands and backgrounds to record an album of new songs composed by the participants, individually or as a group. I became the keyboard player. Wow, I was playing with Chiwoniso, how cool is that?

We called ourselves *The Collaboration*, met a few times a week in the beautiful house of Jules Parsons, whose living room doubles as a fully equipped rehearsal space. Everyone brought in ideas. Willie Hillman, the drummer, naturally emerged as the master of ceremonies and within a few months we had sufficient material for an album. We moved into a studio just outside Harare for about five weeks, well-equipped but a claustrophobic experience. In September 2005 we had our album, *Life at Home/Hupenyu Kumusha/Impilo Ekhaya*, full of stories about life in Zimbabwe at the time. Everyone was pleased with the result.

There was a massively attended official launch in February 2006, we shot a music video[8] in April and were a main stage attraction at the *Harare International Festival of the Arts*. The video played all over Africa for years on the satellite station Channel O. And if that wasn't enough, the South African group *Revolution* recorded a dance version of our song *Urombo* for their new album *4U*.

Meanwhile the crisis in Zimbabwe had reached such proportions that people were struggling to make ends meet, including most of the country's musicians. The two youngest members of *The Collaboration*, Mashasha and Willie, decided to try their luck in the UK. Four years later, they are both still there.

In 2007 we were invited to *the Sauti Za Busara Festival* in Zanzibar, where we got a very receptive crowd on their feet, but that was our swan song. Chiwoniso had started working on a solo album that was released in 2008 by Cumbancha to international acclaim. "Rebel Woman" topped the World Music charts in Europe for several weeks. Busi decided to move to Norway. Rodger, the guitarist, became ill. Charles started his own band and moved to Cape Town. Adam and I were the only ones left.

Adam is a veteran in the Zimbabwe music scene. He has played with all the local greats and has travelled extensively. He is a percussionist and *mbira* player. The *mbira* is the instrument of Zimbabwe and is at the centre of the many traditional ceremonies of Shona culture. The main purpose of the instrument is to, like the *gamelan* in Indonesia, bring the participants into a trance, through its hypnotic sound and endless repetition.

Adam is a true *mbira* master, with an ability to generate structures and rhythms that make your head spin. After 25 years of playing others' music, he had started writing his own. With a wife, three children and the children of his dead brother to support, recording his songs was not

---

[8] Watch the video on http://www.youtube.com/watch?v=REOfjf_bm_g

something he could afford. I might as well help him. And that made me think. Here I was trying to make a living with music and nothing to show for it. I still had some money in the bank. And in another irresistible impulsive moment I decided to build a recording studio in our backyard. Why not? I designed something in traditional local style – three interlocking rondavels of different sizes – operating room, vocal booth and large drum and instrument room. The builders got to work and I went to New York to purchase all the necessary equipment. 18 months later, Thulani Studios (named after our youngest son, Thulani is Ndebele for Peace) officially opened its doors.

Five months later I had produced Adam's album, *Famba Pore Pore*, and an album with Willom Tight, *Kuzangoma*. I had also brought together a group of musicians I called *The Township Survivors* to record a Zimbabwean version of *the Buena Vista Social Club*, called *Zomba By Bus*. These projects were financed by a Belgian NGO and a Spanish Production Company, so the musicians got paid for their efforts. I didn't get a penny.

A few other small recording projects followed. But the country is in chronic crisis. Money is scarce. I joined a pop rock band in late 2009 called *the Tourettes*. Our talented singer, René Swanepoel, writes her own songs that we are currently recording and that we hope will find a following in South Africa.

So here I am, having lots of fun making music but making no money, although at least Assia now has a steady job teaching at the French School. It looks like I have no choice but to return, at least part time, to the poverty industry. Never bite the hand that feeds you. Not much work in Zimbabwe at the moment, but plenty in the region, if I put my mind to it. Hopefully when things finally improve here, the recording studio will provide me with sufficient income. Until then, no worries – I'll make a plan.

THE SUMMER SONG OF THE YELLOW WEAVERS

The December air
feels harsh
and scary.
Hot
it is
and every tone
and every sound
every move
seems
hot.

Weavers
In my waving
palm tree.
Each dancing
palm leaf
ends
in countless
weavers' nests
where
weavers
weave.

Have you seen
how yellow-black weavers
weave?
Fluttering
sharp
in the evening dusk.
Weaving together
their
weaver's nest.

In the
weaverless evening rest.
And on all
those invisible strings
of happiness
hang
the nests
in solitude.

Do these weavers
wait
for the secret
of the night?

What are
weavers
waiting for?

Wait!

For rain.

As no other!

PARTY TIME

Thursday night we leave for Amanzi with Sheila and Paolo. There is no electricity and nobody wants to cook outside over a gas or wood fire after a long day of work. We escape the droning of the big generators around us. On top of that, next Saturday, I have a sit down diner with at least twenty six adults and five children, so there we go, "down the road" to Amanzi for a spell.
Let us enjoy life outdoors for a bit longer because when the infamous "dollarization" is complete, we might not be able to afford these places anymore. This restaurant, the big villa and all the terraces surrounding the house, with a view on a wonderful sloping garden with old, indigenous trees and unique water features. Amazing Amanzi!
After the last heavy rain shower has stopped, hundreds of frogs already treat us to a Thursday night concert, right before a new African music group will perform. The stylishly African ethnic interior changes regularly. The new rooms have been painted in harsh turquoise colours that remind me of the upmarket and trendy restaurants in Cape Town. I am more in favour of the traditional warm earthy tones in the original old rooms of this mansion, with its large collection of our local pottery and traditional baskets.
Zimbabwean artists, selected by Andrew Mama, can display and sell their work here. All the wooden terrace doors with the charming small windows are open everywhere. We have a view on a beautiful giant fern that is still trickling after the wonderful evening shower. All the tables are occupied, inside and outside. There are new, fresh Nigerian table cloths and the mood is cheerful, everyone seems relieved.
About what?
On a night like this, nothing seems to be wrong in this country.
We feel merry, peaceful and avoid politics tonight. But we are all aware things are far from right.
We let the waiter open the wine we brought along.
Paolo puts a good bottle of Sicilian wine in the cooler.
So what do I think about?

I look at the art on the walls and count the number of acquaintances in this circle who have all died, all young and promising.
I tell Sheila: my assistant, artist Beaulah, died at 25, while I was in bed sick with a mysterious African virus on my birthday. The school Principal

called me that morning and again during hours thereafter. I floated back and forth in feverish dreams. Beaulah appeared and just smiled.
A beautiful, slender, happy Shona colleague whom I collected three months earlier from a small clinic. There she gave birth to Matisse, alone. Beaulah had no family nearby, her parents died long time ago and she had no transport. A wonderful baby son and a proud mother, who, nine hours after giving birth, merrily hopped into her jeans and whom I would drop off an hour later at her little flat in town with some fresh vegetables, milk and bread. She would never live to see Matisse grow four months old. *Life is rough in Africa!*

The day after the wonderful Amanzi dinner party, I reported to my friend and art colleague, Maria. We both remember the talented Beaulah, asking ourselves where little Matisse is today and with whom.
Maria happily talks about her "lost day" in Zimbabwe: she tried to pay three bills at three separate places, but either the office was closed – we have gone to lunch –, (an elastic concept) or – try tomorrow, we are on strike –.
Nowadays, all the stores give change in kind, because there is a huge lack of loose dollar bills. Those one dollar notes will be sold for a lot of money one of these days, you'll see.

We continue talking about the change we receive at the cashiers: sweets, bread rolls, bananas, tomato plants, condoms, pens, pencils, disgusting cough drops, an avocado. So we may suggest Hans to start producing chocolate coins, no?
The country is waiting, paralysed.
Which political deal will be made?
Where will we go?
Luctor et emergo.
We keep hoping.
We stay positive.
Friday after work until Sunday I cannot be bothered anymore.
I study the three possibilities of three different kinds of *potjekos* in the *potjekos* cookbook and let Daniel chop a lot of wood. We are counting on 28 adults and five children. An ideal opportunity to get the cast iron three legged cauldrons from the shed!
The South African cookbook talks about my most favourite dish: *waterblommetje poikie.* Unfortunately, the Cape I hold so dear is too far away to pick some *waterblommekies.*
I decide with Sheila that we will have to make do with a vegetarian curry, a leg of pork roast and marinated stew *poikie*. It is served with lentils, beans, butternut and preferably six different kinds of fresh vegetables, heaps of tomatoes as a base, lots and lots of dried and fresh herbs and a supply of Indonesian spices.

Pamela, friend of our Alies, brought a wonderful melange of curry spices and *garam massalas* from Nairobi with her last visit.
I will have to thank her again for that!
These fragrant spices in combination with fresh ginger and coriander!
I cannot wait!

The traditional cooking method in three legged pots is not new, however it is still very popular and also not really South African.
"The hardy cast-iron pot actually originated from Europe: early records suggest that it was first used in cooking during the protracted religious wars of the seventeenth century, when food was scarce and almost anything edible was slowly stewed in a large, communal pot.
The potjie accompanied the early immigrants to the Cape; later it was an essential part of the nomadic trekboers' equipment, and it made its way into African tribal culture as the porridge pot. For the nomads and transport riders of the eighteenth and nineteenth centuries in southern Africa, potjiekos was a necessary way of life. The toughest and often inexpensive meat with addition of almost any available vegetable and a minimal quantity of liquid could be transformed into a meal that was tender, succulent and extremely flavoursome. Only fairly recently potjiekos meals, simmering slowly or frying and baking, gained wide popularity. Cape Malay people love to add apricots, sambals, natural yoghurts and cardamom into the traditional curries."
A universal concept, *potjekos*. The *kos* or the *food in one pot*.
I also still remember the wonderful *Eintopf* meals my mother used to make when I was a child. Layers of fresh beans, potatoes and other vegetables on top of a piece of meat, usually pork. Magnificent!
You could just put all that in a giant pan on the gas stove!

Three long tables with white cotton and orange roses in twelve crystal glasses in a long row are ready by two o'clock. Laid out with a view on the three black cauldrons. The food is simmering for at least two hours now. According to the sacred laws of the *potjekos* gurus, you must never take the lid of the pot nor mix the layers during preparation!
You can only do this just before serving.
And so that's what we will do.

By six o'clock, everybody starts trickling in: Sheila, Paolo, Mia, Granny Betty and Gary, Claire, Charity, Bruno and Thomas, Olga and Luc, Bengt and Assia, Marijke, Hans and his three kids, Graham, Mark and Paddy. We miss about five people, but like this, we can use the big, long table. It is great to see everyone this Saturday, the final day of January!
We all laugh and during a loud thunderclap, we crawl together on our small patio when the sky opens up. Heavy rain!
Luckily, there is an orange sun umbrella over the *poikies*.

The fire smoulders on lazily, beer and wine are opened at the long table. Friends put down the salads and desserts they brought along and start chatting.
We are happy to be together and to catch up on the news of the last weeks!

The kids eat pancakes on a table cloth on the floor. Aad took care of chocolate sprinkles, so they are on cloud nine! After our first toast and before we start eating, everyone is asked to, within three minutes, write on a piece of paper what Zimbabwe means for him or her.

Zimbabwe is: My home, it's the place where I learnt what it was to be human, what it is to live life that always challenged in extremes, never simple, never easy, experiences and lessons never taken for granted.

Zimbabwe is? Intriguing.

Zimbabwe is not as it was before. It is going down like a rock.

Zimbabwe is totally unpredictable.

Zimbabwe is my friends, the best part of my life, my children's home. My heart belongs there.

Zimbabwe is truly a land that God made, in its entirety. I have been blessed to have been born and raised amongst its wonderful people and to be known to all as a Zimbabwean.

Zimbabwe is...
Being inspired in everyday circumstances.
It's the sun shining.
It's making all things possible!!
Zimbabwe is the land that we hope in the future will be as good & fruitful as it was in the past.

Zimbabwe is ...
Heartbreakingly beautiful
Heartbreakingly sad.

Zimbabwe is an example to the rest of southern Africa.

Zimbabwe is changing its name to Zimbobwe.

Zimbabwe is... A country that reminds me of that Chinese curse: "May you live interesting times!"

Zimbabwe is a temporary home.

Zimbabwe is a country where I heard the joke: "Bad news and good news: you will have only half the food of yesterday but double of tomorrow!"

Zimbabwe is...
Amazing, frustrating, lost, hopeless and hopeful at the same time, inflating, in the spotlight for the wrong reasons, contradictory, rich, poor, beautiful, Mugabe.

Zimbabwe is...
And sometimes it isn't. Zimbabwe is a big house of stone.

Zimbabwe is painful, horrible, adorable, lovely, love and hate together.

Zimbabwe is...
A downpour of half an hour followed by a wonderful meal with friends in the garden, accompanied by Belgian beer. And candlelight.
Whatever more can a man – or woman – wish for.

Zimbabwe is...
My passion, my heartache.
Almost like an errand husband. Caught with conceit and deceptive corruption, but deep clenching roots with generations of patriotic devotion.

Zimbabwe is a cure for optimists.

Zimbabwe is real life – positive and negative intertwined – rich in human drama and natural beauty.

Zimbabwe is my home, with smiling people, relaxed people, waiting for a great future!

Z ero
I ncome
M ainly
B ecause
A ll
B usiness
W as
E radicated.

Zimbabwe!
It feels so very, very special to be together.

Here we are, the rain has stopped, the evening is beautiful and we are celebrating our get together and our communal love for our country Zimbabwe .

Zimbabwe is
the place where
the sun and the grass
never stop singing together!

Zimbabwe is... a never ending story!
Zimbabwe
for me: the place to be.

When I closely look at the writings, this last sentence can only come from my Aad, the sailor, the glider pilot, the true Zimbabwean of us two!
The thing is, I cannot ask him yet, because he is already fast asleep.

What I do not know at that moment is that in this deep sleep of ours, a number of people have decided that they have been hungry for long enough, have seen the cars drive away and have managed to cut open the fence and dense hedge. The smallest window is forced; a child has been pushed through who then opens the doors of the small cottage. All the clothes, shoes, microwave, blankets, sleeping bags, covers, duvets, a computer screen, washing powder, a mobile phone, beer surpluses and the complete contents of the deep freezer are moved to a new destination.
The alarm was not activated.
Bad luck.
But I only know all this much, much later, the next day.
We will sleep straight through the half five morning song of the Heuglin's Robin.

When Aad goes to fetch the police (the boys have no transport), he jokes about the situation: "Consider it welfare tax!"

That night, I stay and sit outside for a while.
Near twelve soft beige Dutch candles
in the blanket of the early night.
The things a person brings along nostalgically.
The frogs are quiet and the crickets sing.
A lone nightjar screeches.
It is only half past one in the morning, now.
I reread all the Zimbabwe quotes with pleasure
with a last glass of wine...
Where did I put my small cigar?
I muse and ponder.

Tomorrow, I will see my friend Charlotte again!
She combines living and working in Flanders and living in Chisipite with her Zimbabwean partner Ashley. A global relationship!
The best of two worlds.
Is it an option?
I think.
Wishing that my beautiful three children were here.
As in the old days.
With their very best friends
with their very best girlfriends, who, according to
the extended family system,
are my children too.
Wishing my brother was sitting here.
And all my four sisters.
And my mother.
And
my father.

AND NOW WHAT?
JUNE 2010

Not even one year after writing the original book with all of us.
Zimbabwe remains to be a floating Titanic. For a few among us it is a godsend that we jump into a speed boat now and again visit other places often to retain our sanity and inner balance.
Cape Town, Johannesburg, the islands close to Mozambique, Dar el Salaam...
Still, we know we will wake up from a necessary vacation and return to our country of beauty filled with pain.

We continue.

While respecting Zimbabwean women, I certainly have the same share if not more respect for my Flemish and Dutch friends and women. All are enterprising, all self made. In every new homeland: starting from scratch: moving, adapting, landscape the garden, find jobs and most of all create jobs. A lot of determination and courage I have witnessed in this very country!
I have a lot of respect for the Dutch and Belgians who have made this their permanent residence.

Marijke of the Pangolin Lodge witnessed ten years of life and hard work destroyed by flames in a matter of hours. As predicted: "Phoenix, thou shall arise from these ashes." And that is how it went. She pulled through! She rebuilt the entire lodge, but more beautiful and stronger than ever, as Marijke herself, the single mum of us all.

At full moon, we know where to go!
We shall toss the Hakata stones and read the future.
And like always, we stand together in good times and mostly bad times...

Hans has opened up a second *Veldemeers Chocolates* store, this time in the centre of one of the better suburbs: Mount Pleasant.

Assia has continued with her well-known Arabic courage and perseverance: she now teaches English at the official French school.

Bengt has completed his wonderful music studio and has brought out yet another new CD.

Esther opened *Kiki's* in the great suburb of Umwinsidale: you will find unique furniture, antiques, ceramics, paintings and glass objects from local artists and all sorts of interesting collectibles, all in a setting with a breathtaking view. One of the dreams coming true!

Graham is doing well as a managing director in the tobacco industry and, at my last exhibition in our garden, met Swedish Anna whom he married not long after. Both very happy! Together they now have a family with four special children.

These are a few examples of friends who have settled here for a long or indefinite period, and who command admiration and respect.

A few examples of some of our Zimbabwean friends:
Snowy, the *home study director*, now teaches practically all courses at O and A level and his house is filled with students. This type of home tuition is the best solution for a lot of parents!
After coming home from Scotland, Paddy is where she once started: education. She guides many teachers at the classic Hellenic school towards what could be called an "enlightened vision".
New, young idealistic volunteers and expats are also coming to Zimbabwe. Their partners, mostly without jobs, go for it with positive attitude.
Thus, a fresh wind blows through Harare.
Life gets more and more expensive every day, despite the dollarization.
So, we make our own pâtés, yoghurts, pies and bake our daily bread if there is electricity. We exchange recipes over a glass of wine and admire the latest: classic clay ovens in the garden in which you can bake bread and roast meat when there is no electricity, just like most of the Greeks do. And if we really do not want to go to our home chores after work, we just go to Chocolate Hans and feast on pralines, croissants and chocolate rolls. That is what Africa owes us.
Do they count double, these tropical years? Yes they do.

My gratitude goes out to my brothers and sisters of the Maastricht Oost Rotary Club. For years, I have been in my begging role and thanks to their regular support and the modest proceeds from this book I was able to start new women employment projects at ten different units in between April and early June with fourteen Chinese Singer hand sewing machines.

Very special thanks for extra financial support go to Jan Wijnen, Jacqueline Habermehl, Max Darley, (Fellow Rotarians) and Jose de Goede. Thanks to the support coming from Maastricht, nine street children go to school for an entire year and two extra smart students go to an affordable boarding school in the rural areas! Others, like Henry and Richard just survive on the streets behind the Monomatapa hotel and let others convince us that

they had tragically passed away. Trying to squeeze money out of us! Like this, we are sometimes swindled with smart, but unforgivable tricks.
I would like to thank Kelly Adams en Colin Kay for their special support.
I warmly thank Bram Vermeulen for his presence and introduction at the presentation of the Dutch edition of this book!

At the right moment in your life, you meet the right people.
My publishers Liliane Schoonbrood and René Bouman once again worked on the new changes, questions and adjustments with endless patience.
They guided me through minor and major crises these last months like guarding angels.

Right now, I throw myself into helping 75 year old Jack Chidzero with tracking down and restoring colonial and post-colonial furniture, the final remains and I learn to listen to an old man without teeth.
He is older than that man on the bus.
Today, he sands the past of a Danish shrink sofa with the patience of an angel, while, outside, I fall asleep in the winter sun next to him on the terrace, because it is warmer outside than inside.

The autumn is over; we slide into winter underneath a steel blue sky.
The last blue hydrangeas blossom and the bright orange African tulip trees shine against the evening light which has become dear to us in this existence.

"Jack, tell me about Nyanga. About the fairies and the spirits and the mysteries in the forests of the Vumba. And what happened in the mountains during the war."
And so he does.
And I believe everything he tells me.

Mein schwacher Geist ruht!

END OF 2012

BENGT POST
THERE IS A CRACK IN EVERYTHING
That's how the light gets in[9]

Optimism is a strategy for making a better future. Because unless you believe that the future can be better, you are unlikely to step up and take responsibility for making it so.
Noam Chomsky

November 2012 – We're a US$ economy: Zimbabweans now pledge allegiance to the United States Dollar, that symbol of the Washington Consensus and Western Economic Imperialism. For those with a taste for irony, does it get any better? It is also the currency in which Zimbabwe's foreign debt is denominated. Currently, it owes US$ 8 billion to various foreign creditors, US$ 1 billion more than GDP.

2009 was a good year, or so we hoped. The Zimbabwe Dollar's *From Zero to Hero* campaign didn't work. Our bills were too small to accommodate the zeros and larger, more heroic bills would be impractical, so the local currency was laid to rest and replaced by that of the USA. And, God bless America, the economy started to grow again.

The Government of National Unity, formed in the same year, gave people some hope that they could start reclaiming their future. Life did seem to get easier, for us at least – no more fuel queues, overflowing supermarket shelves. Sure, no electricity for most of the day on most days, but at least the glass seemed to be going from half empty to half full.

You could be excused for believing that merely switching from your local currency to the US dollar is enough to revive an economy that has been more or less vandalised over ten years. If you lived in Harare's lush Northern Suburbs, that is. But you would have to believe in miracles.

Imagine you cut your hair to 4 millimeter. The next day, it will grow by 100%, the day after by 50%, the day after that by 33% and so on, until eventually slows to near zero. You don't have to do anything, it just happens. The same applies to economies – destroy them and at some

---

[9] Leonard Cohen, *Selected Poems*, 1956-1968

point they will start to grow all by themselves, only to slow down again. After shrinking by 40% since 2002, Zimbabwe's economy grew 9% in 2010, 6% in 2011 and the 2012 forecast has been revised downwards from 9.4% to 4.7%. That's what happens when nothing happens.

Miracles remain as elusive for the overwhelming majority of Zimbabweans as ever. Economies simply have no capacity for self-healing, they need competent governments that put the interests of their people ahead of those of the rich and powerful. Alas, Zimbabwe is like everywhere else, some variations on the theme, but essentially the same.

Which means our economy will go nowhere unless it manages to attract significant investment, unlikely to happen anytime soon – having Cabinet Ministers proclaim that all businesses in the country should be indigenised may not sit well with your average foreign investor. The prevailing political uncertainty precludes any possibility of an economic revival. Zimbabwe is like everywhere else, we may have a different financial crisis than the West, but it is a financial crisis all the same.

Petty fights are being fought over the backs of 12 million well-meaning, deserving, innocent people by a ruling elite conditioned by animosity, conflict, corruption, discrimination, envy, fear, hate, hostility, lawlessness, lies, money, oppression, power, propaganda, slander, strife and violence. Zimbabwe is like everywhere else, a few tweaks here and there, but essentially the same – the world over, petty fights are being waged over the backs of 7 billion people, one for every dollar of Zimbabwe's GDP.

Or is it the same? Back in my native Holland, life expectancy is 81. In Zimbabwe it's 40. GDP per capita in Holland is $42,000, in Zimbabwe $500, which means that a Zimbabwean has to work for a year for what a Dutchman earns in three days. HIV prevalence in Holland is 0.2% of the adult population, in Zimbabwe it's 15%.

My friend Adam Chisvo passed away last year from diabetes, 47 years old, leaving behind a wife and 3 children. A career spanning 25 years playing with Zimbabwe's best-known bands, performances and workshops in Europe, Africa and Japan: yet his family didn't have enough money for his funeral. Imagine their feeling of impotent shame. They must have forgotten to read *The Secret*, simply not have realised that they had the freedom to choose their own destiny, to become and have anything they dreamed of. Where did they go wrong?

That gives you an idea of the state of the music business. Although I get the occasional interesting project (I'm putting music to chants for the Buddhist Centre next month), my recording studio is about as busy as Shalom Studios in Jerusalem on Shabbat.

Thank God for luck though. My beautiful wife Assia has completed her mission[10] and is now the librarian and French teacher at St. John's College, our kids' high school. Both are in the pipe band; Daan on pipes, Sander on snare drum. They performed at the wedding of Prime Minister Morgan Tsvangirai in September and are going to the World Championships in Scotland next year. In December, Sander and five other Form 3 students from Zimbabwe are representing the country at the International Junior Science Olympiad in Tehran. I have started consulting again – necessity breeds humility. Back to the old grind and the generous clients, to supporting the system. Paid in US$. No complaints. Thank God for luck – it fills half your cup. Another 17 years in Zimbabwe and ours should be overflowing.

Bengt Post
Harare, November 2012

www.soundcloud.com/bengt-post

---

[10] See chapter Never give up!, page 84

WAITING FOR THE WINDS OF CHANGE...

Another year almost gone.
1992 to 2012 makes it exactly 20 years that we have been living in Zimbabwe.
2012 for sure, did somehow sound better than 2013. But, who knows, the number 13 might bring the country luck? Will it be the year where the luster will enhance the pearl again? Will the people be determined and vote without fear for a possible dramatic change?

After our long break this summer (winter in Zimbabwe) one notices a few things: the cost of living here in Zimbabwe increased again within two months' time. Food is now much more expensive than in the Netherlands or Flanders. Ever since the introduction of the US$, there was a hope for stabilization. However, the price of the fuel, for energy, the goods and the food went up drastically. Zimbabwe is for sure the only country in the world where the value of the US$ keeps on changing, devaluating.
Yes, the shops are full. 'There is nothing to get', the people moan in despair, the so called "have not's". The shops are full for the "haves", the expats, the diplomats, the well-to-do, the successful businessmen or businesswomen. Not for the masses, and frankly, the sight of all the unnecessary luxury imported products in all the new supermarkets is disgusting and embarrassing to those who cannot afford a simple loaf of bread, a bag of maize meal, flour, sugar or salt.
Imported goods coming from South Africa, Italy, New Zealand, Turkey and Egypt kill most of our local products, and although brave local people keep trying their best to come up with something new, often the import produce remains cheaper to buy. Disheartening, saddening....
Not to mention of how the rural people get the cash together for the school fees of their children every term... Not to mention the new elite driving around in the latest Hummer, Mercedes, Porches 4X4 or Ferrari.

There is the one clever child, Rudo, aged 9, sitting in front of the hut, never getting a chance to get a place at a rural school. There is the other child in town, Cherish, also 9, who spends more time with her private nanny, her cook and her private driver than with her father and mother....
This is Zimbabwe today.
The crisis affects right now more than the majority of the people. In this new era however, we seem to move back to a certain situation of years ago: the care for one another when one finds something at an affordable

price, the socializing and cooking with friends at home when one now has declared the restaurant food prices ridiculous, assisting one another technically to avoid getting ripped off, the simple and warm solidarity of watching each other's destiny, success, dips, next steps, next plan....
One fate we all share: we all face problems with water, we all suffer from daily power cuts and we all got used to them in the end...
Again, business is thriving, they say. Investors galore. More cars than ever during office hours, but also: street kids back at the traffic lights, even old and sick ones begging in most of the suburbs and the heart of the Sunshine city...
The Chinese are the most important partners on the scene.
Prices for houses, on sale or to let have never been this high. Ugly castles and huge mansions are built.
They do get sold, they do get let. That is a fact. Provided there is a generator on the plot. AND, a borehole to provide water every day.

Here, people talk openly about HOW to make ends meet. And how difficult it is and what the next step and chance may be. *Sans gene!*
What is more: they keep on smiling! Zimbabweans are knows for their creativity and ingenuity.
In the Netherlands, more and more people need the support of the Food Bank at their backdoor, active for the last ten years in eight Dutch regions, *(Voedselbank)* and dare not to mention it to their own close friends or good neighbours. The young ones feel embarrassed to have to attend school without clothes and shoes of their former favourite brand name...
Der kleine Unterschied?
But yes, crisis in the Netherlands. Crisis in Belgium. Crisis in Europe.
In the Netherlands more than ONE million of the 16, 7 million inhabitants live in poverty of which 380.000 children! The Food Bank promotes redistribution of food instead of our continuous spilling and despite their success for the first time they published waiting lists. Eighteen million Europeans out of 20 countries receive wheat, potatoes, rice, paste, dairy products, meat and fish from the European Union Food Bank program! Quite rightly so, at the discussion on a late summer's night at the local Rotary Club Maastricht Oost, some fellow Rotarians ponder whom to support in the near future: Zimbabwe, or any other African country, Asia or the increasing underprivileged in and around the town of Maastricht.
And I warmly respect this!

On a more positive note: thanks to all co-writers and this book I am able to build the Library at Chengeta Primary, a rural school in the Ngezi area. The books and textbooks arrived in February; we are eagerly waiting for the first academic results in December....
On the very positive note, Zimbabwe seems to be re discovered! The B&B's are fully booked, Backpackers' Lodges shoot up, and consultants

flock into the Guesthouses to avoid city hotels. Small business corners with annex coffee shops, and new cafes, bars and restaurants are opened daily. (e.g *l'O de Vie*, in the Newlands suburb of Harare, the first Belgian restaurant offers whatever you dreamt of!)

One the most positive note, thanks to top education here in Africa, our three children – my best pieces of art ever – work on their future most successfully, after the best schooling they enjoyed ever, in Harare.
Alies, our first born, is back in Africa, in Maputo. She studies Portuguese intensely in order to offer her services and did research for the Dutch embassy, next to various other projects as typical creative and inventive expat-wife and partner. She married Italian economist Vasco and became the proud mum of our olive skinned Maximilien!
Sanna, her sister, is currently working for the company Neurensic in Amsterdam, as a research psychologist, using scans for understanding economic behaviour.
Sytse, our son, works at the AMC, the Academical Hospital in Amsterdam to combine his skills for a thesis and his internship in one of the most challenging IT Masters: Grid computing.
All three look back fondly of their youth in Africa, their unique upbringing in Zimbabwe and cannot wait to come home for the Christmas holidays!

As already mentioned: Zimbabwe is slowly being rediscovered.
The new visitor does like expensive Zimbabwe, discovering all the various regions even when it means to some of them living on less than half a shoestring! Those with a critical mind understand the daily sufferings of the local people.

As for my ceramic designs, I need to throw up the four bones at full moon, to hope for ten hours of continuous power, to fire my work at nights. This will not kill my biggest challenge: designing coral and oyster art work, as thin as porcelain, applying our Zimbabwean clay only.
In the meantime, we harvest at home the heavy weight of our avocado tree, the spinach and the lettuce from a small vegetable garden. We water it sparsely as the borehole has run dry.
The Jacaranda trees are still blooming, shamelessly and intensely purple.
The weavers weave, the Huegelin's robin sings early before sunrise.
It is hot, windy, and dry.
I wait for the rains to come; I wait to be drenched in the first showers, full of the rich smell of November flowers.
And, last but not least, of hope.

Patrice Delchambre, November 2012

2015

AAD VAN GELDERMALSEN
AND NOW, SO MANY YEARS AFTER THE BEGINNING...

Almost six years after the initiative for this book was started I feel there should be an end to the story, otherwise it will drag on like an out-of-date soap opera and it will become a chronicle rather than a well-rounded account of people's life in Zimbabwe at the beginning of the 21st century. Anything after this edition should be a new book, with a different story and title. Considering the present prospects of Zimbabwe, that story may be completely different from what we have seen. Not where it concerns the character of the people, the beautiful nature or the change of seasons with its different scents and colours so nicely illustrated by all the contributors to this book. That will remain the same for a long time to come. No, the change will be with its politics, that is, by whom and perhaps also how the country will be led and the way the economy is guided. As I am writing this, we often hear: "Now everything will *really* change. The ruling party is not able to maintain its unity, the struggle for power by individuals and their factions is ripping it apart. This time something will change and though it may get even worse for a while, it must get better soon." The eternal optimistic Zimbabwe spirit prevails. Things have never been so dire and the party and its elites that rule the country will be seriously shaken. Well, in the meantime this has taken place and many of the old comrades in the ruling party have been purged by the 'old man' and there is a new team of ministers and although the real successor is unknown the role of the president's wife will be more prominent in the months to come. Who am I you may think to make such bold predictive statements? After all, prophecies like this have been expressed for the last 12 years. It is I, husband of Patrice Delchambre, Aad van Geldermalsen, earlier introduced as the epidemiologist cum sailor and glider pilot. Some of these qualifications can be slightly downscaled now, especially since I wrecked my beautiful plane, but a lover of Zimbabwe and its people I still am and of course the proud father of a family that, even if it is spreading over the globe, will still remain what it is: a close-knit family unit, partially thanks to the blessings of the modern communication technology such as Skype, Viber, Whatsapp, etc..

The main reason to make my small contribution is to reflect on how much has changed and still, how much has remained the same. As indicated above, first of all there are the people with their optimistic hope for a better future. That spirit never abated, albeit that much hope is now sought in prophets and their different, often weirdly varying sorts of religion. Praying and hoping has always been the most practiced approach to life's problems for most people. And the hope of deliverance for the severely tested people of Zimbabwe has always been put more in ever sterner beliefs than in building civic organisation or political structures. And for sure, it has been the safer option!

Over the years there have been some interesting proofs of the gullibility of people living on hope and divine intervention. These range from belief in refined diesel fuel oozing from rocks (some of the most powerful politicians believed it and paid their respect to the prophet who claimed to make it possible; she was later charged for unclear crimes), to prophets who literally(!) promised money in people's pockets and even on their bank accounts through the miraculous hand of God. The flocks that prophets can muster during their monster sessions of spiritual healing are many times bigger than what the most popular politician can achieve even though the godly promises for solutions are greatly more unrealistic than those of the political leaders. But those worldly problems that they deal with, are much harder to tackle. Most of Zimbabwe's political leaders are influenced by the many prophets, both the religious and the more pagan ones, and they consult them, often secretly as the story of the diesel-from-the-rocks showed. The profession of prophet can be a very profitable one. Most recently many people gaped at the latest model Mercedes that one of them showed off in the middle of town. Many people were offended by this display of opulence while his followers approved of this show of 'example of being blessed'. But the profession of prophet can be a difficult one to start off in. A wannabe prophet who tried his luck at one of the busy bus stations had to flee for his life when a 'suddenly miraculously healed wheel-chair bound crippled' was recognised by some bystanders as a notorious and bothersome but otherwise very healthy tout! For once the crowd realised how it had been fooled and bade for his blood. Apart from, or could it indeed be?, because of the increased religiosity, the kindness, politeness and generosity of the people has remained the same and is still the most appealing quality noticed by visitors to Zimbabwe.

Obviously, the seasons and the weather are the other great unchanged assets of the country. But it has to be said, the natural environment is under threat, both from the population pressure and the new land and resource use.

What *has* changed is the value of money, the economic situation and the means of dealing with it.

Looking back, that is where the changes have taken place. That's why the stories of all the authors who contributed reflect so nicely this special and painful episode in the history of Zimbabwe. It was the period of the great inflation and the scarcity of the most basic products. To me the situation reminded me of the stories of my parents who had gone through WW II in Europe and who experienced similar periods of shortage in which the search for food was the main occupation and topic of conversation.

At one stage in a fit of self-depreciation many Zimbabweans called their currency *'Zim kwacha'* referring to their neighbour Zambia's currency that went through a period of inflation, while some people referred to US dollars as *'Yussa'*. During the time of inflation I kept a diary (easy enough with the smartphone handy) of every exchange I made, mostly US dollars against the Zimbabwe dollar. There were different rates for dollars *and* for the people that changed currencies. The well-connected who had access to foreign exchange for Zim dollars at the 'official rate' often started multiple exchange mechanisms called 'carrousels' using both rates. It has been the source of wealth of those who knew 'how to play the system' and has resulted in some of the extravagant houses that can be seen in the northern suburbs of Harare. Consequently it meant that all the other Zimbabweans became collectively so much poorer. *Inflation is the thief of the poor man*, I read somewhere. Below is the graph I was able to draw up with the number of Zim dollars I used to be able to get for 1 *'Yussa'* over the time.

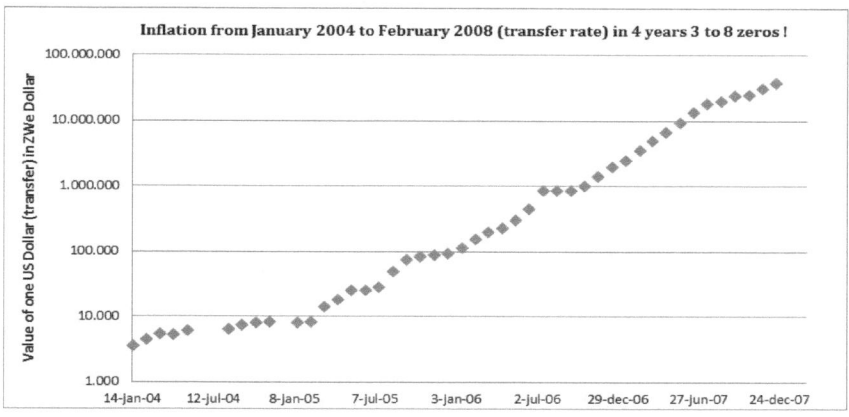

Every bullet is an interaction at a specific date with a purchase of Zim dollars, most often at the bank (via ATM, the maximum amount allowed for that day), but for greater amounts with the dealer who imported fuel (don't asked me how he operated) and sometimes with the guys in the street.

Much has been written and published in economic textbooks on the topic of hyperinflation. But these two graphs show most of it in a nutshell and most importantly, how the rise in inflation is exponential. That is why the trend line on this logarithmic scale is almost straight. It teaches you that one should never change too much money at a time, the next day you might get more for your buck and necessarily so, because prices go up equally.

But that was only the start. In the next graph the timescale has been stretched showing only the year 2008. This was the year when everything came to a head. There were elections with, what was euphemistically called campaigning, but afterwards proved to be gross violence throughout the country. Once it became impossible to fit all the zeroes on the banknotes and the computers and billing systems could no longer cope with the enormous figures, ten zeroes were scrapped and beautiful crisp new notes appeared starting with the value Z$1. The whole exercise was introduced and publicised under the ludicrous slogan *From Zero to Hero* as if something great had been achieved.

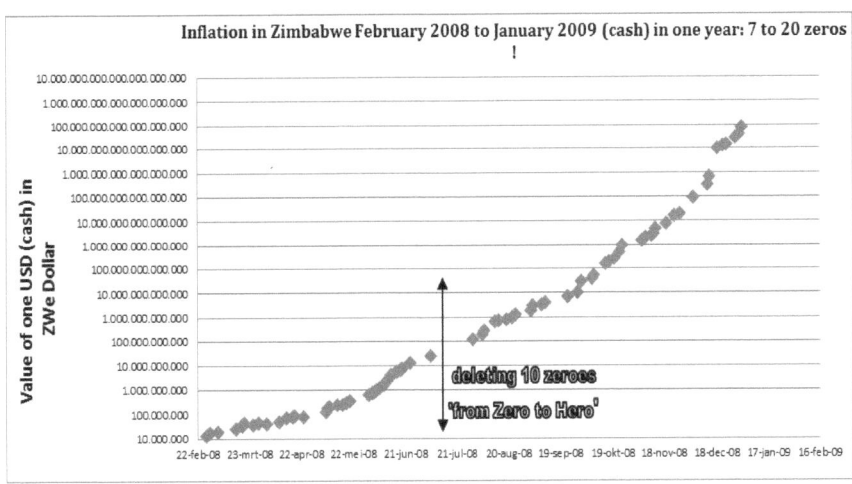

Apparently the new notes had been printed much earlier and were stored for a long time. The printing, watermark and safety features were of high quality and the fact that they didn't have so many zeroes on them made them somehow feel more valuable. Earlier, in order to produce more banknotes of ever bigger denominations, some notes had been put through the printers again with an additional digit printed in a slightly different size(!), in front of the previous value. That is how we had Z$ 750.000 notes for a while, a severe problem for shoppers and sellers who were already in the habit of using a calculator to add up simple amounts like 80 and 60. But after the *Zero to Hero* campaign, we had brand new notes.

Another consequence of the scrapping of 10 zeroes was that even the long forgotten coins could be used again and everybody started looking in drawers and old pots. The value of a loaf of bread could be found in a discarded wallet or the pockets of an unused jacket in the wardrobe. But that was not to last long. Initially there seemed to be no need to change money for a while as is indicated by the gap in the blue graph bullets (or was it because I went to The Netherlands for a few weeks?), but soon enough we were back to the old routines; the Reserve Bank printing money and we changing money almost daily. The streets around the Holiday Inn close to the Government offices where I worked, were called *Wall Street* because of all the black market money traders. It was rumoured they got the freshly printed money, often wrapped with the original bands and nicely numbered (easy for the counting!) straight from the boss of the Reserve Bank a few blocks away.

One of the most interesting features of Zimbabwe's hyperinflation is that it has not led to a radical political collapse as it usually does in other similar situations. Of course there were some political changes. We got a 'Government of National Unity' with a new minister of the new 'coalition party' at my Ministry of Health, but the main actors remained in power. Although US dollars were already used as the standard to calculate prices for many transactions for scarce goods or big purchases, the Zimbabwe dollar was officially abolished only in February 2009 and all other major currencies were allowed as legal tender. I once bought something small in the *Bon Marché* and handled Pula, Pounds and Dollars in one transaction.

So some things *did* change. Looking back it surprises me how little these negative developments influenced the enjoyable things in Zimbabwe. We still went to the pub on Friday night to round off the week with a TGIF beer. We used to go to *the Fife* hotel bar where the Zimbabwean wife of the Swedish husband/proprietor of the establishment always managed to get beer from the breweries, something not everybody was able to do. And it seemed that a 350ml bottle of *Castle* always cost more or less the equivalent of 50 US cent.

That was one sad thing that became different after the dollarisation! Things became available again, but prices went up instantly. Now there are very few pubs selling beer for under 2 dollars!

We can still go on a Sunday morning walk with the birding club *Birdlife Zimbabwe* and see over 60 species of birds within the span of a few hours leisurely stroll around Mukuvisi, the game park within the boundaries of Harare city. We can still sail the May Regatta with 25 cabin cruisers on Lake Kariba. The experiences from this traditional annual event could easily fill some cheerful chapters of this book. Every year the community of Zimbabwe sailors, an almost completely white *(Ie Rhodesian)* affair, organises a nine-day long event. Up to 30, mostly rather tatty, sailing yachts compete in a seven day race in a spirit of camaraderie and general jolliness along the Zimbabwean shores of Lake Kariba as far as 100 km up this 300 km long lake. The racing, only taking place in the mornings, is serious with strict rules and follows regulations and scientifically calculated handicaps. The mooring, camping and socialising on the shores of the Matusadona National Park is most enjoyable. Hippos, elephants, crocodiles and even lions are regularly encountered. Sailing and camping in that beautiful wild area with the hot sun during the days and only the stars at night is an unforgettable experience. The children at the International School who do a catamaran sailing trip on Kariba in their last year always mention it as their most memorable experience in Zimbabwe. For many of the Zimbabwean sailors it is the highlight of the year. As for the 'one-colouredness' of this sailing event, and it has to be said for sailing in general, I have done my slight bit. On two occasions I brought a darker skinned friend as crew member on the regatta and for all parties it was a most memorable and positive event. Both Zo Tsapayi and Oscar Orange were good company and eager crew. They were most graciously received by the sailors and were praised respectively for their sense of humour and their singing and social skills. As for the social skills of Oscar 'Come-and-join-us-for-a-drink' Orange I can vow; the singing is something else, but he *does* it and it works like a charm.

Some other of these outdoor activities for which Zimbabwe is known have declined for want of the minimal threshold of active club members. The gliding club of which I was a member was chased off its fields in Concession. Many of the old club members have passed away, others emigrated, new young amateurs and possible prospective members are scarce. The field is now derelict, the road there hardly passable. On the last visit I found the hangar to be a storage shed for a meagre crop of maize. An old glider and the winch were used as climbing tools and the club grounds were occupied by a 'new farmer' who was absent because of serving a prison term. He tried to grow the more profitable *mbanje* (marihuana) rather than food staple. Some dwindling group of gliding club members have maintained some planes and do occasionally fly, but it has all been a lot of effort by too few people. And money is tight. The less social sport of flying micro-lights is still doing well however, there is a club with a field in Komani, just north of Harare but I hear they have issues of tenure and the rising price of lease agreements.

So yes, things change *and* stay the same.
We live in this wonderful country where in all the suburbs of Harare trenches are being dug and optic fibre cables are being laid, sometimes in

duplicate by two different companies at the same time. Even our little close with only four potential customers got dug open to lay an empty tube that can be filled with an optic fibre cable to branch at our gate. Lovely ladies arrived some months later at the gate to offer us an 'excellent package' of superfast internet access, "connection is free". But subscriptions come to 150 dollars per month, so "no thank you", we still use ADSL via the good old telephone wire. And there we are, massive infrastructural development, privately financed, while we haven't received municipal water for over five years now and everyone in our neighbourhood relies on their borehole for water. Imagine what that does to the region's water table. Already an arms race is taking place where one neighbour sucks out the water from under the other. We feel bad to have been forced to join that race. When we bought our plot, we found a dried up shallow well with a 50 year old rusted rod-driven pump. So later, when the city's supply became erratic, we drilled a 20 meter deep hole finding water at 13 meters. It served us well for some years until recently, when during the dry months it stopped delivering. Our neighbours, with a 40 meters deep hole, happily continued watering their lawn, advising us to buy water from the water vendors (another business shamelessly exploiting everybody's resource for private benefit). So we were also forced to go the extra depth, to 40 meters, fortunately striking water just below 20. Recently the water started to contain far more iron, another sign that the water table is sinking. We had it tested for faecal contamination and no problems there, but the taste has changed.

Still, as if there is no tomorrow, or in fact *because* there is a tomorrow, we have decided to make better use of our little plot and I have finally fulfilled my dream to build that cottage I always had in mind.

I wanted it to have round forms and it has! It is shaped like two attached *rondavels* pulled two meters apart. It should have a balcony for Patrice to have G & Ts on, so it has! Making two stories is another mission altogether, but it creates a beautiful high and spacious veranda, the other requirement for our dream house. The whole exercise grew a bit bigger than initially anticipated and while getting carried away, a separate cottage was erected. We call it 'the small house', in the Zimbabwean context meaning more than just a separate bedroom, but rather the mistress that is put up in it (with the added responsibility to maintain her). Now we have something to be proud of, a grass thatched cottage with all the amenities of a house. We also see it as our 'pension plan' because we can't live in all our three little houses on the plot simultaneously so we will rent out part of it. Which part to whom and under which conditions is a matter of choice and discussion.

So there is no end to *our* story in Zimbabwe yet and we still hope to live *long and happily*, even if not *for ever after* in Zimbabwe.

Harare, Zimbabwe January 2015.

CHENGETA PRIMARY SCHOOL
THE BUILDING OF A LIBRARY

Doris Lessing has written extensively about communities with and without literature. Books on a table, books under the lampshade, torn books near candlelight. And, above all, what it does when this is part of childhood, anywhere whether it is Africa or Europe...

I remember the world of books was one of the worlds I decided to withdraw into, when my father Lucien Delchambre was tragically killed far too young. In that other world I was hiding, imagining I belonged somewhere else, and no one was going to hurt and damage me that deeply anymore as happened in the real world. My poor and brave mother understood this but had to regularly, when it came to meals and chores and homework, shout me back into reality. At school I was told I was daydreaming too much and instead of writing essays I could often only produce cryptic poetry.

One fact remains: all six of us Delchambres were stimulated to read, poverty or no poverty. Up to now I recall a childhood surrounded by literature, at home and certainly at school as well. Being rich and happy in an imaginary world where everything was possible and everybody was met: fairies, Indians, Alice in her Wonderland, Jack and the beanstalk, *Hansel und Gretel, Struwel Peter*, gnomes and dwarfs, cowboys, flying carpets, witches and queens... a world without boredom and duties, at least for the reader!

Zimbabwe was not the first country where building a library in a rural setting was done, next to mothering and working. I look in awe at all these teachers, at all these schools time and again, who try to make the best of it, in empty classrooms, with broken windows. They have to make do with insufficient materials and the fear of the annual paper One and paper Two. Who will make it?? Very few.

The story in short?
In 2006 I started supporting a group of orphans, mentioned earlier in our book. Very early 2010 I met the kind family of Phil and Lorraine Dobinson, and their Irish mum Mary Theresa Dobinson. I discovered we were all supporting the same children and students at Chengeta Primary School. This school enrolled 300 children this new term, of which 75 are orphans now. Phil and Lorraine and Mary, together with friends, supporters and donors rebuilt all the dilapidating classrooms of this governmental school.

Me, the royal beggar, up to today got slowly but surely a similar warm support from Rotary Clubs in Harare and in Maastricht, support from my publishers, relatives, friends and acquaintances, funding from private friends and donors and we build..... brick by brick. It took us all more than one year, but slowly we will get there, one day...

We build brick by brick on a possible future of these children.
The children of tomorrow. The community should get this multipurpose hall, the students deserve a similar world of literature, resource materials, dictionaries with lively pictures, picture books and above all.... the right to dream, the right to withdraw in an imaginary world, where everything is possible, where they can learn proper English and dream of a future.

I thank Lorraine and Phil and Mary Theresa Dobinson.
I dream of the young Zimbabweans, writers of tomorrow.

THE JACARANDA TREE OF ZIMBABWE

Every October, with Jacaranda trees displaying their striking purple blossoms, Zimbabwe's capital Harare, could easily be described as charming.
Since British settlers imported these trees from South America at the end of the 19th century, their appearance heralds the arrival of summer and whole avenues are awash with masses of mauve blooms.
Josiah Chinamano Avenue – Chinaman to the locals – is located in a central Harare suburb called The Avenues. It was obviously laid out in colonial times with streets running north south intersected in a grid pattern by wide avenues lined on both sides by jacaranda trees.
Walking down Chinaman in springtime, you will be struck by the breathtaking splendour of the view. The violet carpet of fallen Jacaranda blooms and an arched canopy of unearthly beauty.

Postcards from the 1960s show this as a prosperous and well-laid-out town with flowerbeds and tidy streets. Like most other cities in Africa, Harare has not escaped the impact of population growth. But viewed from the hill that overlooks the city, it still remained a pretty and well-ordered town laid out in a grid pattern. Luckily the main artery through the city centre contains some of the finest examples of 1950s street lamps surviving in Africa with their typical "Chinese hats".

With the increase of the heat so does the prospect of rain.
The starting of the rains marks the end of the Jacaranda's brief reign. It is soon replaced by flame trees whose flowering branches provide a scarlet-red canopy across the city.
It is to be said that Harare has one of the finest climates in the world. At 5,000 feet it is never too hot or humid and the winter months of May, June, July and August are filled with cloudless blue skies while the rain keeps a discreet distance.
However, with the global climate change, Zimbabwe has also changed!
Windy August has become windy September!
October can be unbearable! It is called the suicidal month for more than 15 years now, and the Jacaranda snow purple faster, it seems.
Temperatures of 35 degrees are not rare anymore. The winters are getting colder and colder over the last years as well. Fleeing into the mountains of Nyanga or Chimanimani is the way to cool down and to behold the last of the Jacaranda over there, blossoming later into the season and even into November!

THE FLAME LILY OF ZIMBABWE

The flame lily, is native to Zimbabwe and most of tropical Africa and parts of Asia. It was the national flower of Rhodesia, as Zimbabwe was known before independence from Britain in 1980, and has retained that special status.

The flame lily is adapted to high summer rainfall and a dormant dry season, and flowers between December and March every year in Zimbabwe. It can grow to about a metre in height, stands out in the wild because of its pinkish-red petals which resemble a flame or the head of a cockerel, hence its vernacular name, *jongwe* (cockerel in the local Shona language). The plant contains a substance called colchicine, which is dangerous to ingest.

In Zimbabwe, the flower occurs mainly in the higher rainfall areas of Marondera, Hwedza, Rusape, Goromonzi and Domboshava – generally east of Harare. Roadside flower vendors are a common sight in these areas. Environmentalists say, in addition to breaking the law by simply harvesting and selling the flame lily, poachers uproot the flower, which makes its regeneration impossible and its extinction a genuine possibility. Sheunesu Mupepereki, chairman of the statutory Environmental Management Authority board, described the harvesting of the special flower as "rampant".

'It is our national flower', Prof Mupepereki, a professor of soil science at the Harare University, said. 'So when it is harvested as rampantly as is the case now, sometimes with no chance of regeneration, we become concerned. Because of its beauty and monetary value that can be derived from it, the rate of its harvesting, if unchecked, might lead to its extinction.'

The flame lily is listed as a protected plant under the Parks and Wildlife Act, so unlicensed cultivation, harvesting and trade in it is illegal. The law also makes it an offence to destroy, possess, or exchange the flower.

"No person shall sell any specially protected indigenous plant except in terms of a permit issued", Section 52 of the Parks and Wildlife Act reads in part. *"The authority, in concurrence with the ministry of environment, may issue a permit to a cultivator of specially protected plants."*

The act further says people can buy the flame lily only from *"an individual who is a licensed dealer in specially protected indigenous plants or unless one is a member of a recognized horticultural society and the sale is to a member of the same or any other recognized horticultural society".*

Anyone who contravenes the act is liable to a fine and/or imprisonment up to six months.

THE NDORO OF ZIMBABWE

The *Ndoro* has a fascinating history within Zimbabwe's material culture and indeed, this is an intriguing story in its own right.
The original *Ndoro* is a marine mollusc of the Genus *Conus Virgo* of large snails. They are made of a heavy white substance and have a deep spiral groove on one side, the other side being smooth.
The earliest written reference of the *Ndoro* can be found in the journals of a sixteenth century Portuguese chronicler who observed that: "The Munhumatapa and the Mararangas and their vassals wear on their foreheads a white shell, as a jewel, strung from their hair, and the Munhumatapa wears another large shell on his chest. They call these shells Andoros."

According to a colourful legend, the *Ndoro* played a dramatic role in the early history of Zimbabwe. At some time in the seventeenth century, it helped in a major battle. The story is that a descendent of Mutota, the apparent founder of the Munhumatapa dynasty, was trying to subjugate a rival king named Karuva. Discovering through a spy that Karuva held the *Ndoro* in great awe and respect, he ordered that all his warriors should wear *Ndoros* upon they foreheads and they marched into battle against Karuva's forces. On seeing the soldiers, all ornamented with *Ndoros* approach him, Karuva became confused and the tide of the battle turned against him.

The Portuguese, having established themselves on the Mozambique coast and starting trade links with the interior, learned of the value placed on the *Ndoro*. Because of its scarcity it became much sought after. The Portuguese took advantage of this demand, using the natural mollusc, and later, mass producing copies of the marine seashell. Traders are believed to have exchanged *Ndoro* for gold, ivory and other valuable goods. In Zimbabwe, *Ndoros* are used by chiefs in the Shona society as symbols of rank authority. They are also a sign of great wealth. Old spirit mediums wore them as well. At present the *Ndoro* is used and popular again as design. It appears on pieces of jewellery and in decorational art and fashion design. Eternal life and eternity are nowadays connected to the *Ndoro*, as well as fortune and good luck.

Useful Addresses

www.bedandbreakfast.com/harare-zimbabwe.html
Some great places to stay in and around Harare.

www.jacana-gardens.com
Enjoy genuine and uncomplicated hospitality in this Feng Sui Lodge. The Dutch Rian and Wim Landman own and run this beautiful place, situated on a quiet and secure one acre property within the Golden Triangle of Harare's Northern suburbs.

www.wilderness-safaris.com - enquiry@wilderness-safaris.com
Setting up eco-villages, education of local population en conserving wilderness areas.

www.shearwateradventures.com
The Victoria Falls adrenalin company. Wild water rafting, canoeing, bungee jumping, elephant safaris.

www.africaalbidatourism.com
Luxury safari lodges in Victoria Falls.

www.africansunhotels.com
Hotels in Zimbabwe's most important cities and safari destinations.

www.cresta-hospitality.com
Hotels in the most important cities.

www.rtg.co.zw
Hotels and safari lodges throughout Zimbabwe.

www.innsofzimbabwe.co.zw
Guest houses in the most important destinations of Zimbabwe's Eastern Highlands.

www.wildzambezi.com
A tour operator specialised in safaris on and around the Zambezi River.

www.europcar.co.zw and www.avis.com
Car rental in Zimbabwe.

http://www.minbuza.nl/reizen-en-landen/reisadviezen/z/zimbabwe.html
Travel advice for Zimbabwe by the State Department.

www.zimbabwetourism.co.zw
The Zimbabwe Tourism Authority.

www.azta.co.zw
AZTA – Association of Zimbabwe Travel Agents.

www.itoza.co.zw
ITOZA – Inbound Tour operators of Zimbabwe Association.

www.vardensafaris.com
Extraordinary horseback safaris in the Mavuradonha Wilderness Area and in Hwanga National Park. Also canoeing safaris in the Zambezi.

www.classicsafaricamps.com
The Hide on the edge of Hwange National Park. Especially well organised camp, fantastic for watching large and small game.

primspa@soothingview.co.zw
Luxury spa on a hill with an extraordinary view.

www.zimbabwesituation.com
Extensive, politically tinged Website on Zimbabwe with a lot of information and interesting links.

www.kubatana.net
The NGO Network Alliance Project, an online community for Zimbabwean activists.

www.zamsoc.org – projects@zamsoc.org
The Zambezi Society is the ONLY conservation group devoted solely to looking after the Zambezi, the finest and wildest river in Africa. Mukuvusi Environment Centre, Glenara Ave/Hillside Rd., Harare, Zimbabwe.

www.patricedelchambre.com
Ceramic art, the passion of the author.

pdelchambre@gmail.com
For information concerning the development project Chengeta Primary and this book.

RECOMMENDABLE WEBSITES ABOUT MUSIC

www.youtube.com/watch?v=REOfJf_bm_g
In downtown Harare filmed music video, starring Bengt Post on keyboards.

www.zimaudio.com
Large database containing Zimbabwean music and artists, including artists with which Bengt Post has worked: Chiwoniso Maraire, Busi Ncube, Adam Chisvo, *The Collaboration*, Willom Tight, Andy Brown, *Township Survivors, Mokoomba, Too Open, Gwarimba*.

www.dandemutande.org
American website with a lot of information and discussion forums about traditional Zimbabwean music.

www.mbira.org
Website containing information about traditional Zimbabwean music and the national instrument: the *mbira*.

www.zimbojam.com
Our aim is simple: To talk about Zimbabwean entertainment, entertainers, showbiz and lifestyle as if there was no tomorrow; to find talent and to showcase it; to take the best of Zimbabwean showbiz to the world.
So let's Jam.

RECOMMENDABLE RESTAURANTS IN HARARE:

Amanzi Restaurant (****)
158 Enterprise Road, Highlands
The owner is half Nigerian and half English and you can tell by the excellent menu: a fusion of everything you can eat in Africa.
Here, bourgeois and common people dine communally.
Wonderfully decorated (African Ethnic).
On Thursday nights, there is a live band that plays everything ever thought of in Africa.
There are also 12 luxury private lodges.
www.amanzi.co.zw – restaurant@amanzi.co.zw

Victoria 22 (****)
22 Victoria Avenue, Newlands
Owners are Italian-German
Classic chic. Wonderful decoration. 5 course menu.

La Fontaine
54 Park Lane Street

The Pavilion
Meikles Hotel
Corner Jason Moyo Ave/3rd Street

The Pointe (*)
A Portuguese restaurant in Third Street between Josiah Chinamano Avenue and Baines Avenue. Noisy, unsightly and low-priced, good food.
A people's restaurant in which everyone is seen and will be seen.
Famous for the loud Karaoke Friday night. Here, you forget your daily troubles in good tempered company consisting of a cross section of the "Avenues" inhabitants.
Do not forget to have a drink before or after the gamba and good fries dinner at the bar on the first floor. There is no other place in Harare where there is as much useless political philosophising as here.

The Sitar (*)
No. 2 Cecil Rhodes Drive, Highlands
An Indian restaurant that, after having been at Newlands Shopping Centre for 30 years, has moved about 700 metres to the Patel family home in Cecil Rhodes Drive.

The Bookcafe (*)
FIFE Avenue Shopping Centre.
Everyone who is young and makes music, writes poetry or thinks about starting an artistic career is embraced here, also due to owner Paul Brickhill's vision.
A room shaped like a tent, sizzling-hot in the summer and ice-cold in winter, a must for everyone who believes in a future made by the youth. Older people are certainly welcome, if not only to increase the bar's revenue.
After closing, you visit the neighbours of course: good jazz in the **Mannenberg.**

Veldemeers Chocolates (****)
Belgian top quality chocolates and pastries, available at three locations:
Doon Estate, Msasa
Arundel shopping centre, Mount Pleasant, Harare
Nush, Iranian restaurant, Avondale
hans@veldemeers.com

Pamuzinda and Chengeta Luxury Safari Lodges (****)
For a real African bush experience, an hour away from Harare, on the Bulawayo road.
www.pamuzindasafarilodge.com
www.chengetasafarilodge.com
reservations@chengeta.com
phil@chengeta.com